Better Homes and Gardens®

Best Recipes YEARBOOK

© Copyright 1995 by Meredith Corporation, Des Moines, Iowa.
All Rights Reserved. Printed in the United States of America.
First Edition. Printing Number and Year: 5 4 3 2 1 99 98 97 96 95
ISSN: 8755-3090
ISBN: 0-696-20063-5

Better Homes and Gardens® Books

An Imprint of Meredith® Books

Best Recipes Yearbook

Project Manager: *Jennifer Darling*
Associate Art Director: *Lynda Haupert*

Vice President and Editorial Director: *Elizabeth P. Rice*
Executive Editor: *Kay Sanders*
Art Director: *Ernest Shelton*
Managing Editor: *Christopher Cavanaugh*
Test Kitchen Director: *Sharon Stilwell*

President, Book Group: *Joseph J. Ward*
Vice-President, Retail Marketing: *Jamie L. Martin*
Vice-President, Direct Marketing: *Timothy Jarrell*

Better Homes and Gardens® Magazine

Food Editor: *Nancy Byal*
Senior Editor: *Joy Taylor*
Associate Editors: *Lisa Holderness, Julia Malloy, Kristi Fuller R.D.*

Meredith Corporation

Chairman of the Executive Commitee: *E.T. Meredith III*
Chairman of the Board and Chief Executive Officer: *Jack D. Rehm*
President and Chief Operating Officer: *William T. Kerr*

Our seal assures you that every recipe in the *Best Recipes Yearbook*
has been tested in the Better Homes and Gardens® Test Kitchen.
This means that each recipe is practical and reliable, and meets
our high standards of taste appeal. We guarantee your satisfaction
with this book for as long as you own it.

WE CARE!

All of us at Better Homes and Gardens® Books are dedicated to
providing you with the information and ideas you need to create tasty foods.
We welcome your comments and suggestions.
Write us at:
Better Homes and Gardens® Books,
Cookbook Editorial Department,
RW-240, 1716 Locust St.,
Des Moines, IA
50309-3023

*If you would like to order additional copies of any of our books,
call 1-800-678-2803 or check with your local bookstore.*

Contents

Introduction

While testing and tasting the recipes for this collection of 1994 magazine stories, we often found ourselves reminiscing about our own personal pasts. It's interesting how quickly the aroma of cinnamon and nutmeg or the taste of mashed potatoes can summon a pleasing childhood memory that captures the link between food and family. Each of us fondly recall memories as different and personal as our taste buds.

Long before the fondue craze, my family would gather around a waffle iron that claimed center stage for many a Saturday-night dinner. Only seconds after I'd hear the sizzle of the batter hit the hot waffle grids, I'd ask impatiently, "Is it done yet?" and Mother would answer calmly, "When you can't see any more steam rising from the iron, that's when it's done." — Nancy Byal, standing left

Whenever my mother made Swedish rice pudding, it was its own holiday, with all the fanfare. We kids would ceremoniously watch the huge, blue-and-white bowl of pudding as it cooled on the counter, and wait eagerly. Often, rice pudding, with candles propped in the custard layer, replaced the more conventional birthday cake. — Lisa Holderness, standing center

My grandmother commandeered a fire-breathing wood stove called "the beast" at our lakeside cabin. A relic of bygone days, it kowtowed to no one save Grandma. I can still hear the stove clatter and hiss as she added another log. Totally subdued, the beast let her grill Norwegian pancakes to lacy, golden perfection, and then we'd pile on wild berries and whipped cream. — Julia Malloy, standing right

I remember my mother making dough for "cabbage burgers" (a German concoction); I was assigned dough-rolling duty. When I thought Mom wasn't looking, I'd pinch off little pieces of buttery, yeasty dough and pop them into my mouth. — Kristi Fuller, sitting left

One of my most treasured possessions is a stand-up electric mixer, inherited from my grandmother. When I visited her small-town Iowa home as a child, I'd anxiously watch her mix up fabulous breads from that mixer. Now the same special appliance connects me and my daughter Anna with those earlier times, as we create yummy baked goods together. — Joy Taylor, sitting right

There is nothing as priceless as time spent with our families. Please join us in our vow to redouble our efforts and pass the joys of home cooking on to our children and grandchildren. They will thank us many times over in years to come.

The Editors — *Nancy, Lisa, Julia, Kristi, and Joy*

January

Resolution Recipes

I resolve to eat more healthful foods.

(but only if they taste great!)

Prize Tested Recipes

Mocha Cheesecake Dreams, Mediterranean Chicken, Spicy Garlic Chicken Pizza, Apricot Nut Bars

Resolution Recipes

BY KRISTI FULLER, R. D.

Out with the old, in with new! If your New Year's resolution is to eat smarter to feel better, begin the new year with these 12 great-tasting, good-for-you recipes. From breakfast starters to healthful munchies, all recipes go easy on the fat and calories.

Resolve to eat a good breakfast every day. Why? You'll stay more alert and concentrate better. And, you can skip that midmorning caffeine urge.

Refrigerator Pear-Almond Muffins

DON'T LET HECTIC WEEKDAY MORNINGS SQUELCH YOUR RESOLUTION. JUST KEEP THE REFRIGERATED DOUGH READY FOR BAKING FRESH, WARM MUFFINS.

1¼ cups all-purpose flour
¾ cup packed brown sugar
1 tablespoon baking powder
½ teaspoon ground ginger or
1 tablespoon finely chopped
   crystallized ginger
¼ teaspoon salt
1 cup chopped pear (about
   1 medium), such as
   Bartlett or Anjou
1 cup whole bran cereal

1 cup skim milk
¼ cup frozen egg product,
   thawed, or 1 beaten egg
¼ cup cooking oil
Nonstick spray coating
2 tablespoons finely chopped
   almonds
1 recipe Ginger-Cream Spread

In a large mixing bowl stir together flour, brown sugar, baking powder, ginger, and salt. Add pear, stirring to coat with flour mixture.

In a medium bowl combine cereal and milk; let stand 5 minutes. Stir egg product or egg and oil into cereal mixture. Add cereal mixture to pear mixture; stir just till moistened. Place the muffin batter in an airtight container. Cover and seal. Refrigerate for up to 3 days, if desired, or bake muffins immediately.

To bake, spray a muffin pan with nonstick coating or line with paper bake cups. Spoon batter into cups, filling cups ¾ full. Sprinkle tops with almonds. Bake in a 400° oven for 18 to 20 minutes or till done. Cool slightly on a wire rack. Serve warm with Ginger-Cream Spread. Makes 14 to 16 muffins.

Microwave directions: Prepare batter as directed. Line 6-ounce custard cups or a microwave-safe muffin pan with paper bake cups. For each muffin, spoon 2 slightly rounded tablespoons of batter into each cup. Top with almonds. For custard cups, arrange cups in a ring on a microwave-safe plate. Micro-cook, uncovered, on 100% power (high) for specified time (see below) or till done, giving the plate a half-turn every minute. (To test for doneness, scratch muffin's top with a toothpick. The muffin should look cooked underneath.) If using custard cups, remove muffins from the oven as each tests done. Remove muffins from the cups or pan. Let stand on a wire rack 5 minutes.

For 1 muffin: Cook on high for 30 to 60 seconds. For 2 muffins: Cook on high for 1 to 2 minutes. For 4 muffins: Cook on high for 1½ to 2½ minutes. For 6 muffins: Cook on high for 2 to 3½ minutes.

Ginger-Cream Spread: In a small bowl mix ⅔ cup *nonfat soft-style cream cheese product*, 1 tablespoon *honey*, and 1 tablespoon finely chopped *crystallized ginger or* ¼ teaspoon *ground ginger*. Stir till mixed. Makes about ¾ cup.

Nutrition facts per muffin: 166 cal., 5 g total fat (1 g sat. fat), 1 mg chol., 144 mg sodium, 30 g carbo., 3 g fiber, and 4 g pro. Daily Value: 10% vit. A, 6% vit. C, 5% calcium, 13% iron.

◆ Refrigerator Pear-Almond Muffins

I resolve to start the day with a good breakfast.

◆ Dutch Babies with Farmer's-Style Eggs

Dutch Babies with Farmer's-Style Eggs

ON LEISURELY WEEKENDS SERVE THIS PUFFY POPOVER, OVERFLOWING WITH ALL THE THINGS YOU LOVE FOR BREAKFAST, WITHOUT GUILT. THE LOW-FAT INGREDIENTS SAVE THE DAY.

Nonstick spray coating
½ cup frozen egg product,
thawed, or 1 whole egg plus
1 egg white
¼ cup skim milk
¼ cup all-purpose flour

1 tablespoon cooking oil
½ teaspoon dried thyme, crushed
1 cup loose-pack frozen hash brown
potatoes with onion and peppers
2 ounces fully cooked ham, cut into
julienne strips (scant ½ cup)
1¼ cups frozen egg product,
thawed, or 3 whole eggs plus
3 egg whites
¼ teaspoon salt
¼ teaspoon dried oregano, crushed
⅛ teaspoon pepper
Shredded low-fat cheddar
cheese (optional)
Fresh thyme (optional)

For Dutch Babies, spray four 4¼-inch pie plates or 4½-inch foil tart pans with nonstick coating. Set aside.

In a medium mixing bowl use a rotary beater or whisk to beat the ½ cup egg product, milk, flour, oil, and thyme till smooth. Divide batter among prepared pans. Bake in a 400° oven for 25 minutes or till brown and puffy. Turn off oven; let stand in oven 5 minutes.

Meanwhile, spray a large nonstick skillet with nonstick coating. Cook potatoes over medium heat for 7 to 8 minutes or till tender, stirring often. Stir in ham; heat through.

In a medium mixing bowl use a wire whisk or rotary beater to beat the 1¼ cups egg product or 3 eggs and 3 egg whites, salt, oregano, and pepper till combined. Add to potatoes in skillet. Cook, without stirring, till mixture begins to set on the bottom and around edge. Using a large spoon or spatula, lift and fold partially cooked eggs so uncooked portion flows underneath. Continue cooking over medium heat for 2 to 3 minutes or till eggs are cooked throughout but are still glossy and moist. Remove eggs from the heat immediately.

To serve, immediately after removing Dutch Babies from oven, transfer to dinner plates. Spoon egg mixture into the center of each Dutch Baby. Top with shredded cheese and garnish with fresh thyme, if desired. Serve immediately. Makes 4 servings.

Nutrition facts per serving: 167 cal., 6 g total fat (1 g sat. fat), 10 mg chol., 526 mg sodium, 15 g carbo., 0 g fiber, 15 g pro. Daily Value: 55% vit. A, 5% vit. C, 5% calcium, 18% iron.

Resolve to eat at least one meatless dinner a week. Generally, meatless-meals fit your healthful lifestyle by being low in fat, cholesterol, and calories, and high in fiber.

Wheat Berry and Pasta Pilaf

WHEAT BERRIES, WHICH ARE WHOLE, UNPROCESSED WHEAT KERNELS, LEND A WHOLE-GRAIN FLAVOR TO A FAMILIAR ITALIAN FAVORITE.

5 cups water
1¼ cups wheat berries
¾ cup orzo
2 cups sliced fresh shiitake or
button mushrooms
2 medium carrots, thinly sliced
(about 1 cup)
1 14½-ounce can pasta-style
chunky tomatoes
1 8-ounce can low-sodium
tomato sauce
½ cup dry white wine
½ teaspoon instant beef or chicken
bouillon granules
½ teaspoon fennel seed, crushed
Dash ground red pepper

◆ Wheat Berry and Pasta Pilaf

For pilaf, in a large saucepan bring the 5 cups water to boiling. Add wheat berries. Reduce heat. Simmer, covered, for 60 minutes. Add orzo. Cook, uncovered, about 10 minutes more or till wheat berries and orzo are tender. Drain off any excess liquid. Cover to keep warm. Set aside.

Meanwhile, for sauce, in a medium saucepan cook mushrooms and carrots, covered, in a small amount of boiling water about 4 minutes or till carrots are crisp-tender. Drain.

Stir undrained tomatoes, tomato sauce, wine, bouillon granules, fennel, and red pepper into the mushroom mixture. Bring to boiling; reduce heat. Simmer sauce, uncovered, about 25 minutes or to desired consistency, stirring occasionally.

To serve, spoon pilaf onto dinner plates. Spoon sauce over. Makes 4 main-dish servings.

Nutrition facts per serving: 437 cal., 2 g total fat (0 g sat. fat), 0 mg chol., 520 mg sodium, 91 g carbo., 5 g fiber, 14 g pro. Daily Value: 98% vit. A, 33% vit. C, 34% iron.

◆ Spinach-Feta Shells with Minted Tomato Sauce

Spinach-Feta Shells with Minted Tomato Sauce

A LITTLE CINNAMON ADDS A NICE SPICI-NESS TO THESE PLUMP, CHEESE-FILLED SHELLS.

12 jumbo shell macaroni
1 10-ounce package frozen chopped
spinach, thawed and well
drained
½ cup crumbled feta cheese
(about 2 ounces)
½ cup low-fat ricotta cheese
¼ cup toasted chopped walnuts
1 slightly beaten egg white
¼ teaspoon salt
¼ teaspoon ground cinnamon
⅛ teaspoon pepper
1 14½-ounce can low-sodium
tomatoes, cut up

½ of a 6-ounce can (⅓ cup) reduced-
sodium tomato paste
2 tablespoons water
1½ teaspoons dried mint, crushed
1 teaspoon sugar
¼ teaspoon garlic powder
¼ cup shredded low-fat
mozzarella cheese (1 ounce)

Cook shell macaroni according to package directions. Drain. Set aside.

For filling, in a medium mixing bowl combine spinach, feta cheese, ricotta cheese, 3 tablespoons of the walnuts, egg white, salt, cinnamon, and pepper. Stir to mix. Set aside.

For sauce, in a medium saucepan, combine undrained tomatoes, tomato paste, water, mint, sugar, and garlic powder. Bring to boiling; reduce heat. Simmer, uncovered, about 5 minutes or till slightly thickened.

Stuff each shell with about 2 tablespoons of the spinach filling. Place in an ungreased 2-quart square baking dish. Spoon sauce over shells. Sprinkle with remaining nuts. Bake, covered, in a 350° oven for 25 minutes. Sprinkle with mozzarella. Bake, uncovered, for 2 to 3 minutes more. Makes 4 main-dish servings.

Nutrition facts per serving: 276 cal., 10 g total fat (3 g sat. fat), 19 mg chol., 466 mg sodium, 35 g carbo., 4 g fiber, 15 g pro. Daily Value: 72% vit. A, 61% vit. C, 21% calcium, 26% iron.

Oven-Baked Split Pea and Lentil Soup

SATISFYING HOMEMADE SOUP IS AN EASY WAY FOR YOUR FAMILY TO "GO VEGETAR-IAN" ONCE IN A WHILE.

½ cup split peas
½ cup lentils
5 cups chicken or vegetable
broth
¾ cup sliced carrot
¾ cup sliced celery
1 medium red sweet pepper,
chopped (about 1 cup)
or ¼ cup chopped roasted
red sweet pepper
1 medium onion, chopped
1 bay leaf
1 teaspoon ground cumin
¼ teaspoon pepper
¼ cup nonfat plain yogurt
¼ cup chopped, unpeeled
cucumber

Rinse and drain split peas and lentils. In a Dutch oven combine peas, lentils, broth, carrot, celery, red pepper, onion, bay leaf, cumin, and pepper. Bake, covered, in a 350° oven about 2 hours or till the lentils and split peas are tender. (Or, bring mixture to boiling on range top. Reduce heat and simmer, covered, for 1 hour or till peas are tender.)

Remove bay leaf. Top each serving with yogurt and cucumber. Makes 4 main-dish servings.

Nutrition facts per serving: 231 cal., 1 g total fat, 0 mg chol., 562 mg sodium, 41 g carbo., 7 g fiber, 16 g pro. Daily Value: 76% vit. A, 125% vit. C, 8% calcium, 32% iron.

◆ Oven-Baked Split Pea and Lentil Soup

I resolve
to make at least one meatless dinner a week.

I resolve to serve more fish and seafood to my family.

◆ Shrimp and Lobster Bouillabaisse

Resolve to serve fish or seafood more often. Here's why: They're low in saturated fat (the type of fat that can raise your blood cholesterol) and high in omega-3 fatty acids (which can help lower your blood cholesterol). You and your family can benefit by eating fish at home two or three times per week. Try a new variety each time you shop.

Shrimp and Lobster Bouillabaisse

FOR THOSE WHO'VE SWORN OFF LOBSTER AND SHRIMP, GO AHEAD AND SPLURGE ON THIS CLASSIC FRENCH DISH. YES, SHELLFISH CONTAINS CHOLESTEROL, BUT IT'S NOT THE KIND THAT WILL RAISE YOURS.

1 14½-ounce can low-sodium
stewed tomatoes
1 cup reduced-sodium chicken broth
1 8-ounce bottle clam juice
3 medium leeks, sliced (1 cup)
½ cup water
1 teaspoon Cajun seasoning
1 teaspoon finely shredded orange peel
8-ounces fresh or frozen lobster tail or
6 ounces cooked lobster, cut into chunks, or
one 8-ounce package frozen lobster-
flavored, lobster-shaped fish pieces (surimi),
thawed
8 ounces fresh or frozen peeled and
deveined shrimp
4 slices French bread, toasted (optional)
Snipped fresh parsley (optional)

In a 4½- or 5-quart Dutch oven combine the first 7 ingredients. Bring to boiling; reduce heat. Cover and simmer for 10 minutes.

Meanwhile, if using lobster tail, thaw lobster, if frozen. Use kitchen shears to cut lengthwise through the lobster shell. Turn tail over and cut through underside shell and meat. Cut each halved tail crosswise through shell and meat 3 or 4 times to make 6 or 8 pieces total.

Add lobster pieces and shrimp to broth mixture. (Do not add cooked lobster or surimi at this point.) Bring almost to boiling, then reduce heat. Simmer gently for 2 to 3 minutes or till shrimp just turn pink.

Add cooked lobster or surimi, if using; simmer about 1 minute more or till heated through.

To serve, place a bread slice into each soup bowl, if desired. Spoon shrimp mixture atop. Sprinkle with parsley. Makes 4 main-dish servings.

Nutrition facts per serving: 151 cal., 1 g total fat (0 g sat. fat), 118 mg chol., 579 mg sodium, 16 g carbo., 5 g fiber, 20 g pro. Daily Value: 19% vit. A, 47% vit. C, 8% calcium, 79% iron.

Zesty Jalapeño Fish Fillets

IT WILL BE EASY TO GET YOUR FAMILY TO EAT MORE FISH WITH THESE MEXICAN-STYLE FILLETS. LOW IN FAT BUT FULL OF FLAVOR, THIS QUICK-TO-FIX DINNER GETS A FINS UP!

3 medium carrots, cut into
julienne strips (1½ cups)
1 medium zucchini, cut into
julienne strips (1½ cups)
1 pound skinless fish fillets, such as
red snapper, flounder, sole,
haddock, or orange roughy
1½ cups water
½ teaspoon instant chicken bouillon
granules
1 cup couscous
⅓ cup jalapeño pepper jelly
1 tablespoon white wine vinegar or
vinegar
1 tablespoon snipped fresh cilantro or
parsley

In a saucepan cook carrots, covered, in a small amount of boiling water for 2 minutes; add the zucchini and cook 2 minutes more or till vegetables are crisp-tender. Drain. Cover; keep warm.

◆ Zesty Jalapeño Fish Fillets

Spray nonstick coating onto the cold rack of a broiler pan. Place fish on an unheated rack. Season with salt and pepper. Measure thickness of fish. Broil fish 4 inches from the heat just till it flakes easily when tested with a fork. Allow 4 to 6 minutes per ½-inch thickness.

Meanwhile, for couscous, in a 1½-quart microwave-safe casserole combine 1½ cups water and the chicken bouillon granules. Micro-cook, uncovered, on 100% power (high) for 3 to 4 minutes or till boiling. Stir in couscous. Cover and let stand for 3 to 5 minutes or till liquid is absorbed.

In a small saucepan stir together jelly and vinegar. Heat and stir over low heat till jelly is melted.

To serve, use a fork to fluff the couscous; stir in the cilantro or parsley. Spoon the couscous onto each dinner plate. Top with a fillet and some of the vegetables. Drizzle with the warm jelly mixture. Makes 4 main-dish servings.

Nutrition facts per serving: 375 cal., 2 g total fat (0 g sat. fat), 60 mg chol., 358 mg sodium, 60 g carbo., 10 g fiber, 28 g pro. Daily Value: 130% vit. A, 5% vit. C, 4% calcium, 9% iron.

January

Resolve to eat 5 servings of fruit and vegetables a day. What an easy way to help lower your risk of heart disease and some types of cancers.

Fruit and Granola Parfaits

USE ANY KIND OF FRUIT IN THIS YUMMY TREAT. THE COMBINATION OF APPLES, PEARS, AND STRAWBERRIES IS A TASTY OPTION. YOU'LL NEED ABOUT 3 CUPS OF FRUIT TOTAL.

½ cup low-fat vanilla yogurt
¼ cup nonfat soft-style cream cheese product
1 tablespoon honey
¼ teaspoon ground cinnamon
2 kiwi fruit, peeled, halved lengthwise, and sliced
1 medium banana, sliced
1 medium orange, peeled, cut into fourths lengthwise, and sliced
1½ cups frozen red raspberries, thawed and drained
1 cup low-fat granola cereal

In a small mixing bowl combine yogurt, cream cheese, honey, and cinnamon; beat with an electric mixer on medium speed till combined. Chill. To assemble, stir together fruit in another small bowl. Divide one-third of the fruit mixture among 4 parfait glasses or wine goblets. Spoon about 2 tablespoons each of cream cheese mixture and granola atop fruit. Repeat. Top with remaining third of fruit. Serve immediately. Makes 4 servings.

Nutrition facts per serving: 243 cal., 3 g total fat (0 g sat. fat), 4 mg chol., 164 mg sodium, 51 g carbo., 3 g fiber, 8 g pro. Daily Value: 14% vit. A, 122% vit. C, 16% calcium, 12% iron.

Orange-Glazed Brussels Sprouts and Carrots

ONE SERVING OF THIS VEGETABLE DYNAMO MEETS ALL YOUR VITAMIN C NEEDS FOR THE DAY. FIX IT QUICKLY ON THE RANGE TOP OR IN THE MICROWAVE.

I resolve to eat 5 servings of fruits and vegetables every day.

◆ Fruit and Granola Parfaits

*2 cups fresh brussels sprouts or one
10-ounce package frozen brussels sprouts
3 medium carrots, cut lengthwise into
quarters, then into 1-inch pieces
⅓ cup orange juice
1 teaspoon cornstarch
½ teaspoon sugar
¼ teaspoon ground nutmeg (optional)
¼ teaspoon salt*

Cut brussels sprouts in half. In a medium saucepan combine sprouts and carrots. Cook, covered, in a small amount of boiling water for 10 to 12 minutes or till crisp-tender. Drain well. Return all of the vegetables to pan.

In a bowl mix the orange juice, cornstarch, sugar, nutmeg (if desired), and salt. Add to brussels sprouts and carrots. Cook and stir the mixture over medium heat till thickened and bubbly. Cook and stir for 1 minute more. Serve immediately. Makes 4 side-dish servings.

Microwave directions: Halve the brussels sprouts as directed. In a 1½-quart microwave-safe casserole, micro-cook fresh brussels sprouts, carrots, and 2 tablespoons water, covered, on 100% power (high) for 6 to 8 minutes or till crisp-tender, stirring once. (Or, if using frozen brussels sprouts, thaw slightly under cold water, then cut in half. Cook with carrots on high for 8 to 10 minutes, stirring once.) Drain. In a small bowl stir together the orange juice, cornstarch, sugar, nutmeg (if desired), and salt. Add to the brussels sprouts and carrots. Micro-cook, uncovered, on high for 2 to 3 minutes or till the mixture is thickened and bubbly, stirring every 30 seconds.

Nutrition facts per serving: 61 cal., 1 g total fat (0 g sat. fat), 0 mg chol., 184 mg sodium, 14 g carbo., 4 g fiber, 3 g pro. Daily Value: 90% vit. A, 100% vit. C, 3% calcium, 8% iron.

◆ Orange-Glazed Brussels Sprouts and Carrots

◆ Peppered Beef Salad

Peppered Beef Salad

LET VEGETABLES AND GREENS BE THE
STARS IN YOUR MAIN-DISH SALAD. SLICE
THE MARINATED BEEF EVER SO THIN.

*¾ pound boneless beef sirloin steak,
cut 1 inch thick
1 cup water
¼ cup white wine vinegar or cider vinegar
1 teaspoon sugar
1 teaspoon coarse ground black pepper
½ teaspoon dry mustard
½ teaspoon dried oregano, crushed
2 cloves garlic, minced
Dash salt
2 tablespoons regular powdered fruit pectin
(about ½ of a 1¾-ounce package)
8 cups mixed greens (such as curly endive,
spinach, and/or romaine)
1½ cups sliced fresh mushrooms
4 radishes, coarsely shredded
1 medium cucumber, sliced
1 red onion, sliced and separated into rings
8 cherry tomatoes, halved, or 2 medium
oranges, peeled, sliced, and halved
Nonstick spray coating
¼ cup crumbled peppercorn feta cheese or
plain feta cheese*

◆ Apricot Cardamom Bar

Trim fat from beef. For salad dressing
and marinade, in a screw-top jar combine the water, vinegar, sugar, pepper,
dry mustard, oregano, garlic, and salt.
Cover; shake well to combine.

Place meat in a shallow 2-quart dish;
pour about half of the vinegar mixture
over the meat (about ⅔ cup). Turn meat
to coat with the marinade. Cover meat;
marinate in the refrigerator for 6 to 24
hours, turning occasionally.

To the remaining vinegar mixture,
add the powdered fruit pectin. Cover
and shake well to combine. Let mixture
stand several minutes and shake again.
Chill dressing till serving time.

For salad, in a large bowl toss together
the mixed greens, sliced mushrooms,
shredded radishes, sliced cucumber, red
onion, and cherry tomatoes or oranges.
Cover and chill till needed.

For meat, drain and discard marinade.
Spray an unheated rack of a broiler pan
with nonstick coating. Broil the meat
about 3 inches from the heat to desired
doneness, turning meat halfway through
cooking. For medium doneness, allow
13 to 17 minutes total broiling time.

To serve, pour some of the reserved
dressing (about ½ cup) over salad; toss to
coat well. Divide salad mixture among 4
dinner plates. Thinly slice meat across
the grain into bite-size strips. Arrange
meat atop salad. Sprinkle with feta
cheese. Serve immediately with remaining dressing. Makes 4 main-dish
servings.

Nutrition facts per serving: 270 cal.,
12 g total fat (6 g sat. fat), 71 mg chol.,
321 mg sodium, 18 g carbo., 5 g fiber,
25 g pro. Daily Value: 52% vit. A, 65%
vit. C, 16% calcium, 36% iron.

R esolve to eat healthful snacks. No, snacks aren't off-limits. But, when the hungries strike, just make wise choices that won't sabotage other good eating intentions.

Apricot-Cardamom Bars

APPLESAUCE HELPS CUT THE FAT IN THESE MOIST AND FLAVORFUL BARS.

1 cup all-purpose flour
½ cup packed brown sugar
½ teaspoon baking powder
¼ teaspoon baking soda
¼ teaspoon ground cardamom or
⅛ teaspoon ground cloves
½ cup apricot nectar or
orange juice
¼ cup unsweetened
applesauce
2 tablespoons cooking oil
1 slightly beaten egg
½ cup finely snipped dried apricots
1 recipe Apricot Icing

In a medium mixing bowl stir together flour, brown sugar, baking powder, baking soda, and cardamom or cloves; set aside. Stir together apricot nectar or orange juice, applesauce, oil, and egg till combined. Add to dry ingredients, stirring till just combined. Stir in the snipped apricots.

Spread batter in an ungreased 11x7x1½-inch baking pan. Bake in a 350° oven about 25 minutes or till a wooden pick inserted near the center comes out clean. Cool in pan on a wire rack. Drizzle with Apricot Icing. Cut into bars. Makes 24 bars.

Apricot Icing: In a small mixing bowl stir together ½ cup *powdered sugar* and 2 to 3 teaspoons *apricot nectar or orange juice.*

Nutrition facts per serving: 67 cal., 1 g total fat (0 g sat. fat), 9 mg chol., 17 mg sodium, 13 g carbo., 0 g fiber, 1 g pro. Daily Value: 3% vit. A, 3% vit. C, 0% calcium, 3% iron.

Butter Pecan Popcorn

WHEN YOU CRAVE CARAMEL POPCORN, REACH FOR THIS BUTTERY TASTING TREAT WITH HALF THE FAT. WHAT'S THE SECRET INGREDIENT? BUTTER PECAN PUDDING MIX.

8 cups popped popcorn (about
⅓ to ½ cup unpopped)
Nonstick spray coating
½ cup broken pecans
2 tablespoons margarine or butter
⅓ cup light corn syrup
¼ cup instant butter pecan
pudding mix
¾ teaspoon vanilla

Discard unpopped popcorn kernels. Spray a 17x12x2-inch roasting pan with nonstick coating. Place the popped corn and pecans in pan. Keep popcorn warm in a 300° oven while making coating.

In a small saucepan melt the margarine or butter. Remove saucepan from heat. Stir in the corn syrup, pudding

◆ Butter Pecan Popcorn

mix, and vanilla. Pour syrup mixture over popcorn. With a large spoon, gently toss the popcorn with the syrup mixture to coat.

Bake popcorn, uncovered, in a 300° oven for 16 minutes, stirring halfway through baking. Remove the pan from the oven. Turn mixture onto a large piece of foil. Cool popcorn completely. When cool, break into large pieces. Store leftover popcorn, tightly covered, in a cool, dry place for up to 1 week. Makes about 9 (1 cup) servings.

Nutrition facts per serving: 157 cal., 7 g total fat (0 g sat. fat), 0 mg chol., 116 mg sodium, 22 g carbo., 1 g fiber, 2 g pro. Daily Value: 3% vit. A, 0% vit. C, 1% calcium, 5% iron.

Prize Tested Recipes

Apricot Nut Bars

TANGY APRICOT AND SWEET ORANGE PAIR UP FOR THIS DELECTABLE NUT-TOPPED FRUIT BAR.

1 cup all-purpose flour
Dash salt
¼ cup margarine or butter
½ cup snipped dried apricots
¾ cup packed brown sugar
2 eggs
1 cup chopped walnuts
½ cup shredded coconut
1 teaspoon vanilla
2 tablespoons all-purpose flour
2 tablespoons margarine or butter
2 teaspoons finely shredded orange peel
1¼ cups sifted powdered sugar
1 to 2 tablespoons orange juice
½ cup chopped walnuts

◆ Apricot Nut Bars

For crust, in a medium mixing bowl combine the 1 cup flour and salt. Cut in the ¼ cup margarine or butter till crumbly; press into the bottom of a lightly greased 11x7x1½-inch baking pan. Bake in a 375° oven 12 minutes.

Meanwhile, in a small saucepan combine apricots and enough water to cover. Bring to boiling; reduce heat. Simmer, covered, for 10 minutes. Drain. In a large mixing bowl stir together brown sugar and eggs till combined. Stir in the drained apricots, the 1 cup walnuts, coconut, and vanilla. Add the 2 table-spoons flour; stir till combined. Spread apricot mixture evenly over baked crust. Bake in a 375° oven 15 minutes. Cool.

For frosting, in a medium mixing bowl, beat the 2 tablespoons margarine or butter and the orange peel with an electric mixer till combined. At low speed, gradually beat in the 1¼ cups powdered sugar. Add orange juice, a little at a time, till of spreading consis-tency. Spread frosting over cooled bars in pan. Sprinkle with the ½ cup walnuts. Makes 32 bars.

Nutrition facts per bar: 121 cal., 6 g total fat (1 g sat. fat), 13 mg chol., 36 mg sodium, 15 g carbo., 1 g fiber, 2 g pro. Daily Value: 4% vit. A, 1% calci-um, 4% iron.

$100 WINNER
Beverly McCabe
Platteville, Wisconsin

Mocha Cheesecake Dreams

A LUSCIOUS MOCHA CREAM CHEESE
LAYER TOPS A CHOCOLATY CRUST.

1¼ cups all-purpose flour
1 cup sifted powdered sugar
½ cup unsweetened cocoa powder
¼ teaspoon baking soda
¾ cup margarine or butter
1 tablespoon instant coffee crystals
1 tablespoon hot water
1 8-ounce package cream cheese, softened
1 14-ounce can (1¼ cups) sweetened
condensed milk
2 eggs
Chocolate syrup (optional)

For crust, in a large mixing bowl stir together flour, powdered sugar, cocoa powder, and baking soda. With a pastry blender or fork, cut in margarine or butter till crumbly; press flour mixture into the bottom of a 13x9x2-inch baking pan. Bake in a 350° oven 15 minutes.

Meanwhile, dissolve instant coffee crystals in hot water. Set aside. In a large mixing bowl beat cream cheese with an electric mixer till fluffy. Gradually beat in the sweetened condensed milk. Add the coffee mixture and eggs; beat till thoroughly combined. Pour over the hot baked crust. Bake in a 350° oven for 20 minutes or till set. Cool on a wire rack. Cover and keep refrigerated. To serve, cut into bars and drizzle with chocolate syrup, if desired. Makes 32 bars.

Nutrition facts per bar: 143 cal., 8 g total fat (5 g sat. fat), 37 mg chol., 94 mg sodium, 14 g carbo., 0 g fiber, 3 g pro. Daily Value: 8% vit. A, 0% vit. C, 4% calcium, 3% iron.

$200 WINNER
Andrea Ray Chandler,
Olathe, Kansas

Spicy Garlic Chicken Pizza

AN ORIENTAL FLAIR AND ZESTY SPICES
GIVE THIS PIZZA ITS WINNING FLAVOR.

12 ounces skinless, boneless chicken
breasts
½ cup sliced green onion
2 cloves garlic, minced

◆ Mocha Cheesecake Dreams, above
◆ Spicy Garlic Chicken Pizza, left

2 tablespoons rice vinegar or white vinegar
2 tablespoons reduced-sodium soy sauce
1 tablespoon olive oil or cooking oil
½ teaspoon crushed red pepper or
¼ teaspoon ground red pepper
¼ teaspoon black pepper
1 tablespoon olive oil or cooking oil
1 tablespoon cornstarch
1 16-ounce (12 inch) Italian bread shell
(Boboli brand)
½ cup shredded Monterey Jack cheese
½ cup shredded mozzarella cheese
2 tablespoons pine nuts or sliced almonds

Rinse chicken; pat dry with paper towels. Cut chicken into ½-inch pieces. In a large bowl combine half of the green onion, the minced garlic, vinegar, soy sauce, the first tablespoon oil, and the red and black peppers. Add the
continued on page 20

continued from page 19

chicken pieces; stir to coat. Let stand 30 minutes at room temperature. Drain, reserving marinade.

Heat remaining oil in a large skillet; add chicken pieces. Cook and stir about 3 minutes or till no longer pink. Stir cornstarch into reserved marinade. Add to skillet. Cook and stir till thickened and bubbly. Spoon evenly atop bread shell. Sprinkle with cheeses. Bake, uncovered, in a 400° oven for 12 minutes. Top with remaining green onion and nuts. Return to oven for 2 minutes more. Makes 6 main-dish servings.

Nutrition facts per serving: 389 cal., 17 g total fat (4 g sat. fat), 47 mg chol., 720 mg sodium, 36 g carbo., 1 g fiber, 25 g pro. Daily Value: 6% vit. A, 3% vit. C, 18% calcium, 16% iron.

$100 WINNER
Kelly L. Delahunty
Inver Grove Heights, Minnesota

Mediterranean Chicken

SERVE THIS TOMATO AND CINNAMON-SPICED CHICKEN ATOP COUSCOUS—A TINY PASTA.

◆ Mediterranean Chicken

2½ to 3 pounds meaty chicken pieces
2 tablespoons cooking oil
1 14½-ounce can tomatoes, cut up
½ envelope regular onion soup mix
1 6-ounce jar marinated artichoke hearts, drained and quartered
½ cup pitted ripe olives, halved
¼ cup dry white wine (optional)
¼ teaspoon ground cinnamon
2¼ cups water or chicken broth
3 tablespoons margarine or butter
1½ cups couscous

Skin and rinse chicken; pat dry. In a 12-inch skillet brown chicken in hot oil. Drain fat. Stir together the undrained tomatoes and soup mix. Add to chicken in skillet. Bring to boiling; reduce heat. Simmer, covered, for 30 to 35 minutes. Add artichokes, olives, wine, and cinnamon. Simmer, covered, 10 minutes or till chicken is no longer pink.

Meanwhile, in a saucepan bring water or broth and margarine or butter to boiling (if using water, add ½ teaspoon salt, if desired). Stir in couscous. Cover;

remove from heat. Let stand 5 minutes. Fluff with fork. Serve with chicken. Makes 6 main-dish servings.

Nutrition facts per serving: 445 cal., 18 g total fat (4 g sat. fat), 66 mg chol., 624 mg sodium, 43 g carbo., 8 g fiber, 28 g pro. Daily Value: 12% vit. A, 27% vit. C.

$200 WINNER
Stella Wolf
Culver City, California

February

Chocolate Hall of Fame

Winter Wonderful Suppers

Prize Tested Recipes

Bavarian Apple Cheesecake, Ham and Lima Bean Salad, Teriyaki Potatoes, Double-Coconut Cream Pie

Fashioned after an all-time favorite, pecan pie, this tart mixes several
kinds of nuts and chocolate pieces in a caramel custard filling.

Chocolate Hall of Fame

By Lisa Holderness

Ultimate Nut and Chocolate Chip Tart

WITH A SCOOP OF RICH VANILLA ICE CREAM, IT'S HEAVEN.

*1 recipe Pastry for Single-
Crust Tart (see recipe,
right) or ½ of a 15-ounce
package folded refrigerated
unbaked piecrust (1 crust)
3 eggs
1 cup light corn syrup
½ cup packed brown sugar
⅓ cup butter, melted and cooled
1 teaspoon vanilla
1 cup coarsely chopped salted
mixed nuts
½ cup miniature semisweet
chocolate pieces
⅓ cup miniature semisweet
chocolate pieces
1 tablespoon shortening
Vanilla ice cream (optional)*

Prepare Pastry for Single-Crust Tart, if using. On a lightly floured surface, flatten dough with your hands. Roll pastry from the center to the edge, forming a circle about 12 inches in diameter. For refrigerated piecrust, let pastry sit at room temperature according to package directions.

Ease pastry into an 11-inch tart pan with removable bottom. Trim pastry

◆ Ultimate Nut and Chocolate Chip Tart

even with the rim of the pan. Do not prick pastry.

For filling, in a large mixing bowl beat eggs slightly with a rotary beater or a fork. Stir in the corn syrup. Add the brown sugar, butter, and vanilla, stirring till sugar is dissolved. Stir in the nuts and the ½ cup chocolate pieces.

Place the pastry-lined tart pan on a baking sheet on the oven rack. Carefully pour filling into pan. Bake in a 350° oven for 40 minutes or till a knife inserted near the center comes out clean. Cool on a rack.

To serve, cut tart into wedges and transfer to dessert plates. Place the ⅓ cup chocolate pieces and the shortening in a small heavy saucepan over very low heat, stirring constantly till it begins to melt. Immediately remove from heat and stir till smooth. Cool slightly. Transfer chocolate mixture to a clean, small, heavy plastic bag. Snip a very small hole in one corner of the bag. Drizzle the melted chocolate in zigzag lines across each piece of tart, overlapping onto the plate (see photo, above right).

Serve each piece with a scoop of ice cream, if desired. Cover and chill any leftover tart for up to 2 days. Makes 8 to 10 servings.

Nutrition facts per serving: 616 cal., 34 g total fat (9 g sat. fat), 100 mg chol., 340 mg sodium, 74 g carbo., 1 g fiber, 8 g pro. Daily Value: 10% vit. A, 7% calcium, 25% iron.

Use a small plastic bag to drizzle melted chocolate over each wedge of the tart.

Pastry for Single-Crust Tart

USE THIS PASTRY FOR THE ULTIMATE NUT AND CHOCOLATE CHIP TART OR ANY SINGLE-CRUST 9-INCH PIE OR 11-INCH TART.

*1¼ cups all-purpose flour
¼ teaspoon salt
⅓ cup shortening or butter
3 to 4 tablespoons cold water*

In a bowl stir together flour and salt. Cut in shortening or butter till pieces are size of small peas. Sprinkle 1 tablespoon of water over part of the mixture; gently toss with a fork. Push to side of bowl. Repeat till all is moistened. Form dough into a ball. Use immediately or cover and chill till needed.

Nutrition facts per ⅛ pastry recipe: 141 cal., 9 g total fat (2 g sat. fat), 0 mg chol., 67 mg sodium, 14 g carbo., 0 g fiber, 2 g pro. Daily Value: 0% vit. A, 0% vit. C, 0% calcium, 5% iron.

Chocolate-Hazelnut Cookie Torte

To save time, bake the large cookies and wedges up to a month ahead; place them in a freezer container and freeze. Thaw before using. Or, store the cookies and wedges, covered, for up to 2 days at room temperature.

2 cups shelled whole hazelnuts
or almonds
⅔ cup sugar
1 cup all-purpose flour
¾ cup butter, cut in pieces
½ teaspoon salt
1 egg yolk
Sugar
1 cup whipping cream
1 tablespoon sugar
1 teaspoon vanilla
1 recipe Chocolate Mousse
(see recipe, opposite page)
2 cups sliced strawberries
2 to 3 ounces semisweet chocolate, chopped
1 teaspoon shortening
Whole strawberries (optional)

Chill two medium mixing bowls and the beaters of an electric mixer.

Place hazelnuts or almonds on a baking sheet in a single layer. Toast in a 350° oven for 8 to 10 minutes, watching carefully and stirring so they don't burn. Cool. In a food processor bowl* (see blender note, opposite page), cover and process toasted nuts and the ⅔ cup sugar till nuts are finely ground (do not overprocess). Add flour, butter, and salt. Process till combined. Add egg yolk. Process till thoroughly combined. Divide dough into four equal balls. Cover and chill two balls till needed.

◆ Chocolate Hazelnut Cookie Torte

Grease and lightly flour two baking sheets; place each sheet on a towel to prevent slipping while rolling dough. On each baking sheet, draw an 8-inch round with your finger using an 8-inch cake pan as a guide. On one of the prepared baking sheets, roll one portion of the dough to fit the circle, trimming edges of dough with a knife to make an even circle. Repeat with another portion of dough on the second baking sheet. Score one dough round into 8 to 12 wedges, keeping circle intact. Sprinkle both rounds with sugar.

Bake the dough rounds in a 375° oven for 10 to 12 minutes or till browned around the edges. Cool the cookies on baking sheets for 5 minutes. Cut the warm, scored cookie into wedges. Carefully transfer cookie and wedges to a wire rack; cool completely. Allow baking

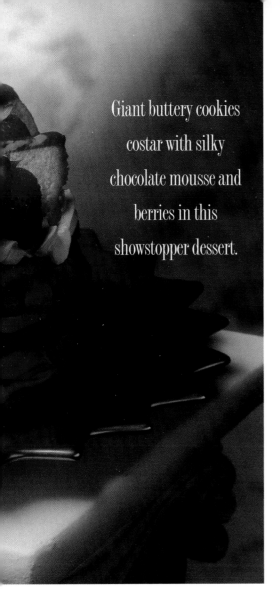

Use one of the chilled mixing bowls to prepare Chocolate Mousse; chill (for no more than 2 hours). In another chilled mixing bowl, beat whipping cream, the 1 tablespoon sugar, and vanilla on medium speed just till stiff peaks form. Spoon whipped cream into a pastry bag fitted with a large star tip.

To assemble torte, place a whole cookie on a serving platter. Spread with half of the Chocolate Mousse and top with half of the sliced strawberries. Place another cookie atop. Repeat with remaining Chocolate Mousse and sliced strawberries. Top with the remaining whole cookie.

Pipe large dollops of the sweetened whipped cream atop torte, covering the whole top. Cover and chill about 2 hours to soften the cookies.

Just before serving, place the chocolate (use the 3 ounces if also dipping berries) and shortening in a heavy small saucepan over low heat, stirring constantly till it is partially melted. Immediately remove from the heat and stir till smooth. Dip one long side of each cookie wedge into melted chocolate mixture (see photo, above right). Set aside on waxed paper till chocolate is set. If desired, dip whole strawberries in remaining melted chocolate. (If your saucepan is not small, you may need additional chocolate to dip.)

Arrange chocolate-dipped cookie wedges atop the sweetened whipped cream, placing chocolate-dipped edges up and tilting slightly in a pinwheel pattern. Pipe a large star of whipped cream in the center where the cookie wedges meet. If using chocolate-dipped strawberries, place between wedges and on top

Brush off any loose cookie crumbs before dipping the cookie wedge into the warm chocolate.

of the whipped cream star in the center. Serve immediately. With a serrated knife, cut into wedges. Serves 12.

*Blender method: In a blender container place half of the nuts. Cover and blend till finely ground. Transfer nuts to a mixing bowl; repeat with remaining nuts. In a mixing bowl beat butter and sugar till combined. Beat in egg yolk. Beat in ground nuts and half of the flour. Beat or stir in remaining flour. Continue as directed.

Chocolate Mousse: In a chilled mixing bowl combine ¼ cup *sugar* and 3 tablespoons *unsweetened cocoa powder*. Add 1½ cups *whipping cream*. Beat with the chilled beaters of an electric mixer on medium speed just till stiff peaks form. Chill till needed. Makes 3 cups.

Nutrition facts per serving: 536 cal., 45 g total fat (21 g sat. fat), 117 mg chol., 226 mg sodium, 34 g carbo., 3 g fiber, 6 g pro. Daily Value: 35% vit. A, 24% vit. C, 7% calcium, 10% iron.

sheets to cool completely. Grease and flour baking sheets again. Repeat shaping and baking the remaining two portions of dough except do not score either portion.

(To make ahead, layer the cookies, with waxed paper between each, in a covered storage container. Keep the cookies at room temperature for 2 days or freeze for up to 1 month. If frozen, thaw the cookies before using.)

Mocha Java Ice-Cream Bombe

LOOK FOR LADYFINGERS IN THE COOKIE AISLE OR REFRIGERATOR CASE IN YOUR LOCAL GROCERY STORE. OR, TRY A BAKERY OR AN ITALIAN FOODS SHOP. BRUSHING THEM WITH THE COFFEE MIXTURE ADDS A RICHER FLAVOR AND A SOFT CARAMEL COLOR.

*¼ cup hot strong coffee
(optional)
1 tablespoon coffee liqueur (optional)
1 teaspoon sugar (optional)
18 to 20 ladyfingers, split in half
horizontally
1 8-ounce package cream cheese,
softened
¼ cup sugar
1 teaspoon vanilla
1½ cups vanilla ice cream
½ cup miniature semisweet
chocolate pieces
1 pint coffee ice cream
1 recipe Coffee-Hot Fudge
Sauce (see recipe, right) or 1½ cups fudge
ice cream topping (optional)*

Chill two small mixing bowls. Line a 5-cup round-bottomed bowl or mold with plastic wrap; let edges of wrap hang over sides of bowl or mold.

If desired, in a bowl mix hot coffee, coffee liqueur, and the 1 teaspoon sugar; stir to dissolve sugar. Brush rounded sides of ladyfingers with coffee mixture.

Line the bottom and sides of the bowl or mold with ladyfingers, placing the rounded side outward. Fill any gaps with ladyfinger trimmings so that the lining is solid. Drizzle with any remaining coffee mixture, if using. Reserve remaining ladyfingers. Cover and chill the lined bowl or mold till needed.

Use a flexible metal spatula or spoon to spread the cream cheese mixture over the ladyfingers in the bowl.

In a medium mixing bowl beat cream cheese, the ¼ cup sugar, and vanilla with an electric mixer on medium speed till fluffy; set aside.

In a chilled mixing bowl, stir vanilla ice cream, pressing it against the side of the bowl with a spoon, just till softened (do not let the ice cream get too soft).

Immediately fold the softened vanilla ice cream and chocolate pieces into the cream cheese mixture; cover and freeze for 3 to 4 hours or till stiff, stirring mixture occasionally so chips don't sink. Spread cream cheese mixture over the ladyfingers in the bowl or mold, spreading up the sides, to make a lining (see photo, above). Cover with heavy foil and freeze for 2 to 4 hours or till firm.

Soften coffee ice cream as directed for the vanilla ice cream. Spoon atop the cream cheese mixture, spreading smoothly. Cover surface of the bombe completely with the remaining ladyfingers. Fold excess plastic wrap over the surface. Cover tightly with heavy foil. Freeze till firm or for up to 1 month.

To serve, remove foil and invert bombe onto a serving platter; remove bowl or mold and plastic wrap. Let stand

at room temperature for 20 to 30 minutes to soften slightly before cutting.

Meanwhile, in a small saucepan heat and stir the Coffee-Hot Fudge Sauce or fudge ice-cream topping. Cut the bombe into wedges and transfer to dessert plates. Drizzle each wedge with some of the sauce, if desired; pass any remaining sauce. Makes 8 to 10 servings.

Nutrition facts per serving without sauce: 322 cal., 20 g total fat (10 g sat. fat), 83 mg chol., 162 mg sodium, 34 g carbo., 0 g fiber, 6 g pro. Daily Value: 18% vit. A, 0% vit. C, 8% calcium, 5% iron.

Coffee-Hot Fudge Sauce

SERVE WITH THE MOCHA JAVA ICE-CREAM BOMBE, THEN ENJOY ANY LEFTOVERS SPOONED OVER PLAIN ICE CREAM.

*¾ cup miniature semisweet
chocolate pieces
¼ cup butter
⅔ cup sugar
4 teaspoons instant coffee crystals
1 5-ounce can evaporated milk*

Place the chocolate and butter in a small heavy saucepan over very low heat, stirring constantly till smooth. Add the sugar and coffee crystals. Gradually stir in the evaporated milk. Bring to boiling; reduce heat. Boil gently over low heat for 8 minutes, stirring frequently. Remove from heat. Makes 1½ cups.

Nutrition facts per tablespoon: 71 cal., 3 g fat (1 g sat. fat), 7 mg chol., 29 mg sodium, 10 g carbo., 0 g fiber. Daily Value: 2% vit. A, 0% vit. C, 2% calcium, 0% iron.

◆ Mocha Java Ice Cream Bombe

You'll melt hearts with this chocolate and coffee ice-cream dream.
Busy romantics can make it up to a month ahead.

Chocolate takes on a whole new meaning
with this triple white chocolate and raspberry cake.
One forkful and you'll be smitten.

White Chocolate Fantasy Cake

FOR DIRECTIONS ON HOW TO MAKE THE WHITE CHOCOLATE CURLS THAT COVER THIS SPECTACULAR CAKE, SEE THE OPPOSITE PAGE.

4 egg whites
1¾ cups all-purpose flour
1 tablespoon finely shredded lemon peel
2 teaspoons baking powder
¼ teaspoon salt
3 ounces white baking bar, chopped
¾ cup half-and-half, light cream, or milk
⅓ cup margarine or butter
1 cup sugar
1 teaspoon vanilla
4 egg yolks
1 cup fresh raspberries or sliced strawberries
3 tablespoons raspberry liqueur (optional)
1 recipe White Chocolate Frosting (see recipe, opposite page)
⅓ cup seedless raspberry jam
1 recipe White Chocolate Curls (optional) (see recipe, opposite page)
½ cup fresh raspberries or sliced strawberries (optional)
Powdered sugar (optional)

In a medium mixing bowl let egg whites stand at room temperature for 30 minutes. In a small mixing bowl stir together flour, lemon peel, baking powder, and salt. Set flour mixture aside.

Melt the 3 ounces white baking bar with ¼ cup of the half-and-half, light cream, or milk in a small heavy saucepan over very low heat, stirring constantly till

◆ White Chocolate Fantasy Cake

baking bar starts to melt. Immediately remove from heat and stir till baking bar is completely melted and smooth. Stir in remaining half-and-half, light cream, or milk; cool.

In a large mixing bowl beat the margarine or butter with an electric mixer on medium to high speed about 30 seconds or till softened. Add sugar and vanilla; beat till combined. Add the egg yolks, one at a time, beating till combined. Alternately add the flour mixture and the white baking bar mixture, beating on low to medium speed after each addition just till combined.

Wash beaters. In a medium mixing bowl beat the egg whites with an electric mixer on high speed till stiff peaks form. Gently fold the egg whites into the batter. Spread batter into 2 greased and lightly floured 8x1½-inch round baking pans.

Bake in a 350° oven for 25 to 30 minutes or till a wooden toothpick inserted near the center of cakes comes out clean. Cool cakes in pans on wire racks for 10 minutes. Remove from pans. Cool cakes completely on racks.

In a small bowl combine the 1 cup berries and raspberry liqueur, if using. Set aside till needed.

Prepare the White Chocolate Frosting. To assemble cake, place one cake layer on a cake plate. Drain liqueur from berries, if using, and drizzle liqueur over cake layer on plate. Stir jam to soften. Spread jam over cake layer. Top with one-third of the White Chocolate Frosting. Spoon the 1 cup berries atop.

Top the berries with remaining cake layer. Frost top and sides with the

Gradually add the melted white chocolate to the whipped cream, beating just till peaks form.

remaining frosting. Gently place the White Chocolate Curls on the frosting on top of cake or all over top and sides of the cake (as shown on page 28). At this point, you can carefully cover the cake loosely with plastic wrap and chill for up to 24 hours. Just before serving, sprinkle cake with the ½ cup berries and sift powdered sugar lightly over cake, if desired. Makes 10 servings.

White Chocolate Curls: Carefully draw a vegetable peeler across the broad surface of two or three 2-ounce *white baking bars* (or a 4- to 6-ounce chunk of white baking bar). This works best if baking bar is at warm room temperature (see photo, opposite page). Use immediately or carefully place on paper towels in a covered storage container in a single layer. Store at room temperature or chill.

Nutrition facts per serving: 532 cal., 29 g total fat (15 g sat. fat), 141 mg chol., 193 mg sodium, 62 g carbo., 1 g fiber, 7 g pro. Daily Value: 38% vit. A, 7% vit. C, 9% calcium, 9% iron.

White Chocolate Frosting

USE THIS FLUFFY FROSTING FOR THE WHITE CHOCOLATE FANTASY CAKE. FIX IT JUST BEFORE FROSTING THE CAKE.

4 ounces white baking bar, chopped
1½ cups whipping cream
1 tablespoon cold water
½ teaspoon unflavored gelatin
3 tablespoons sugar

Chill a medium mixing bowl and the beaters of an electric mixer.

Place the white baking bar and ¼ cup of the whipping cream in a small heavy saucepan over very low heat, stirring constantly till baking bar starts to melt. Immediately remove from heat and stir till smooth. Cool completely.

In a 1-cup glass measure combine the cold water and unflavored gelatin. Let stand for 2 minutes. Place cup in saucepan of boiling water. Heat and stir till gelatin is completely dissolved.

In the chilled mixing bowl beat the remaining 1¼ cups whipping cream and sugar with the chilled beaters on medium speed while gradually drizzling gelatin over the whipping cream mixture. Beat till soft peaks form. Continue beating, gradually adding cooled baking bar mixture till stiff peaks form (see photo, above left). Do not overbeat. Use immediately to frost cake. Makes about 2½ cups frosting.

Chocolate Hearts with Honey-Caramel Sauce

THESE RICH, CREAMY HEARTS TASTE LUSCIOUS, BUT FOR A REAL TREAT, SERVE THEM WITH HONEY-CARAMEL SAUCE, WHIPPED CREAM, AND CANDIED ORANGE PEEL. THE HEARTS CAN BE MADE AND FROZEN UP TO ONE MONTH AHEAD OF SERVING.

8 ounces bittersweet or semisweet
chocolate, chopped
2 ounces unsweetened chocolate, chopped
1 cup whipping cream
3 slightly beaten egg yolks
⅓ cup milk
¼ cup sugar
2 tablespoons coffee or orange liqueur
¾ teaspoon ground cinnamon
Unsweetened cocoa powder (optional)
1 recipe Honey-Caramel
Sauce (optional) (see recipe, right)
Whipped Cream (optional)
1 recipe Candied Orange Peel (optional)
(see recipe, right)

Chill a medium mixing bowl and the beaters of an electric mixer.

Place chocolate in a medium heavy saucepan over low heat, stirring constantly till partially melted; immediately remove from heat and stir till smooth. Cool slightly.

In the chilled mixing bowl beat whipping cream with the chilled beaters on medium speed till stiff peaks form. Cover; chill till needed.

In a heavy small saucepan stir together egg yolks, milk, and sugar. Bring to a gentle boil over low heat, stirring constantly. Reduce heat. Cook and stir for

For a finishing touch, sprinkle cocoa powder over each heart, using paper strips to make a lattice pattern.

2 minutes. Remove from heat and pour mixture into a medium mixing bowl; add liqueur and cinnamon. Stir to combine. Add the melted chocolate, 2 tablespoons at a time, to the hot mixture, beating with an electric mixer on low speed till combined (mixture will be thick). Add ½ cup of the whipped cream and continue beating on low speed till smooth. Gently fold in the remaining whipped cream.

Line 6 individual heart-shaped pans (about 3 inches in diameter) or 6-ounce custard cups with plastic wrap, allowing edges to hang over sides. Spoon chocolate mixture evenly into pans. Cover with heavy foil; freeze till firm (about 4 hours) or for up to 1 month.

Before serving, remove pans or cups from freezer. Invert onto a baking sheet. Remove plastic wrap. Smooth tops of desserts with a knife that has been dipped in hot water. Let desserts stand for 15 minutes at room temperature.

If desired, for the cocoa design, cut several ¼-inch-wide strips of paper, making each strip slightly longer than one of the heart-shaped or round desserts. Place the strips atop one of the desserts in a lattice design. Sift cocoa atop (see photo, left). Carefully remove strips. Repeat with the remaining desserts.

To serve, spoon Honey-Caramel Sauce atop 6 dessert plates, if desired. With a spatula, transfer the desserts to the dessert plates, placing them atop sauce. Dollop with whipped cream and top with Candied Orange Peel, if desired. Serve immediately. Makes 6 desserts.

Honey-Caramel Sauce: In a small heavy saucepan cook and stir ⅓ cup *honey* over medium-high heat till bubbly and foamy. Reduce heat to medium. Continue to cook and stir till foam is dark golden brown (the color of a penny). This should take about 6 minutes. Remove from heat and stir in ¾ cup *whipping cream*. Return to heat. Cook and stir about 2 minutes or till slightly thickened. Cover surface with plastic wrap. Cool. Makes about 1 cup.

Candied Orange Peel: With a vegetable peeler or small knife, cut strips of peel from 1 large *orange,* leaving the white pith behind. Use the rest of the orange for another purpose. Cut the strips of orange peel into thin julienne strips (about ⅛ inch wide).

Place peel in a small pan of boiling water for 2 minutes; drain. Remove peel. In same pan combine ½ cup *water* and ¼ cup *sugar.* Bring to boiling, stirring till

◆ Chocolate Hearts with Honey Caramel Sauce

Woo true chocolate loyalists with valentine hearts of creamy chocolate pâté scented with orange.

sugar is dissolved. Reduce heat. Add peel. Simmer, uncovered, 12 to 15 minutes or till the peel is transparent; drain.

With a fork, transfer peel to a sheet of buttered foil; cool thoroughly. Use immediately or transfer to a tightly covered storage container and store in a cool, dry place for up to 1 week.

Nutrition facts per Chocolate Heart: 445 cal., 34 g fat (20 g sat. fat), 162 mg chol., 27 mg sodium, 37 g carbo., 3 g fiber, 6 g pro. Daily Value: 34% vit. A, 16% iron.

CHOCOLATE LOVER'S HANDBOOK

SHOPPING FOR CHOCOLATE

Browsing through the chocolate section in grocery stores, candy shops, and gourmet shops will show you that there are many types and brands of chocolate available. If your recipe specifies a type of chocolate, such as semisweet, you're best off purchasing that type.

Even within types of chocolate, the flavor, sweetness, and color can vary from one manufacturer to another. Try several different brands and settle on the one you like best. Prices vary too; usually the imported chocolates and cocoas cost the most.

To check the quality of a chocolate, look for a glossy appearance and a chocolaty aroma. The chocolate should break with a snap. Also, it should melt on your tongue without waxiness or graininess.

Unsweetened chocolate has no sugar added, resulting in a strong, bitter flavor. Sometimes called baking or bitter chocolate, it is almost exclusively used for baking and cooking.

Unsweetened cocoa powder is pure chocolate with most of the cocoa butter removed. Some cocoa powders labeled as Dutch-process or European-style have been treated to neutralize the naturally occurring acids. This gives the cocoa powder a more mellow flavor and a darker, redder color.

Semisweet chocolate is pure chocolate with added cocoa butter and sugar. It is also referred to as bittersweet chocolate. Bittersweet chocolate is usually darker and less sweet than chocolate labeled as semisweet. However, there are no legal specifications for either term. Some European bittersweet chocolates are labeled as dark chocolate. Use dark chocolate, semisweet chocolate, and bittersweet chocolate interchangeably in recipes.

Milk chocolate is pure chocolate with added cocoa butter, sugar, and milk or cream. It's similar to semisweet and bittersweet chocolates, but generally contains less pure chocolate and added milk solids. Milk chocolate has a creamier texture, lighter color, and milder flavor than semisweet or bittersweet chocolates.

White baking bars and pieces and vanilla-flavored candy coatings are often referred to as white chocolate. However, this is a misnomer. Because these products lack pure chocolate, they can't legally be labeled as chocolate in the United States. Some of these products do contain cocoa butter for extra flavor.

STORAGE

Keep chocolate in tightly covered containers or sealed plastic bags in a cool, dry place. Ideal storage conditions are between 60° and 78°, with less than 50% relative humidity.

MELTING CHOCOLATE

When melting chocolate, make sure all of your equipment is completely dry. Any moisture on the utensils or in the container may cause the chocolate to stiffen. If this happens, stir in ½ to 1 teaspoon of melted shortening for every ounce of chocolate.

Before melting, chop chocolate bars and squares into smaller pieces. Always stir chocolate, melting over low heat to avoid scorching.

Some candy recipes call for tempering chocolate before using, which enables the chocolate to stay glossy and firm at room temperature without the addition of wax or refrigeration. If tempering is desired, refer to a candy-making book.

Choose from the following methods for melting chocolate, white baking bars, and candy coatings. Also use one of these methods when a recipe calls for melting chocolate with another ingredient, such as butter or whipping cream.

Direct heat: Place the chocolate in a heavy saucepan over low heat, stirring constantly till partially melted. Immediately remove the chocolate from the heat and stir till smooth.

Double boiler: Place water in the bottom pan of a double boiler so that the top of the water is ½ inch below the upper pan. Place the chocolate in the upper pan. Then place the double boiler over low heat. Stir the chocolate constantly till it is melted. The water in the bottom of the double boiler should not come to boiling.

Microwave oven: Place up to 12 ounces of chopped chocolate or chocolate pieces in a microwave-safe bowl or glass measure. Micro-cook, uncovered, on 100% power (high) for 1½ to 2 minutes or till soft enough to stir smooth. Stir every minute during heating.

Winter Wonderful Suppers

BY LISA HOLDERNESS

Come in from the blustery days of winter and cozy up to a hearty, soul-soothing dinner. Choose from chunky chowders and stews, simmering one-pot dinners, and oven-baked dishes—each guaranteed to satisfy.

Deep-Dish Steak and Vegetable Pie

AS PICTURED AT RIGHT, YOU CAN SHAPE THE DOUGH SCRAPS INTO INTERESTING DESIGNS, SUCH AS MINI VEGETABLES, TO DECORATE THE TOP CRUST.

1 recipe Whole Wheat Pastry
(see recipe, page 34)
1½ pounds boneless beef sirloin steak,
trimmed and cut into ¾-inch pieces
2 tablespoons cooking oil
½ cup beef broth
¼ cup dry white wine or beef broth
2 cloves garlic, minced
1¼ teaspoon dried marjoram, crushed
1 bay leaf
¼ teaspoon salt
¼ teaspoon pepper

◆ Deep-Dish Steak and Vegetable Pie

2 medium parsnips, peeled and
cut into ½-inch pieces
2 tablespoons margarine or butter
1 medium red or green sweet pepper, cut
into ½-inch pieces
2 small carrots, thinly sliced

1 onion, chopped (½ cup)
⅓ cup all-purpose flour
1 cup half-and-half or light cream
¾ cup loose-pack frozen peas
1 beaten egg
continued on page 34

continued from page 33

Prepare the Whole Wheat Pastry and set aside.

In a large skillet brown meat, half at a time, in oil. Drain fat, if needed. Return all of the meat to the skillet. Stir in broth, wine, garlic, marjoram, bay leaf, salt, and pepper. Bring to boiling. Add parsnips. Reduce heat; simmer, covered, for 10 minutes.

Meanwhile, in a large saucepan melt margarine or butter. Add sweet pepper, carrot, and onion. Cook and stir till onion is tender but not brown. Stir in flour. Add half-and-half or cream; cook and stir till thickened and bubbly. Stir in the meat mixture; add the peas. Heat through. Transfer the mixture to a 2-quart casserole; set aside.

On lightly floured surface, roll the Whole Wheat Pastry into a circle 2 inches larger than the diameter of the top of casserole and about ¼ inch thick. Prick pastry a few times with a fork. Center pastry over top of casserole. Trim pastry 1 inch beyond edge of the casserole. Turn pastry edge under and press gently to adhere to edge of casserole. If desired, use pastry scraps to make small vegetable decorations. Brush crust with beaten egg. If using pastry decorations, place atop crust and brush again with egg.

Bake in a 400° oven for 25 to 30 minutes or till crust is golden brown. Makes 6 main-dish servings.

Whole Wheat Pastry: In a mixing bowl stir together ¾ cup *all-purpose flour,* ½ cup *whole wheat flour,* and ¼ teaspoon *salt.* Cut in ½ cup *butter* till pieces are the size of small peas. Sprinkle 1 tablespoon *cold water* over part of the mixture; gently toss with a fork. Push to side of bowl. Repeat till all is moistened,

◆ Roasted Rosemary Chicken with Garlic Mashed Potatoes

using 1 to 2 tablespoons additional *cold water.* Form dough into a ball. Cover with plastic wrap till needed.

Nutrition facts per serving: 627 cal., 37 g total fat (17 g sat. fat), 165 mg chol., 570 mg sodium, 38 g carbo., 6 g fiber, 34 g pro. Daily Value: 96% vit. A, 48% vit. C, 8% calcium, 35% iron.

Roasted Rosemary Chicken with Garlic Mashed Potatoes

FOR MORE FRESH LEMON FLAVOR, QUARTER A LEMON RIND, SQUEEZE OUT THE JUICE, AND PLACE IT IN THE CAVITY OF THE CHICKEN BEFORE ROASTING.

10 cloves garlic
2 tablespoons snipped fresh rosemary or
2 teaspoons dried rosemary, crushed
2 tablespoons olive oil
2 tablespoons lemon juice

¼ teaspoon pepper
⅛ teaspoon salt
1 2½- to 3½-pound whole broiler-
fryer chicken
1½ cups peeled and trimmed baby
carrots (6 ounces)
1 large onion, cut into wedges
1 medium red and/or green sweet pepper,
cut into 1-inch strips
1 recipe Garlic Mashed Potatoes
1 recipe Homemade Gravy

In a small saucepan cook garlic cloves and rosemary in hot olive oil over low heat for 8 to 10 minutes or till garlic is soft (watch garlic closely to avoid burning). Remove garlic with a slotted spoon and set aside, reserving the oil mixture. Let oil mixture cool. Stir lemon juice, pepper, and salt into oil.

Wash the chicken thoroughly; pat dry with paper towels. Season body cavity with salt. Pull the neck skin to the back and fasten with a small skewer. If a band of skin crosses the tail, tuck the drumsticks under the band. If there is no band, tie the drumsticks securely to the tail. Twist wing tips under the back.

Place the chicken, breast side up, on a rack in a shallow roasting pan. Cut five slits randomly in the chicken skin, large enough to insert a garlic clove under the skin. Insert five garlic cloves. Reserve remaining garlic for Garlic Mashed Potatoes. Brush chicken with some of the olive oil mixture. Insert meat thermometer into the center of one of the inside thigh muscles. The bulb should not touch the bone.

Roast in a 375° oven for 1¼ to 1¾ hours or till thermometer registers 180° and drumsticks move easily in their sockets, brushing occasionally with drippings. When the bird is two-thirds done, cut the band of skin or string between the drumsticks so thighs will cook evenly. When chicken is done, remove it from the oven; cover with foil till carving time. Reserve pan drippings for the Homemade Gravy.

Meanwhile, in a 9x9x2-inch baking pan, toss carrots and onion with remaining olive oil mixture. Roast, uncovered, alongside chicken till vegetables are tender and brown on the edges. Allow about 45 minutes total cooking time for vegetables, adding sweet pepper after 30 minutes and stirring twice. Prepare Homemade Gravy.

Carve chicken and serve with the roasted vegetables, Garlic Mashed Potatoes, and Homemade Gravy. Makes 4 main-dish servings.

Garlic Mashed Potatoes: Finely chop the 5 reserved garlic cloves; set aside. In a large saucepan cook 5 unpeeled medium *potatoes* (about 1½ pounds), quartered, in boiling water for 20 to 25 minutes or till tender; drain.

Mash unpeeled potatoes with a potato masher or beat smooth with an electric mixer on low speed. Add the reserved finely chopped garlic, 1 tablespoon *olive oil*, ½ teaspoon *salt*, and ¼ to ½ teaspoon *pepper*. Gradually beat in enough *milk* (¼ to ⅓ cup) to make light and fluffy. Makes 4 side-dish servings.

Homemade Gravy: Pour pan drippings from chicken roasting pan into a 2-cup glass measure. Also scrape the browned bits from pan into the cup. Skim and reserve fat from pan drippings.

Place 2 tablespoons of reserved fat in a medium saucepan (discard remaining fat). Stir in 2 tablespoons *all-purpose flour*. Add enough *chicken broth* to drippings in the measuring cup to equal 1 cup. Add chicken broth mixture all at once to flour mixture. Cook and stir over medium heat till thickened and bubbly. Cook and stir for 1 minute more. Season to taste with salt and pepper. Makes 1 cup gravy.

Nutrition facts per serving with Garlic Mashed Potatoes and Homemade Gravy: 671 cal., 33 g total fat (8 g sat. fat), 105 mg chol., 606 mg sodium, 55 g carbo., 3 g fiber, 38 g pro. Daily Value: 28% vit. A, 108% vit. C, 8% calcium, 39% iron.

Lamb and Squash Stew

1¼ pounds boneless lean lamb,
cut into 1-inch pieces
2 teaspoons cooking oil
2 14½-ounce cans beef broth
½ cup dry red wine
¼ cup quick-cooking tapioca
2 teaspoons dried thyme, crushed
2 bay leaves
¼ teaspoon salt
¼ teaspoon pepper
1 pound butternut squash, peeled and
cut into chunks
2 medium potatoes (12 ounces), cut
lengthwise into thin wedges
½ of a 16-ounce package frozen whole
small onions
1 10-ounce package frozen lima beans
1 recipe Buttermilk-Chive Biscuits
(optional) (see recipe, right)

In a large skillet cook the lamb, half at a time, in hot oil till brown on all sides; drain. In a 4-, 5-, or 6-quart electric slow crockery cooker* stir together beef broth, red wine, tapioca, thyme, bay leaves, salt, and pepper. Add lamb, squash, potatoes, and onions. Cover; cook on low-heat setting for 8 hours or on high-heat setting for 4 hours.

Rinse lima beans in strainer under cold water to thaw slightly; drain. Remove bay leaves from stew; stir in lima beans. If stew was cooked on low-heat, turn cooker to high-heat setting. Cover; cook 45 to 60 minutes more or till meat and vegetables are tender. Meanwhile, prepare Buttermilk-Chive Biscuits, if desired. Makes 6 main-dish servings.

*Note: This recipe was tested only in cookers with heating elements that wrap around the sides of the pot. These pots have very low wattages and the elements remain on continuously during cooking. They are identified by the heat control with two fixed settings: Low and High.

Nutrition facts per serving: 352 cal., 13 g total fat (5 g sat. fat), 53 mg chol., 606 mg sodium, 37 g carbo., 6 g fiber, 21 g pro. Daily Value: 45% vit. A, 34% vit. C, 6% calcium, 27% iron.

Buttermilk-Chive Biscuits

⅔ cup all-purpose flour
1 tablespoon snipped chives
¾ teaspoon baking powder
¼ teaspoon baking soda
⅛ teaspoon salt
⅛ teaspoon pepper
¼ cup buttermilk or sour milk
2 tablespoons cooking oil

In a bowl mix flour, chives, baking powder, baking soda, salt, and pepper. Stir together buttermilk or sour milk and oil; pour into flour mixture. Stir with a fork till combined. Drop onto a greased baking sheet in 6 mounds. Bake in a 450° oven for 8 to 10 minutes or till golden. Serve warm. Makes 6 biscuits.

Nutrition facts per biscuit: 95 cal., 5 g total fat (1 g sat. fat), 0 mg chol., 92 mg sodium, 11 g carbo., 0 g fiber, 2 g pro. Daily Value: 0% vit. A, 0% vit. C, 1% calcium, 4% iron.

Seafood-Fennel Chowder

¾ pound fresh or frozen salmon steak
⅓ pound fresh or frozen bay scallops
8 fresh or frozen large shrimp
1 medium fennel bulb with tops
½ cup sliced green onion
2 tablespoons margarine or butter
3 tablespoons all-purpose flour
2 cups milk
2 cups half-and-half or light cream
1½ teaspoons instant chicken
bouillon granules
¼ teaspoon seafood seasoning or
seasoned salt
⅛ teaspoon ground red pepper
1 10-ounce package frozen whole
kernel corn
Paprika (optional)

Thaw the salmon, scallops, and shrimp, if frozen. Cut salmon into ½-inch pieces, discarding skin and bones; set aside. Peel and devein shrimp, leaving tails intact, if desired.

Remove green tops from fennel; cut into sprigs and reserve. Cut bulb into wedges; remove core and discard. Chop fennel wedges (you should have about 1¼ cups). In a large saucepan cook fennel and green onion in margarine or butter till tender. Stir in flour. Stir in milk, cream, bouillon granules, seafood seasoning, and ground red pepper. Cook and stir till thickened and bubbly. Stir in frozen corn. Cook and stir for 2 minutes. Stir in salmon, scallops, and shrimp; cook and stir for 2 minutes more or till shrimp turn pink and salmon flakes easily with a fork.

Ladle soup into bowls and top with fennel tops. Sprinkle with paprika. Makes 4 main-dish servings.

Nutrition facts per serving: 469 cal., 23 g total fat (11 g sat. fat), 117 mg chol., 760 mg sodium, 33 g carbo., 2 g fiber, 33 g pro. Daily Value: 33% vit. A, 18% vit. C, 28% calcium, 17% iron.

◆ Lamb and Squash Stew with Buttermilk Chive Biscuits, bottom, and Seafood Fennel Chowder, top

◆ Country-Style Cassoulet

Country-Style Cassoulet

1 pound assorted dry beans (2½ cups)
4½ cups cold water
1 tablespoon instant beef bouillon granules
Dash ground cloves
4 bay leaves
1 5-pound domestic duckling or one
3- to 3½-pound broiler-fryer chicken,
cut up and skinned, if desired
1 to 2 tablespoons cooking oil (optional)
¾ pound boneless lean pork, cut into
bite-size pieces

¾ pound boneless lean lamb or beef,
cut into bite-size pieces
2 large onions, cut into thin wedges
2 medium carrots, sliced (1 cup)
3 cloves garlic, minced
1¼ cups dry white wine
1 14½-ounce can tomatoes, cut up
2 teaspoons dried thyme, crushed
1 teaspoon pepper
¾ cup dry bread crumbs
3 tablespoons margarine or butter, melted
2 tablespoons snipped parsley

In an 8- to 10-quart Dutch oven, combine beans with enough water to cover. Bring to boiling; reduce heat. Simmer for 2 minutes. Remove from heat. Cover; let stand for 1 hour. Drain beans; rinse.

In the same Dutch oven combine drained beans, the 4½ cups cold water, bouillon granules, and cloves. Add bay leaves. Bring to boiling; reduce heat. Simmer, covered, for 1½ hours. Discard bay leaves.

Meanwhile, in a large skillet brown the duckling or chicken, in hot oil (omit oil if duckling or chicken is not skinned) over medium-high heat about 10 minutes or till brown, turning occasionally. Remove duckling or chicken from skillet, reserving drippings in pan.

Cook pork in the reserved drippings for 5 to 6 minutes or till no longer pink; remove pork. In the same skillet cook lamb or beef for 8 to 10 minutes or till brown. Remove meat; drain any fat from the skillet.

In the same skillet cook onions and carrots about 5 minutes or till tender. Add garlic; cook for 30 seconds more. Add pork, lamb, and onion mixture to bean mixture in the Dutch oven; stir to combine.

To the same skillet add ¼ cup of the white wine. Heat and stir to scrape up browned bits in bottom of skillet. Add to Dutch oven along with the remaining 1 cup wine, undrained tomatoes, thyme, and pepper. Arrange duckling or chicken pieces atop. Bring to boiling; reduce heat. Cover and simmer for 1 hour. (At this point, mixture can be cooled, then stored in the refrigerator, covered, for up to 3 days.)

Bake, covered, in a 375° oven for 45 minutes (1 hour, if chilled). Combine bread crumbs, margarine or butter, and parsley. Sprinkle atop cassoulet; bake, uncovered, 15 to 20 minutes more or till crumbs are brown. Makes 10 servings.

Nutrition facts per serving: 591 cal., 31 g total fat (10 g sat. fat), 93 mg chol., 503 mg sodium, 40 g carbo., 4 g fiber, 34 g pro. Daily Value: 45% vit. A, 17% vit. C, 8% calcium, 41% iron.

Kielbasa with Kraut

⅓ cup chopped onion
2 slices bacon, cut up
1 cup beer
1 cup water
2 tablespoons cornstarch
2 tablespoons coarse-grain brown mustard
2 tablespoons molasses
2 teaspoons caraway seed
½ teaspoon ground allspice
¼ teaspoon pepper
1 large rutabaga, peeled and cut
into 1-inch cubes
1 pound fully cooked kielbasa (Polish
sausage), bias-sliced into 2- to
2½-inch pieces
2 medium cooking apples, cored and cut
into 8 wedges each
1 16-ounce can sauerkraut, drained
and rinsed
1 recipe Soft Pretzels (optional)
(see recipe, right)

In a Dutch oven cook onion and bacon till onion is tender but not brown; drain off fat. Stir in beer. In a 2-cup glass measure combine the water, cornstarch, brown mustard, molasses, caraway seed, allspice, and pepper; stir into bacon mixture. Cook and stir till thickened and bubbly. Add rutabaga; cover and cook 15 minutes. Stir in the kielbasa, apples,

◆ Kielbasa and Kraut with Soft Pretzels

and sauerkraut. Cook, covered, 15 to 20 minutes more or till apples are tender. Serve with Soft Pretzels. Serves 6.

Nutrition facts per serving: 375 cal., 24 g total fat (9 g sat. fat), 65 mg chol., 1,167 mg sodium, 26 g carbo., 4 g fiber, 12 g pro. Daily Value: 0% vit. A, 56% vit. C, 7% calcium, 14% iron.

Soft Pretzels: Unroll one package (8) *refrigerated breadsticks* so breadsticks lay flat. Gently pull each breadstick into a 16-inch rope. Shape each rope into a pretzel by crossing one end over the other to form a circle, overlapping about 4 inches from each end. Take one end of

dough in each hand and twist once at point where dough overlaps. Carefully lift each end across to the edge of the circle opposite it. Tuck ends under edges to make pretzel shape. Moisten ends; press to seal. Place on a greased baking sheet. Brush with a mixture of 1 beaten *egg white* and 1 tablespoon *water*. Sprinkle with *poppy seed*. Bake in a 375° oven for 12 to 15 minutes or till golden. Makes 8.

Nutrition facts per pretzel: 103 cal., 2 g total fat (1 g sat. fat), 0 mg chol., 237 mg sodium, 17 g carbo., 0 g fiber, 4 g pro.

Prize Tested Recipes

◆ Teriyaki Potatoes

Teriyaki Potatoes

THESE FLAVORFUL POTATOES LOOK
OVEN-BROWNED, BUT THEY'RE COOKED
IN THE MICROWAVE OVEN.

1½ pounds tiny new potatoes (about 10)
or medium red potatoes (about 5)
1 tablespoon margarine or butter,
cut into pieces
1 tablespoon teriyaki sauce
¼ teaspoon garlic salt
¼ teaspoon Italian seasoning, crushed
Fresh snipped rosemary (optional)

Wash potatoes; scrub thoroughly with
a vegetable brush. Cut tiny new potatoes
into quarters or the medium potatoes
into 1-inch pieces. Place potatoes in 1½-
quart microwave-safe casserole. Add
margarine or butter, teriyaki sauce, garlic
salt, Italian seasoning, dash black pepper,
and dash red pepper. Toss to combine.

Cover; micro-cook on 100% power
(high) 12 to 15 minutes (14 to 16 minutes for low-wattage ovens) or till tender,
stirring twice during cooking. Stir before
serving. Garnish with rosemary and serve
with sour cream, if desired. Makes 5
side-dish servings.

Nutrition facts per serving: 155 cal.,
2 g total fat (0 g sat. fat), 0 mg chol.,
277 mg sodium, 31 g carbo., 1 g fiber, 3
g pro. Daily Value: 2% vit. A, 29% vit.
C, 1% calcium, 15% iron.
$100 WINNER
Karen Winchell,
Fort Collins, Colorado

Ham and Lima Bean Salad

JOANNA'S DELICIOUS TOP-NOTCH SALAD
CAN EASILY BE HALVED FOR SMALLER
FAMILIES.

2 10-ounce package frozen lima beans
2 cups sliced fresh mushrooms
1 cup chopped red onion
½ cup finely chopped fully cooked ham
⅓ cup chopped ripe olives
¼ cup snipped parsley
1 4-ounce jar diced pimiento, drained
⅓ cup tarragon vinegar or
white wine vinegar
¼ cup olive oil or salad oil
2 cloves garlic, minced
½ teaspoon sugar
½ teaspoon salt
½ teaspoon lemon juice
⅛ teaspoon pepper

◆ Ham and Lima Bean Salad

Cook lima beans according to package
directions. Drain. Rinse with cold water;
drain again. In a mixing bowl combine
beans, mushrooms, onion, ham, olives,
parsley, and pimiento. For dressing, in a
screw-top jar combine vinegar, oil, garlic, sugar, salt, lemon juice, and pepper.
Cover; shake to combine. Pour over
bean mixture. Toss to coat. Cover; chill
3 to 24 hours before serving, stirring
once or twice. Serves 8 to 10.

Nutrition facts per serving: 168 cal.,
8 g total fat (1 g sat. fat), 2 mg chol.,
264 mg sodium, 18 g carbo., 6 g fiber, 7
g pro. Daily Value: 25% vit. C, 2% calcium, 13% iron.
$200 WINNER
Joanna Manoogian
San Francisco, California

◆ Bavarian Apple Cheesecake

Bavarian Apple Cheesecake

GOLDEN BAKED APPLE SLICES, CINNA-
MON, AND SUGAR TOP THIS DELICIOUS
CHEESECAKE.

⅓ cup sugar
⅓ cup margarine or butter
1 tablespoon shortening
¼ teaspoon vanilla
1 cup all-purpose flour
⅛ teaspoon salt
*4 cups peeled, cored, and sliced
cooking apples (such as Golden
Delicious or Granny Smith)*
*2 8-ounce packages cream
cheese, softened*
½ cup sugar
½ teaspoon vanilla
2 eggs

⅓ cup sugar
1 teaspoon ground cinnamon
¼ cup sliced almonds

In a medium mixer bowl beat the first
⅓ cup sugar, margarine or butter, shortening, and ¼ teaspoon vanilla on
medium speed of an electric mixer till
combined. Blend in flour and salt till
crumbly. Pat onto the bottom of a
9-inch springform pan. Set aside.

Place apple slices in a single layer in a
shallow baking pan. Cover with foil.
Bake in a 400° oven for 15 minutes.
Meanwhile, for filling, in a large mixer
bowl beat the cream cheese, the ½ cup
sugar, and the ½ teaspoon vanilla with
an electric mixer till fluffy. Add the eggs

all at once, beating on low speed just till
combined. Pour into dough-lined pan.
Arrange warm apple slices atop filling.
Combine the remaining ⅓ cup sugar
and cinnamon. Sprinkle filling with
sugar mixture and the almonds. Bake in
a 400° oven for 40 minutes or till gold-
en. Cool. Remove sides and place cake
on a serving plate. Cover; chill 4 to 24
hours before serving. Makes 12 servings.

Nutrition facts per serving: 293 cal.,
20 g total fat (10 g sat. fat), 42 mg chol.,
195 mg sodium, 27 g carbo., 1 g fiber, 4
g pro. Daily Value: 22% vit. A, 0% vit.
C, 3% calcium, 6% iron.

$200 WINNER
Christine A. Purich
Indianapolis, Indiana

◆ Double Coconut Cream Pie

Double-Coconut Cream Pie

COCONUT FANS WILL ENJOY THIS LUS-
CIOUS PIE WITH CREAM OF COCONUT IN
THE FILLING.

⅓ cup sugar
¼ cup cornstarch
¼ teaspoon salt

2 cups milk
1 8-ounce can cream of coconut (¾ cup)
3 beaten egg yolks
2 tablespoons margarine or butter
1 cup flaked coconut
2 teaspoons vanilla
1 9-inch baked pastry shell
3 egg whites

½ teaspoon vanilla
¼ teaspoon cream of tartar
⅓ cup sugar
2 tablespoons flaked coconut

For filling, in a medium saucepan combine the first ⅓ cup sugar, cornstarch, and salt. Stir in milk and cream of coconut. Cook and stir over medium heat till thickened and bubbly. Cook and stir 2 minutes more. Gradually stir about 1 cup of the hot milk mixture into the beaten egg yolks, stirring constantly. Return all of the mixture to saucepan. Cook and stir till bubbly. Cook and stir 2 minutes more. Remove from heat. Stir in margarine or butter till melted. Stir in the 1 cup coconut and 2 teaspoons vanilla. Pour filling into baked pastry shell.

For meringue, let egg whites stand at room temperature for 30 minutes. In a mixing bowl beat egg whites, ½ teaspoon vanilla, and cream of tartar on medium speed of an electric mixer till soft peaks form (tips curl). Gradually add ⅓ cup sugar, 1 tablespoon at a time, till stiff peaks form. Evenly spread meringue over hot filling; seal to pastry edge. Sprinkle with the 2 tablespoons coconut. Bake in a 350° oven for 15 minutes. Cool for 1 hour on a wire rack. Cover and chill 3 to 6 hours before serving. Serves 8.

Nutrition facts per serving: 561 cal., 38 g total fat (12 g sat. fat), 84 mg chol., 233 mg sodium, 49 g carbo., 1 g fiber, 7 g pro. Daily Value: 19% vit. A, 7% calcium, 10% iron.

$100 WINNER
Teresa Cicchella
Englewood, Florida

March

A World of Flavors

Healthful and Delicious Cooking

Prize Tested Recipes

*Mocha and Cherry Cake, Spicy Shrimp and Noodle Soup,
Smoked Sausage and Bean Soup, Raspberry Mousse Cake*

A World of Flavors

You only have to see the vegetables in a stir-fry or the beans in a tortilla to know that cooks worldwide have been making healthful meals for centuries. Now, you can learn their secrets and sample their recipes for the world's healthiest and tastiest dishes. There's nothing fancy, nothing strange about our collection of international recipes, just good home cooking that's good for you.

BY JULIA MALLOY

The Near and Far East: Temptingly Spicy

Red Pepper Pork And Noodles

YOU CAN BUY RICE STICKS IN THE PASTA SECTION OF SOME SUPERMARKETS OR IN ORIENTAL FOOD SHOPS.

12 ounces boneless lean pork
1 cup chicken broth
2 tablespoons reduced-sodium soy sauce
2 teaspoons cornstarch
5 ounces rice sticks or noodles, angel hair pasta, or vermicelli
2 tablespoons reduced-sodium soy sauce or oyster sauce
2 tablespoons finely chopped fresh lemongrass or ¾ teaspoon finely shredded lemon peel
1½ teaspoons toasted sesame oil
½ to 1 teaspoon crushed red pepper
1 tablespoon cooking oil

2 cloves garlic, minced
8 green onions, bias-sliced into 1-inch lengths
1 medium red, yellow, orange, or green sweet pepper, cut into thin strips
2 ounces pea pods, halved crosswise diagonally (1 cup)
1 medium orange, peeled, cut crosswise into ½-inch-thick slices, and halved
Orange wedges (optional)
Green onions (optional)

Trim fat from pork. Partially freeze meat. Thinly slice across the grain into bite-size strips. Set aside.

For sauce, in a small mixing bowl stir together broth, 2 tablespoons soy sauce, and cornstarch; set aside.

Soak rice sticks for 15 minutes in enough warm water to cover. Drain well. Cut into 2- to 3-inch lengths, if desired. Set aside. (Or, break pasta into 2- to 3-inch lengths; cook according to package directions.)

◆ Red Pepper Pork and Noodles

In another mixing bowl combine pork strips, 2 tablespoons soy sauce or oyster sauce, lemongrass or lemon peel, sesame oil, and crushed red pepper. Cover and let stand for 20 minutes.

Pour cooking oil into a wok or 12-inch skillet. (Add more oil as necessary during cooking.) Preheat over medium-high heat. Stir-fry garlic in hot oil for 15 seconds. Add green onion, pepper strips, and pea pods; stir-fry for 2 minutes or till vegetables are crisp-tender. Remove vegetables from wok.

Add meat mixture to the hot wok. Stir-fry for 2 to 3 minutes or till no pink remains. Push meat to sides of wok. Stir sauce; add to center of wok. Cook and stir till thickened and bubbly. Add

◆ Curried Peas,
Cauliflower, and Potatoes

The scent of citrus and sesame oil accents this simple stir-fry of Japanese rice noodles. Turn up the heat a little or a lot with fiery dried peppers.

soaked rice sticks or cooked pasta and vegetables; stir to coat. Stir in orange slices. Serve immediately. If desired, garnish with orange wedges and green onions. Makes 4 main-dish servings.

Nutrition facts per serving: 253 cal., 11 g total fat (4 g sat. fat), 39 mg chol., 784 mg sodium, 21 g carbo., 2 g fiber, 17 g pro. Daily Value: 20% vit. A, 106% vit. C, 3% calcium, 14% iron.

Curried Cauliflower, Peas, And Potatoes

KEEP GARAM MASALA, THE HOMEMADE INDIAN-STYLE SPICE MIX USED IN THIS RECIPE, ON HAND FOR SEASONING POULTRY, FISH, AND VEGETABLES.

6 to 8 tiny new potatoes, quartered (1 to 1½ pounds)
1 medium onion, chopped (½ cup)
1 tablespoon cooking oil
1 cup water
1 teaspoon Garam Masala (see recipe, right) or curry powder
¾ teaspoon salt
½ teaspoon ground coriander
½ teaspoon ground turmeric
¼ teaspoon ground cumin
⅛ teaspoon crushed red pepper
2 cups cauliflower flowerets
¾ cup frozen peas

In a large skillet cook potatoes and onion in hot cooking oil till the edges start to brown. Add water, Garam

In India, curry powder translates to garam masala, a no-fat blend of spices and peppers. Use it to pique the taste of simple vegetables.

Masala or curry powder, salt, coriander, turmeric, cumin, and crushed red pepper. Bring to boiling; reduce heat. Cover and simmer for 10 minutes.

Add cauliflower; cook about 5 minutes more or till vegetables are tender, stirring occasionally. Add frozen peas; heat through, adding more water, if necessary. Transfer vegetables to a bowl. Makes 4 to 6 side-dish servings.

Garam Masala: In an 8x8x2-inch baking pan combine 2 tablespoons *whole black peppercorns*, 4 teaspoons *cumin seed*, 2 teaspoons *whole cloves*, 1 teaspoon *coriander seed*, 1 teaspoon *whole cardamom seed* (pods removed), and 3 inches broken *stick cinnamon*. Roast in a 350° oven for 15 minutes. In a blender container place roasted spices. Cover tightly; blend till very fine. Cool to room temperature. Store in a covered container in a cool, dry place. Makes ⅓ cup.

Nutrition facts per serving: 238 cal., 4 g total fat (1 g sat. fat), 0 mg chol., 449 mg sodium, 46 g carbo., 4 g fiber, 7 g pro. Daily Value: 2% vit. A, 72% vit. C, 4% calcium, 25% iron.

Serve small individual bowls of Soy Dipping Sauce so guests can dip their own Beef Steamed Dumplings.

The Near and Far East

Beef Steamed Dumplings

STEAMING, A TIMELESS ORIENTAL COOK-
ING TRADITION, KEEPS THE FAT IN THESE
APPETIZER BUNDLES TO A MINIMUM.

2 cups all-purpose flour
½ teaspoon salt
⅔ cup boiling water
¼ cup cold water
2 tablespoons hoisin sauce or
reduced-sodium soy sauce
1 teaspoon cornstarch
1 cup finely chopped bok choy
1 medium carrot, shredded (½ cup)
2 tablespoons thinly sliced green onion
2 tablespoons snipped fresh cilantro
¼ teaspoon salt
¾ pound lean ground beef
1 recipe Soy Dipping Sauce
Fresh cilantro (optional)

For dough, in a medium mixing bowl combine flour, the ½ teaspoon salt, and the boiling water, stirring constantly with a fork. Add the cold water; mix with hands till dough forms a ball. (The dough will be sticky.) Cover and set aside.

For filling, in a medium mixing bowl stir together hoisin or soy sauce and cornstarch. Stir in bok choy, carrot, green onion, cilantro, and the ¼ tea-spoon salt. Add ground beef; mix well.

Bring the dough up and around the filling, allowing a small portion of filling to show at the top. Press the dough firmly around the filling, pleating to fit.

Using about 1 tablespoon for each, shape filling into 30 balls. Set aside.

Divide dough in half. Return one portion to the bowl; cover and set aside. Divide the other portion into 15 balls. On a well-floured surface, roll each dough ball into a 3-inch circle. Place a meatball in the center of each circle. Fold the dough up and around filling, allowing the filling to show at the top. Press dough firmly around filling, pleating to fit (see photograph, above). Gently flatten the bottom of each dumpling. Repeat with remaining dough and filling to make 30 dumplings total.

In a steamer or Dutch oven bring water to boiling. Place dumplings, open side up, on a greased steamer rack so the edges don't touch. (If all the dumplings won't fit on a steamer rack, refrigerate remainder till ready to steam.) Place rack over, but not touching, boiling water. Cover and steam dumplings for 16 to 18 minutes or till no pink remains in meat. Serve warm with Soy Dipping Sauce.

If desired, garnish with cilantro. Makes 30 dumplings.

Soy Dipping Sauce: Combine ¼ cup *rice vinegar or white vinegar* and ¼ cup *reduced-sodium soy sauce*. Sprinkle with 1 teaspoon thinly sliced *green onion*.

Nutrition facts per dumpling: 54 cal., 1 g total fat (1 g sat. fat), 7 mg chol., 201 mg sodium, 7 g carbo., 0 g fiber, 3 g pro. Daily Value: 7% vit. A, 4% vit. C, 0% calcium, 4% iron.

Tandoori-Style Chicken

ROAST CHICKEN MARINATED IN SPICES AND YOGURT IS AN AROMATIC SPECIALTY OF INDIA. IT'S MOIST, DELICIOUS, AND EASY TO MAKE.

1 2½- to 3-pound whole broiler-fryer
chicken
1½ teaspoons ground coriander
¾ teaspoon ground cumin
½ teaspoon salt
½ teaspoon ground cardamom
½ teaspoon pepper
¼ teaspoon ground cinnamon
⅛ teaspoon ground cloves
2 8-ounce cartons plain nonfat yogurt
1 tablespoon paprika
1 tablespoon grated gingerroot
1 tablespoon lemon juice
⅓ cup finely chopped onion
2 cloves garlic, minced
2 tablespoons water
½ cup chopped, seeded cucumber
1 tablespoon diced pimiento, drained
Fresh cilantro (optional)
Lemon wedges (optional)
Onion wedges (optional)

Remove skin and giblets from chicken. Rinse cavity and outside of chicken; pat dry with paper towels. Tie drum-

◆ Tandoori-Style Chicken

Serve spicy roast chicken with a refreshing cucumber yogurt sauce.

sticks to tail; twist wing tips under back. Place chicken in a plastic bag set in a shallow bowl. Set chicken aside. In a small bowl combine coriander, cumin, salt, cardamom, pepper, cinnamon, and cloves; set aside.

For marinade, combine 1 tablespoon of the spice mixture, 1 carton of yogurt, paprika, gingerroot, and lemon juice. Pour over the chicken in the bag. Close bag; chill for 4 to 24 hours.

For sauce, in a small saucepan cook onion, garlic, and remaining spice mixture in the 2 tablespoons water, covered, for 5 minutes. Do not drain. Cool. Stir in remaining carton of yogurt. Cover and chill.

Remove chicken from marinade; discard marinade. Place bird, breast side up, on a rack in a shallow roasting pan. Insert a meat thermometer into the center of one of the inside thigh muscles. The bulb should not touch the bone. Roast, uncovered, in a 375° oven for 1¼ to 1½ hours or till done. The thermometer should register 185° and the juices should run clear.

For sauce, stir cucumber and pimiento into the chilled yogurt sauce. Serve with chicken. If desired, garnish with cilantro, lemon wedges, and onion wedges. Makes 6 main-dish servings.

Nutrition facts per serving: 217 cal., 7 g total fat (2 g sat. fat), 78 mg chol., 219 mg sodium, 9 g carbo., 0 g fiber, 30 g pro. Daily Value: 4% vit. A, 7% vit. C, 14% calcium, 9% iron.

◆ Spicy Red Snapper with Mango Sauce

In the sunny Caribbean, fish is the order of the day. Cool, juicy tropical fruits help relieve the heat of peppery spices rubbed onto red snapper.

The New World: A Satisfying Feast

Spicy Red Snapper with Mango Salsa

WHILE RED SNAPPER IS THE CARIBBEAN FISH OF CHOICE FOR THIS RECIPE, YOU CAN USE OTHER FIRM-FLESHED WHITE-FISH, SUCH AS REDFISH, ORANGE ROUGHY, OR HADDOCK.

1 pound fresh or frozen red snapper fillets
1 tablespoon lime juice
1 tablespoon water
1 teaspoon paprika
½ teaspoon salt
¼ teaspoon ground ginger
¼ teaspoon ground allspice
¼ teaspoon pepper
1 recipe Mango Salsa (see recipe, page 49)
1 medium lime, cut into wedges (optional)
Parsley or cilantro sprigs (optional)

Thaw fish, if frozen. Rinse; pat dry with paper towels. Cut into 4 serving-size portions. Measure the thickness of fish. Brush with a mixture of lime juice and water. In a bowl combine paprika, salt, ginger, allspice, and pepper; rub onto the fish.

Arrange fish in a shallow baking pan. Bake, uncovered, in a 450° oven till fish just flakes easily when tested with a fork. Allow 4 to 6 minutes for each ½ inch of thickness.

To serve, brush fish with pan juices. Serve with Mango Salsa. If desired, garnish with lime wedges and parsley or cilantro. Makes 4 main-dish servings.

Mango Salsa: In a medium mixing bowl combine 1 *mango,* peeled, seeded, and chopped (about 1½ cups); 1 medium *red sweet pepper,* seeded and finely chopped; ¼ cup thinly sliced *green onion;* 1 *Scotch bonnet or hot green chili pepper,* seeded and finely chopped; 3 tablespoons *olive oil;* 2 tablespoons *lime juice;* 1 tablespoon *vinegar;* ½ teaspoon finely shredded *lime peel;* ¼ teaspoon *salt;* and ¼ teaspoon *pepper.* Makes 2 cups.

Nutrition facts per serving: 256 cal., 12 g total fat (2 g sat. fat), 42 mg chol., 453 mg sodium, 14 g carbo., 2 g fiber, 24 g pro. Daily Value: 46% vit. A, 119% vit. C, 4% calcium, 5% iron.

◆ Brazilian Black Beans

Brazilian Black Beans

EACH SERVING OF THIS FULL-FLAVORED COMBO PROVIDES ONE-FOURTH OF THE FIBER, HALF OF THE VITAMIN C, AND THREE-QUARTERS OF THE VITAMIN A YOU NEED FOR THE DAY, PLUS ENOUGH PROTEIN TO MAKE IT A MAIN DISH. NOW THAT'S NUTRITIOUS!

8 ounces dry black beans (1⅛ cups)
3 cups water
½ cup chopped onion
2 cloves garlic, minced
1 bay leaf
¼ cup snipped parsley
½ teaspoon salt
½ teaspoon crushed red pepper
3 cups water
1 medium sweet potato, halved lengthwise and sliced ¼ inch thick
1 16-ounce can diced tomatoes

Though some versions of Brazil's national dish contain meat, you won't miss it in this satisfying entrée. Serve it with sweet potatoes, fresh greens, and rice.

½ teaspoon finely shredded orange peel
3 cups hot cooked rice
Shredded kale, spinach, or flatleaf parsley (optional)

Rinse beans. In a large saucepan combine beans and enough water to cover. Bring to boiling; reduce heat. Simmer for 2 minutes. Remove from heat. Cover; let stand for 1 hour. (Or, soak beans in water in a large saucepan. Cover; set in a cool place for 6 to 8 hours or overnight.)

Drain beans in a colander; rinse. Return beans to the saucepan. Stir in onion, garlic, bay leaf, parsley, salt, and red pepper. Stir in 3 cups fresh water. Bring to boiling; reduce heat. Cover and simmer about 1½ hours or till beans are tender, adding more water, if necessary, and stirring occasionally.

Meanwhile, cook sweet potato in boiling salted water to cover for 15 to 20 minutes or till tender; drain.

Remove bay leaf from beans and discard. Add tomatoes to bean mixture. Uncover and simmer, stirring occasionally, for 15 to 20 minutes more or till a thick gravy forms.

Stir in orange peel. To serve, spoon beans over hot rice. Serve with sweet potato. If desired, sprinkle with shredded kale, spinach, or flatleaf parsley. Makes 4 main-dish servings.

Nutrition facts per serving: 368 cal., 1 g total fat (0 g sat. fat), 0 mg chol., 472 mg sodium, 74 g carbo., 6 g fiber, 16 g pro. Daily Value: 74% vit. A, 49% vit. C, 8% calcium, 33% iron.

◆ Beef and Bean Burritos

A trio of fat-free Mexican vegetables—corn, pinto beans, and jicama—add color, crunch, and fiber to these stuffed tortillas.

The New World

Beef and Bean Burritos

USE LEAN MEAT AND LOW-FAT CHEESE AND SOUR CREAM TO KEEP FAT IN CHECK.

½ pound lean ground beef or turkey
½ cup sliced green onion
½ cup chopped jicama
2 cloves garlic, minced
¼ cup water
4 teaspoons chili powder
1 tablespoon unsweetened cocoa powder
2 teaspoons sugar
1 15-ounce can pinto beans, rinsed and drained
½ cup frozen whole kernel corn
2 to 4 tablespoons diced green chili peppers, drained, or 2 to 4 jalapeño peppers, seeded and chopped
10 8-inch flour tortillas
1 cup shredded reduced-fat sharp cheddar or Monterey Jack cheese (4 ounces)
Shredded lettuce
Salsa
Low-fat dairy sour cream or plain yogurt
Thinly sliced green onion
Scotch bonnets or other fresh hot chili peppers (optional)

For filling, in a large skillet cook ground beef or turkey, green onion, jicama, and garlic till meat is brown and onion is tender. Drain off fat.

Stir in the water, chili powder, cocoa powder, and sugar. Cook for 2 minutes. Remove from heat. Stir in beans, corn, and chili peppers.

Stack tortillas; wrap tightly in foil. Heat in a 350° oven for 10 minutes to soften before filling. When ready to fill tortillas, remove only half at a time, keeping the others warm in the oven.

Spoon a generous ½ cup filling onto each tortilla just below the center. Top each with a generous tablespoon of cheese. Fold the bottom edge of the tortilla up and over the filling just to the center till the filling is covered. Fold in the opposite sides of each tortilla just till they meet. Roll up tortillas from the bottom. Secure bundles with wooden toothpicks.

Arrange burritos on a baking sheet. Bake in a 350° oven for 10 to 12 minutes or till heated through. Remove toothpicks. Serve burritos on lettuce with salsa, sour cream or yogurt, and green onion. If desired, garnish with Scotch bonnets or fresh hot peppers. Makes 10 main-dish servings.

Nutrition facts per serving: 267 cal., 9 g total fat (3 g sat. fat), 24 mg chol., 483 mg sodium, 33 g carbo., 3 g fiber, 15 g pro. Daily Value: 10% vit. A, 22% vit. C, 13% calcium, 17% iron.

◆ Basque Chicken

Savor the ingredients of the peasant-style cooking of southern France—chicken simmered with juicy tomatoes and lean ham.

Europe: Old World Taste

Basque Chicken

KEEP THE FAT CONTENT LOW BY REMOVING THE SKIN FROM THE CHICKEN.

4 small chicken thighs (1 to 1½ pounds)
4 chicken drumsticks (1 pound)
1 large onion, chopped (1 cup)
2 cloves garlic, minced
1 tablespoon olive oil
1 cup chicken broth
3 medium potatoes (1 pound), quartered
½ cup diced fully cooked ham
1 hot red chili pepper, seeded and chopped
1 tablespoon snipped fresh thyme or
1 teaspoon dried thyme, crushed
¼ teaspoon ground black pepper
⅛ teaspoon salt
2 large tomatoes, seeded and chopped
2 medium green sweet peppers,
cut into strips

Rinse chicken; pat dry with paper towels. Remove skin. In a large skillet cook chicken, onion, and garlic in hot oil about 10 minutes or till chicken is light brown, turning to brown evenly.

Remove chicken from skillet; drain off fat. Add chicken broth, potatoes, ham, chili pepper, thyme, pepper, and salt to skillet. Bring to boiling; reduce heat. Arrange chicken pieces on top. Cover and simmer for 35 to 40 minutes or till chicken is tender and no longer pink.

Transfer chicken and potato mixture to a serving platter; cover and keep warm. Stir tomatoes and green peppers into skillet. Simmer, uncovered, about 10 minutes or till peppers are tender and most of the liquid is evaporated. Serve vegetables with chicken. If desired, garnish with fresh thyme. Makes 4 servings.

Nutrition facts per serving: 390 cal., 13 g total fat (3 g sat. fat), 83 mg chol., 551 mg sodium, 38 g carbo., 2 g fiber, 31 g pro. Daily Value: 9% vit. A, 130% vit. C, 4% calcium, 28% iron.

In a large saucepan cook potatoes and rutabaga, covered, in boiling lightly salted water for 10 minutes. Add carrots, turnip, parsnip, and onion. Return to boiling; reduce heat. Cook, covered, for 7 to 9 minutes or till tender. Drain vegetables; return to pan.

Meanwhile, for glaze, in a small saucepan melt margarine. Stir in brown sugar and cornstarch. Stir in water, lemon peel, lemon juice, dill, salt, and pepper. Cook and stir till thickened and bubbly. Cook and stir 2 minutes more.

Pour the glaze over the drained vegetables in the pan. Cook and stir for 3 to 4 minutes or till vegetables are heated through. Makes 6 side-dish servings.

Nutrition facts per serving: 156 cal., 2 g total fat (0 g sat. fat), 0 mg chol., 250 mg sodium, 33 g carbo., 3 g fiber, 3 g pro. Daily Value: 61% vit. A, 42% vit. C, 5% calcium, 11% iron.

Scarlet Salad

BEETS, RED BELGIAN ENDIVE, RED LEAF LETTUCE, AND RED-SKINNED POTATOES COLOR THIS SALAD.

◆ Lemon Glazed Vegetables with Dill

Tender new potatoes, rutabaga, turnips, parsnips, and carrots are all Scandinavian staples that taste great on American tables too.

Europe

Lemon-Glazed Vegetables with Dill

8 tiny new potatoes, halved, or 2 medium red-skinned potatoes, quartered
1 medium rutabaga, peeled and cut into 1-inch pieces (1½ cups)
2 medium carrots, peeled and sliced (1 cup)
1 medium turnip, peeled and cut up (1¼ cups)

1 medium parsnip, peeled and sliced (1 cup)
1 small onion, cut into wedges
1 tablespoon margarine
3 tablespoons brown sugar
1 teaspoon cornstarch
¼ cup water
½ teaspoon finely shredded lemon peel
3 tablespoons lemon juice
2 teaspoons snipped fresh dill or ½ teaspoon dried dillweed
½ teaspoon salt
¼ teaspoon pepper

¾ pound tiny new potatoes, sliced ⅛ inch thick
¾ pound green and/or white asparagus spears
Mixed greens, such as red or green leaf lettuce, red Belgian endive, watercress, radicchio and/or Swiss chard
1 8-ounce can sliced beets, drained
2 ounces fresh pea pods, trimmed (1 cup)
12 ears baby corn,* cut in half crosswise
1 small red onion, chopped (⅓ cup)
¼ teaspoon cracked black pepper
1 recipe Red Wine Vinaigrette
1 recipe Dijon Croutons (optional) (see recipe, page 53)

In a large saucepan cook potatoes, covered, in a small amount of boiling water for 10 minutes. Snap off and discard woody bases from asparagus. Add asparagus spears to potatoes in saucepan. Cover and cook for 4 to 8 minutes more or till potatoes are tender and asparagus is crisp-tender. Drain; cover and chill vegetables for 2 to 24 hours.

To assemble, line 6 salad plates with your choice of mixed greens. Arrange chilled cooked potatoes, asparagus, beets, pea pods, and baby corn atop greens. Sprinkle with chopped onion and black pepper. Serve salads with Red Wine Vinaigrette and Dijon Croutons. Makes 6 side-dish servings.

*Note: Look for either a 14-ounce can of baby corn or an 8-ounce package of frozen baby corn at your supermarket. Cook the frozen corn according to package directions. Drain before using.

Nutrition facts per serving with 2 tablespoons Red Wine Vinaigrette: 190 cal., 10 g total fat (2 g sat. fat), 0 mg chol., 164 mg sodium, 23 g carbo., 4 g fiber, 5 g pro. Daily Value: 6% vit. A, 63% vit. C, 4% calcium, 0% iron.

Red Wine Vinaigrette

THIS VINAIGRETTE USES LESS OIL THAN THE TRADITIONAL FRENCH VERSION, BUT MAKES UP FOR FLAVOR WITH A SPLASH OF HEARTY BURGUNDY AND HERBS.

¼ cup salad oil
¼ cup red wine vinegar or cider vinegar
2 tablespoons burgundy, dry red wine, or water
2 teaspoons sugar
2 teaspoons snipped fresh thyme or ½ teaspoon dried thyme, crushed
2 teaspoons snipped fresh savory or

◆ Scarlet Salad

Turn to food-loving France for exciting fresh greens and exotic vegetables. This salad is splashed with vinaigrette and served with crusty oversize croutons.

½ teaspoon dried savory, crushed
¼ teaspoon salt
¼ teaspoon dry mustard or 1 teaspoon Dijon-style mustard

In a screw-top jar combine oil, vinegar, red wine or water, sugar, thyme, savory, salt, and mustard. Cover and shake well to mix. Store in the refrigerator for up to 2 weeks. Shake well before serving. Makes about ¾ cup.

Nutrition facts per tablespoon: 43 cal., 5 g total fat (1 g sat. fat), 0 mg chol., 46 mg sodium, 0 g carbo., 0 g fiber, 0 g pro. Daily Value: 0% vit. A, 0% vit. C, 0% calcium, 0% iron.

Dijon Croutons

2 tablespoons reduced-calorie mayonnaise or salad dressing
2 teaspoons Dijon-style mustard
6 ½-inch-thick slices French bread (baguette)

Mix mayonnaise or salad dressing and mustard. Spread onto one side of each baguette slice. Arrange slices, mustard side up, in a shallow baking pan. Bake in a 300° oven for 10 to 15 minutes or till dry and crisp. Makes 6 croutons.

Nutrition facts per crouton: 84 cal., 2 g total fat (0 g sat. fat), 2 mg chol., 199 mg sodium, 13 g carbo., 0 g fiber, 2 g pro. Daily Value: 0% vit. A, 0% vit. C, 1% calcium, 4% iron.

Rye Bread and Garlic Cheese Canapés

FOR THIS SIMPLE APPETIZER, SPREAD A CREAMY, LOW-FAT YOGURT DIP ONTO RYE BREAD AND ADD YOUR CHOICE OF TOPPINGS.

1 medium head garlic
2 teaspoons olive oil
1 cup dry cottage cheese
¼ cup plain low-fat yogurt or
dairy sour cream
⅓ cup toasted chopped walnuts*
2 tablespoons snipped parsley
¾ teaspoon lemon-pepper seasoning
¼ teaspoon salt
Dark rye party bread or firm, dark rye bread
Toppings, such as slices of beets, cucumber, pear, apple, pickles, ham, smoked salmon, or herring; caviar; lemon slice quarters; chives; crabmeat; dill sprigs; capers; and/or toasted chopped walnuts

Peel away the dry outer layers of skin from garlic, leaving cloves and skins of garlic intact. Cut off the pointed top portion (about ¼ inch), leaving the bulb intact but exposing the individual garlic cloves. Place the head of garlic, cut side up, in a small baking dish. Drizzle garlic with olive oil.

Bake, covered, in a 400° oven for 35 to 45 minutes or till cloves feel soft when pressed. Allow the bulb to cool. To remove the paste from the garlic head, squeeze the paste from each clove. Discard the skins. You should have about 1 tablespoon of garlic paste.

◆ Rye Bread and Garlic Cheese Canapés

Sandwiches that look as scrumptious as they taste are the hallmark of East European and Scandinavian cooks.

In a blender container combine garlic paste, cottage cheese, yogurt or sour cream, walnuts, parsley, lemon-pepper seasoning, and salt. Cover and blend till smooth. Spread cheese mixture onto rye bread slices; add desired toppings. Makes about 1¼ cups.

*Note: To toast, place walnuts in a shallow baking pan; bake in a 400° oven for 7 to 8 minutes or till nuts start to brown.

Nutrition facts per 2 slices bread without toppers: 74 cal., 2 g fat (0 g sat. fat), 1 mg chol., 189 mg sodium, 12 g carbo., 1 g fiber, 4 g pro. Daily Value: 0% vit. A, 1% vit. C, 3% calcium, 4% iron.

Pasta with Artichokes And Basil

NO MATTER WHAT THE SHAPE OR SIZE, PASTA IS ONE GREAT WAY TO LOAD UP ON CARBOHYDRATES. ACCORDING TO THE USDA FOOD PYRAMID, YOU SHOULD EAT AT LEAST SIX SERVINGS OF CARBOHYDRATE-RICH FOODS, SUCH AS GRAINS, BREADS, CEREALS, AND PASTA, A DAY.

4 ounces tagliatelle, fusilli, or fettuccine,
broken up
1 9-ounce package frozen artichoke hearts, thawed, or one 14-ounce jar or can artichoke hearts, rinsed and drained
2 medium red or green sweet peppers, chopped
⅓ cup finely chopped onion
2 cloves garlic, minced
1 tablespoon olive oil
1 medium tomato, seeded and chopped
¼ cup snipped fresh basil or
2 teaspoons dried basil, crushed
2 tablespoons grated Parmesan cheese

Cook pasta in boiling lightly salted water according to package directions. Immediately drain. Return pasta to pan; keep warm.

Meanwhile, place artichoke hearts in a colander under cold running water to separate. In a large skillet cook and stir artichokes, peppers, onion, and garlic in hot oil over medium-high heat about 5 minutes or till vegetables are tender.

◆ Pasta with Artichokes and Basil

Wrap ribbons of pasta tossed with garden-fresh vegetables and basil around your fork. A dusting of Parmesan adds flavor without much fat.

◆ Fennel-Mushroom Risotto

Italian cooks frequently add a variety of spring-fresh vegetables to risotto, a delectably creamy rice classic from Italy

Stir in tomato and basil; cook and stir about 2 minutes more or till heated through. Add artichoke mixture to pasta. Toss gently to mix. Sprinkle each serving with Parmesan cheese. Makes 4 to 6 side-dish servings.

Nutrition facts per serving: 216 cal., 5 g total fat (1 g sat. fat), 2 mg chol., 124 mg sodium, 36 g carbo., 4 g fiber, 8 g pro. Daily Value: 31% vit. A, 128% vit. C, 7% calcium, 15% iron.

Fennel-Mushroom Risotto

FOR JUST-RIGHT CREAMINESS, USE ARBORIO OR MEDIUM-GRAIN RICE AND DON'T PEEK DURING COOKING. YOU'LL FIND ARBORIO RICE IN ITALIAN SPECIALTY FOOD SHOPS OR IN THE RICE SECTION OF SOME SUPERMARKETS. REGULAR LONG-GRAIN RICE WORKS, TOO, BUT THE MIXTURE WON'T BE AS CREAMY.

1 cup sliced fresh mushrooms, such as shiitake, oyster, morel, or porcini
1 cup sliced fennel bulb
½ teaspoon fennel seed, crushed
1 tablespoon. olive oil
⅔ cup Arborio or medium-grain rice
2 cups water
½ teaspoon salt
⅛ teaspoon pepper
4 asparagus spears,* cut into 1-inch pieces (¼ cup)
⅓ cup thinly sliced green onion
1 tablespoon snipped fennel leaves
Fennel leaves (optional)

In a medium saucepan cook mushrooms, sliced fennel bulb, and fennel seed in hot olive oil till tender. Stir in uncooked Arborio or medium-grain rice. Cook and stir for 2 minutes more.

Carefully stir in water, salt, and pepper. Bring to boiling; reduce heat. Cover and simmer for 20 minutes (do not lift cover).

Remove from heat. Stir in asparagus and green onion. Let stand, covered, for 5 minutes. The rice should be tender but slightly firm, and the mixture should be creamy. If necessary, stir in a little water to reach the desired consistency.

Stir in snipped fennel leaves. If desired, garnish risotto with additional fennel leaves. Makes 4 side-dish servings.

*Note: If using thick asparagus spears, halve the spears lengthwise and cook in a small amount of boiling water till crisp-tender before stirring into risotto.

Nutrition facts per serving: 160 cal., 4 g total fat (1 g sat. fat), 0 mg chol., 285 mg sodium, 28 g carbo., 1 g fiber, 3 g pro. Daily Value: 3% vit. A, 12% vit. C, 3% calcium, and 12% iron.

◆ Grilled Lamb with Rosemary-Lemon Sauce and Spiced Lentil Bulgur Pilaf

Marinate lean lamb in the flavors of Greece—fresh lemon, fragrant rosemary, and sultry garlic—then sizzle it over hot coals. Serve fiber-rich Spiced Lentil-Bulgur Pilaf alongside.

The Mediterranean

Grilled Lamb with Rosemary-Lemon Sauce

TODAY'S LAMB IS LEANER THAN EVER, ESPECIALLY WHEN YOU TRIM OFF ANY VISIBLE FAT AND GRILL OVER COALS SO THE FAT DRIPS OFF.

1 1¼- to 1½-pound lamb rib roast*
(8 to 10 ribs)
1 teaspoon snipped fresh rosemary or
¼ teaspoon dried rosemary, crushed
2 cloves garlic, minced
Salt
Pepper

⅔ cup beef broth
½ teaspoon finely shredded lemon peel
1 tablespoon lemon juice
2 teaspoons cornstarch
1 teaspoon honey
⅛ teaspoon pepper
1 recipe Spiced Lentil-Bulgur Pilaf
(see recipe, page 57)
Steamed baby carrots (optional)

Trim fat from lamb. Rub meat with half of the rosemary and all of the garlic. Sprinkle with salt and pepper. Insert a meat thermometer so it does not touch fat or bone.

In a covered grill arrange medium coals around a drip pan. Test for medium-low heat above the drip pan. (At medium-low heat, you should be able to hold your hand for five seconds where the food will cook over the coals.) Place meat, fat side up, on a grill rack over the drip pan, but not over the coals. Lower the grill hood. Grill to desired doneness, allowing 35 to 40 minutes for medium-rare (150°). (Or, place meat, fat side up, on a rack in a shallow roasting pan. Insert a meat thermometer. Roast in a 400° oven to desired doneness, allowing 30 to 35 minutes for medium-rare.)

For sauce, in a small saucepan stir together broth, remaining rosemary, lemon peel, juice, cornstarch, honey, and pepper. Cook and stir till thickened and bubbly. Cook and stir 2 minutes more.

To serve, cut lamb into 1-rib portions. Serve meat with Spiced Lentil-Bulgur Pilaf and baby carrots, if desired. Top the lamb with the sauce. Makes 4 main-dish servings.

*Note: Instead of a lamb roast, you can use eight 1-inch-thick lamb rib chops. Grill directly over medium coals for 10 to 16 minutes or till of desired doneness, turning once.

Nutrition facts per serving: 112 cal., 5 g total fat (2 g sat. fat), 41 mg chol., 230 mg sodium, 4 g carbo., 0 g fiber, 13 g pro. Daily Value: 0% vit. A, 3% vit. C, 1% calcium, 8% iron.

Spiced Lentil-Bulgur Pilaf

THIS TASTY PILAF IS A SIMPLE WAY TO ADD FIBER TO MEALS. YOU'LL FIND BULGUR OR CRACKED WHEAT IN THE FLOUR OR RICE SECTION OF YOUR SUPERMARKET.

2½ cups water
½ cup lentils
¼ teaspoon salt
¼ teaspoon ground cinnamon
¼ teaspoon ground cumin
¾ cup bulgur
2 tablespoons feta cheese, crumbled
1 tablespoon snipped parsley

In a medium saucepan combine the 2½ cups water, lentils, salt, ground cinnamon, and ground cumin. Bring to boiling; reduce heat to low. Cover and simmer lentils for 10 minutes.

Add the uncooked bulgur to the lentil mixture in the saucepan. Cover and simmer over low heat for 15 to 20 minutes more or till the lentils and bulgur are tender and the liquid is almost evaporated. Spoon the pilaf onto plates. Sprinkle each serving with crumbled feta cheese and snipped parsley. Makes 4 side-dish servings.

Nutrition facts per serving: 202 cal., 2 g total fat (1 g sat. fat), 7 mg chol., 682 mg sodium, 37 g carbo., 8 g fiber, 10 g pro. Daily Value: 3% vit. A, 3% vit. C, 7% calcium, 21% iron.

Sherried Shrimp with Garlic

WITH OLIVES, CAPERS, AND ROASTED PEPPERS, THIS SHRIMP DISH IS A DELICIOUS EXAMPLE OF TAPAS—APPETIZERS THAT TIDE THE SPANISH OVER UNTIL THEIR LATE DINNER HOUR.

1 pound fresh or frozen large shrimp in shells
¼ cup dry sherry or orange juice
2 tablespoons orange juice
1 roasted red or green sweet pepper*, cut into strips, or ½ cup diced pimiento
10 pitted ripe olives, halved (⅓ cup)
2 tablespoons snipped parsley
3 cloves garlic, minced
2 teaspoons capers, drained
2 teaspoons tomato paste
⅛ teaspoon coarsely ground black pepper
1 teaspoon olive oil
French bread

Thaw shrimp, if frozen. Peel and devein, leaving tails intact. Set aside.

In a large skillet combine sherry, orange juice, red pepper strips or pimiento, olives, parsley, garlic, capers, tomato paste, and black pepper. Bring to boiling. Add shrimp. Cook and stir for 1 to 3 minutes or till shrimp turn pink.

◆ Sherried Shrimp with Garlic

Use a crusty piece of French bread to soak up every last drop of Sherried Shrimp with Garlic. Serve with a glass of Spanish sherry, if you wish.

Remove from heat. Stir in olive oil. Serve with French bread. Makes 6 appetizer servings.

*Note: To roast peppers, quarter lengthwise. Remove stem and seeds. Cut small slits in ends so pieces lie flat. Place, skin sides up, on a foil-lined baking sheet. Bake in a 425° oven for 20 to 25 minutes or till dark and bubbly. Place in a clean paper bag. Close the bag tightly; cool to room temperature. Remove skin; cut peppers into strips.

Nutrition facts per serving: 181 cal., 3 g total fat (1 g sat. fat), 87 mg chol., 388 mg sodium, 21 g carbo., 1 g fiber, 13 g pro. Daily Value: 5% vit. A, 25% vit. C, 5% calcium, 19% iron.

Flavors of the World

Each world cuisine owes some of its distinctive characteristics to the different blends of herbs and spices used.

Allspice: The roots of this reddish brown spice lie in Jamaica, where Christopher Columbus likely discovered it. The name allspice was coined by Europeans, who thought the berries tasted like a blend of cloves, cinnamon, and nutmeg. Use versatile allspice with meats, vegetables, and desserts.

Basil: A favorite Italian herb with large green or purple leaves, basil's flavor can vary from peppery and robust to sweet and spicy. It is the classic herb for pesto sauce and goes well with any kind of meat, vegetable, pasta, and rice.

Cardamom: A member of the ginger family, cardamom has a sweet, aniselike flavor mixed with a little clove. Scandinavians love cardamom, especially in baked goods. Cardamom is available as whole pods, whole seeds, and ground.

Chili powder: Mexican cooks rely heavily on this seasoning blend, which consists of mild chili peppers, oregano, cumin, garlic, and salt. The heat and spiciness can vary, depending on the blend. Chili powder flavors meats, chicken, and many Mexican dishes.

Cinnamon: The whole form of this spice, a cinnamon stick, looks like what it is—the bark of a tropical evergreen tree. Use stick cinnamon to flavor beverages and poaching liquid. Use the ground form for baking, desserts, and other foods.

Cilantro: Also known as Chinese parsley, cilantro leaves come from the coriander plant. The snipped leaves add a fresh lemony flavor to many Mexican and Oriental dishes. Cilantro leaves are available fresh, freeze-dried, or dried.

Cloves: This dark, nail-shaped spice adds a strong, pungent flavor to foods. You can use whole cloves in ham or beverages and ground cloves in baked foods.

Coriander: A popular seasoning in curry powder and Mideastern or Indian dishes, coriander seeds taste like lemon and sage combined. They may be purchased either whole or ground.

Cumin: The tiny, amber-colored seed of a plant in the parsley family, cumin has a pungent, spicy, and slightly bitter flavor. It is a mainstay in both chili and curry powders. Cumin is available whole or ground.

Dill: Dillweed comes from the feathery green leaves of the dill plant. Its distinct evergreen flavor is popular in Scandinavian cooking, particularly with fish and vegetables. You can purchase dillweed fresh or dried.

Fennel seed: The small, yellowish-brown seeds of the fennel plant have a mild, licorice-like flavor and aroma. The seeds are used in Italian cooking, often as a pizza topping, and in Oriental cooking as an ingredient in five-spice powder. You can buy fennel seed whole or ground.

Garam Masala: Cooks in northern India use this relative of curry powder in many classic dishes. The blend of seasonings varies by cook, but typically combines pepper, cumin, coriander, cloves, cardamom, and cinnamon.

Gingerroot: The root of a semitropical plant, ginger adds a slightly hot flavor to many Oriental dishes. European cooks use the ground dry spice in baking.

Lemongrass: This lemon-flavored plant, used to flavor many Oriental and Thai dishes, resembles a fibrous green onion. If fresh or dried lemongrass is unavailable in Oriental markets, use lemon peel as a substitute.

Prize Tested Recipes

◆ Mocha and Cherry Cake

Mocha and Cherry Cake

2 cups granulated sugar
1¾ cups all-purpose flour
¾ cup unsweetened cocoa powder
2 teaspoons baking soda
1 teaspoon baking powder
½ teaspoon salt
2 eggs
1 cup buttermilk or sour milk
1 cup strong coffee, cooled
½ cup cooking oil
2 teaspoons vanilla
2½ cups ricotta cheese
½ cup granulated sugar
½ cup miniature semisweet chocolate pieces
½ cup chopped maraschino cherries,
well drained
⅔ cup margarine or butter
½ cup unsweetened cocoa powder
7½ cups sifted powdered sugar
½ to ⅔ cup milk
2 teaspoons vanilla

In a very large mixing bowl combine the 2 cups sugar, flour, ¾ cup cocoa powder, baking soda, baking powder, and salt. Add eggs, buttermilk, coffee, oil, and first 2 teaspoons vanilla. Beat with an electric mixer on low speed for 30 seconds till combined, then for 2 minutes on medium speed. Grease two 9x1½-inch round baking pans; sprinkle with cocoa powder. Pour batter into pans. Bake in a 350° oven for 25 to 30 minutes or till cakes test done. Cool on a rack for 10 minutes. Remove from pans. Cool. Split each cake horizontally to make 4 layers total. For filling, combine the ricotta cheese, ½ cup sugar, and chocolate pieces. Gently stir in cherries. Place one cake layer on a serving plate. Spread ⅓ of the filling on the bottom layer of cake. Top with another cake layer. Continue layering the filling and cake, ending with cake.

For frosting, in a bowl beat margarine or butter till fluffy. Gradually add the ½ cup cocoa and half of the powdered sugar. Slowly beat in half of the milk and the remaining vanilla. Beat in remaining powdered sugar. Beat in additional milk till of spreading consistency. Frost cake. Garnish with shaved chocolate and edible flower petals, if desired. Serve immediately or cover and chill up to 12 hours. Makes 14 to 16 servings.

Nutrition facts per serving: 698 cal., 25 g total fat (5 g sat. fat), 45 mg chol., 385 mg sodium, 113 g carbo., 1 g fiber, 10 g pro. Daily Value: 18% vit. A, 21% calcium.

$200 WINNER
Ms. Brenda Vernon
East Hartford, Connecticut

♦ Spicy Shrimp and Noodle Soup

¼ cup snipped fresh cilantro
1 green onion, thinly sliced
Shredded cheddar cheese (optional)
Fresh cilantro (optional)

Thaw shrimp if frozen. Peel and devein shrimp.

In a medium mixing bowl combine lemon juice, chili powder, cumin, and pepper; add shrimp. Toss to coat. Let shrimp stand for 20 minutes at room temperature, stirring occasionally. Meanwhile, in a large saucepan bring water to boiling. Stir in one noodle flavor packet (reserve remaining flavor packet for another use). Break noodles into pieces and add to saucepan. Return to boiling and cook 1 minute. Add the shrimp and cook for 1 to 2 minutes more or till shrimp turn pink. Stir in salsa, beans, corn, snipped cilantro, and green onion. Heat through. To serve, if desired, top each serving with cheese and garnish with cilantro. Makes 4 to 6 main-dish servings.

Nutrition facts per serving: 419 cal., 14 g total fat (2 g sat. fat), 137 mg chol., 1,296 mg sodium, 57 g carbo., 6 g fiber, 30 g pro. Daily Value: 26% vit. A, 77% vit. C, 12% calcium, 35% iron.

$200 WINNER
Roxanne E. Chan
Albany, California

Spicy Shrimp and Noodle Soup

FRESH SHRIMP TEAMED WITH NOODLES, BEANS, AND ZESTY SPICES MAKES THIS SOUP TOPS.

1 pound fresh or frozen medium shrimp in shells
1 tablespoon lemon juice
¼ teaspoon chili powder
¼ teaspoon ground cumin
⅛ teaspoon pepper
3 cups water
2 3-ounce packages shrimp- or oriental-flavored ramen noodles
1 16-ounce jar salsa (2 cups)
1 15-ounce can black beans, rinsed and drained
1 8¾-ounce can no-salt-added whole kernel corn, drained

Smoked Sausage and Bean Soup

TO SAVE TIME, JACQUELINE USES PRESHREDDED CABBAGE FOUND IN THE PRODUCE SECTION.

◆ Smoked Sausage and Bean Soup

1 medium onion, finely chopped
1 teaspoon bottled minced garlic
2 tablespoons margarine or butter
6 cups water
2 medium potatoes, chopped (2 cups)
1 pound fully cooked smoked
turkey sausage, sliced
1 15-ounce can red kidney beans,
rinsed and drained
1 teaspoon instant beef bouillon granules

2 cups chopped cabbage or preshredded
cole slaw mix
¼ cup tomato paste or catsup
3 tablespoons vinegar

In a 4-quart Dutch oven cook the onion and garlic in margarine or butter till tender but not brown. Add the water, potatoes, sausage, beans, and bouillon granules. Heat to boiling. Reduce heat; simmer, covered, for 15 minutes. Add the cabbage or coleslaw mix, tomato paste or catsup, and vinegar. Simmer, covered, 10 minutes more. Makes 6 main-dish servings.

Nutrition facts per serving: 298 cal., 13 g total fat (4 g sat. fat), 51 mg chol., 933 mg sodium, 30 g carbo., 6 g fiber, 20 g pro. Daily Value: 7% vit. A, 29% vit. C, 8% calcium, 22% iron.

$100 WINNER
Jacqueline R. Abels
Skokie, Illinois

● Raspberry Mousse Cake

Raspberry Mousse Cake

1 cup all-purpose flour
2 tablespoons cornstarch
1¼ teaspoons baking powder
4 egg yolks
½ cup sugar
1 teaspoon lemon juice
4 egg whites
½ cup sugar
2 cups frozen red raspberries,
thawed
¼ cup sugar

¼ cup orange juice or orange-flavored
liqueur
1 envelope unflavored gelatin
3 cups whipping cream
3 tablespoons sugar
3 cups fresh red raspberries

Grease and flour two 9x1½-inch round baking pans. Stir together the flour, cornstarch, baking powder, and ¼ teaspoon salt. In a medium bowl beat yolks with an electric mixer on high speed for 5 minutes. Beat in first ½ cup sugar on low; beat in lemon juice and 3 tablespoons water. Clean beaters. In a mixing bowl beat egg whites on medium speed till soft peaks form. Add second ½ cup sugar; beat at high speed till stiff peaks form. Fold in the yolk mixture. Fold the flour mixture into the egg mixture. Divide batter between pans. Bake in a 325° oven for 25 to 35 minutes or till top springs back when touched. Remove from pans immediately. Cool. Split layers in half horizontally. Place thawed berries in a blender container. Cover; blend till smooth. Strain to remove seeds. Stir in the ¼ cup sugar. Set aside. In a 1-cup heat-safe measure combine juice or liqueur and gelatin; let stand 5 minutes. Place measure in a saucepan filled with 1 inch of water. Heat till gelatin dissolves, stirring constantly. Beat whipping cream and 3 tablespoons sugar to soft peaks. Gradually add gelatin mixture, beating to stiff peaks. Reserve 3½ cups whipped cream. To remaining whipped cream, fold in berry puree and 2 cups fresh berries. Place a cake layer on a platter; top with ⅓ of berry mixture. Repeat twice. Top with last layer. Frost cake with reserved cream. Cover; chill 6 hours or overnight. To serve, garnish with remaining berries. Makes 12 servings.

Nutrition facts per serving: 401 cal., 25 g total fat (14 g sat. fat), 153 mg chol., 90 mg sodium, 41 g carbo., 3g fiber, 5g pro. Daily Value: 37% vit. A, 27% vit. C, 5% calcium, 7% iron.

$100 WINNER
Kathleen Roberts
West Sayville, New York

April

50 Nifty Homemade Basics
Simple ways to add style to your family dinners

Prize Tested Recipes
Cheese and Vegetable Chowder, Rhubarb-Raspberry Pie,
Rhubarb-Pineapple Crumble, Curry-Cajun Spiced Chicken

50 Nifty Homemade Basics

Kiss mundane meals good-bye. With our deliciously simple recipes, you can jazz up your mealtime standbys and serve something nifty every time. Start with one of these quickie sauces for pasta and work your way up to number 50—a ten-minute dessert sauce. Whoever said good home cooking can't be fun?

By Kristi Fuller

◆ Garden Vegetable Sauce

1 Garden Vegetable Sauce

1 14½-ounce can stewed tomatoes
2 tablespoons tomato paste
1 tablespoon snipped fresh mint or
1½ teaspoons dried mint, crushed
½ teaspoon sugar
2 small yellow summer squash and/or
zucchini, halved lengthwise
and thinly sliced
5 ounces asparagus spears, cut into 1-inch
pieces (1 cup)
Hot cooked pasta (such as fettuccine
or spaghetti)

In a large saucepan combine un-drained tomatoes, tomato paste, mint, and sugar. Bring to boiling; reduce heat. Simmer, uncovered, for 5 minutes. Add squash and asparagus. Cook, covered, for 5 to 7 minutes more or till squash and asparagus are tender. Serve over hot pasta. Makes 3½ cups sauce.

Nutrition facts per ½ cup sauce: 29 cal., 0 g total fat (0 g sat. fat), 0 mg chol., 179 mg sodium, 6 g carbo., 1 g fiber, 1 g pro. Daily Value: 6% vit. A, 26% vit. C, 5% iron.

2 Southwest Vegetable Sauce:

Prepare sauce as above except omit mint and asparagus. Add 1 cup cubed (¼ to ½ inch) *jicama;* one 4-ounce can *chopped green chili peppers,* drained; and 1 teaspoon *ground cumin* along with the squash. Makes about 3½ cups sauce.

Nutrition facts per ½ cup sauce: 40 cal., 0 g total fat (0 g sat. fat), 0 mg chol., 198 mg sodium, 9 g carbo., 1 g fiber, 2 g pro.

3 Wild Mushroom Toss

4 cups sliced fresh mushrooms (such as
shiitake, morel, oyster, and/or cèpes)
2 small red or green sweet peppers,
cut into strips
1 medium onion, cut into thin wedges
¼ cup margarine or butter
¼ teaspoon seasoned salt
¼ teaspoon pepper
Hot cooked pasta
Shaved* or grated Parmesan cheese

In a large skillet cook mushrooms, peppers, and onion in hot margarine or butter till tender. Stir in seasoned salt and pepper. Toss with hot pasta. Top with cheese. Makes about 2 cups sauce.

*To shave Parmesan cheese, draw a

◆ Wild Mushroom Toss

vegetable peeler across the flat side of a block of Parmesan cheese.

4 Tarragon Mushroom Toss: Prepare as directed above except add 1 tablespoon snipped *fresh tarragon or 1 teaspoon dried tarragon,* crushed, along with vegetables.

Nutrition facts per ¼ cup Wild Mushroom Toss or Tarragon Mushroom Toss: 77 cal., 6 g total fat (1 g sat. fat), 1 mg chol., 128 mg sodium, 4 g carbo., 1 g fiber, 2 g pro. Daily Value: 14% vit. A, 30% vit. C, 2% calcium, 5% iron.

5 Madeira-Mushroom Toss: Prepare Wild Mushroom Sauce as directed except add ¼ cup *Madeira or dry sherry* to mushroom mixture after cooking. Bring to boiling. Boil gently till sauce is reduced by half.

Nutrition facts per ¼ cup sauce: 84 cal., 6 g total fat (1 g sat. fat), 1 mg chol., 128 mg sodium, 4 g carbo., 1 g fiber, 2 g pro. Daily Value: 14% vit. A, 30% vit. C, 2% calcium.

◆ Asparagus Cheese Sauce

6 *Asparagus Cheese Sauce*
10 ounces fresh asparagus, trimmed and cut into 2-inch pieces
1 8-ounce package light cream cheese (Neufchâtel)
½ cup milk
⅛ teaspoon white or black pepper
2 tablespoons grated Parmesan cheese
2 teaspoons snipped fresh thyme, tarragon, basil, or chives
Hot cooked pasta (such as bow ties, rigatoni, or rotini)

Fresh snipped thyme, tarragon, basil, or chives (optional)
Cracked pink peppercorns or toasted sliced almonds (optional)

In a medium saucepan cook asparagus, covered, in a small amount of lightly salted boiling water for 5 to 10 minutes or till crisp-tender. Drain.

Meanwhile, in a medium saucepan heat the cream cheese, milk, and pepper over low heat till cream cheese is softened. Stir in Parmesan cheese and the 2 teaspoons desired herb; heat through. (If mixture seems too thick, stir in additional milk to desired consistency.) Toss hot cooked pasta with cooked asparagus and sauce. Garnish with additional herb and pink peppercorns or almonds, if desired. Makes about 1½ cups.

Nutrition facts per ¼ cup sauce: 130 cal., 10 g total fat (6 g sat. fat), 33 mg chol., 220 mg sodium, 3 g carbo., 1 g fiber, 6 g pro. Daily Value: 17% vit. A, 12% vit. C.

7 *Pepper Cheese Pasta Sauce*

ROASTED PEPPERS AND CHEESE WITH JALAPEÑOS PERK UP A PACKAGE OF HOL-LANDAISE SAUCE MIX.

1 0.9- to 1.25-ounce package hollandaise sauce mix
1 7-ounce jar roasted sweet peppers, drained and chopped
2 teaspoons white wine Worcestershire sauce
½ cup shredded Monterey Jack cheese with jalapeño peppers
Hot cooked pasta (such as mostaccioli, medium shells, or rigatoni)

Prepare hollandaise sauce according to package directions except use only 2 tablespoons margarine or butter. Stir in peppers and white wine Worcestershire sauce. Remove pan from heat. Stir in cheese till melted. Serve over pasta. Makes about 1⅓ cups.

8 Cheddar Cheese Pasta Sauce:

Prepare sauce as directed above except substitute shredded *cheddar cheese* for the Monterey Jack cheese. Omit the sweet peppers.

Nutrition facts per ¼ cup Pepper Cheese or Cheddar Cheese Pasta Sauce: 265 cal., 23 g total fat (11 g sat. fat), 54 mg chol., 1,025 mg sodium, 10 g carbo., 8 g pro.

9 Blue-Cheese Sauce:

Prepare sauce as directed except substitute ¼ cup (1 ounce) crumbled *blue cheese* for all of the Monterey Jack cheese with jalapeño peppers. Omit the sweet peppers. If sauce is too thick, add 1 to 2 tablespoons *milk* to desired consistency. Serve over hot cooked pasta. Sprinkle with ¼ cup toasted *walnuts* before serving.

◆ Herb Mustard Rub

◆ Pepper Cheese Pasta Sauce

Nutrition facts per ¼ cup sauce: 265 cal., 23 g total fat (9 g sat. fat), 42 mg chol., 1,030 mg sodium, 10 g carbo., 6 g pro.

10 *Sorrel Cream Sauce*

⅓ cup dairy sour cream
⅓ cup mayonnaise or salad dressing

1 teaspoon finely shredded lemon peel
1 teaspoon dried thyme, crushed
½ teaspoon prepared mustard
¼ cup whipping cream
¼ cup coarsely chopped fresh sorrel or spinach

In a small saucepan combine sour cream, mayonnaise or salad dressing, lemon peel, thyme, and mustard. Cook and stir over low heat till hot (do not boil). Remove from heat.

In a medium mixing bowl beat whipping cream with an electric mixer on low speed till soft peaks form. Fold whipped cream and sorrel or spinach into sour cream mixture. Serve immediately with fish. Makes 1¼ cups.

11 Lemon Chive Sauce:

Prepare sauce as directed except omit sorrel or spinach. Fold 1 tablespoon snipped *chives* into mixture along with whipped cream. Makes 1 cup.

Succulent Meat, Fish, and Chicken Fix-Ups

CREAMY SAUCES, HERB RUBS, AND WINE MARINADES CARVE YOUR NEXT ENTRÉE INTO A PRIME CUT.

◆ Sorrel Cream Sauce

12 Lemon Cucumber Sauce: Prepare cream sauce as directed except omit thyme and sorrel. Stir ½ cup shredded *cucumber* and ¼ teaspoon *dried dillweed* into prepared sauce. Makes 1½ cups.

Nutrition facts per 2 tablespoons Sorrel Cream Sauce, Lemon Chive Sauce, or Lemon Cucumber Sauce: 70 cal., 8 g total fat (2 g sat. fat), 8 mg chol., 50 mg sodium, 1 g carbo., 0 g fiber, 0 g pro.

13 *Herb Mustard Rub*

A SIMPLE BLEND OF HERBS, ONION, AND MUSTARD MAKES A GOLDEN COATING WHEN RUBBED ON MEAT, THEN ROASTED.

1 small onion, finely chopped
2 tablespoons coarse-grain mustard or Dijon-style mustard
¼ teaspoon dried marjoram, crushed
¼ teaspoon dried rosemary, crushed
¼ teaspoon pepper
Pork, beef, or lamb roast (up to 3 pounds)

In a small bowl combine onion, mustard, marjoram, rosemary, and pepper. With a large spoon, spread herb mixture on all sides of roast. Cover; refrigerate for 2 hours or up to 24 hours. Roast or grill meat.

14 Honey-Mustard Rub: Prepare as directed above except stir 1 tablespoon *honey* into mustard mixture and omit the marjoram.

15 Maple-Mustard Rub: Prepare Herb Mustard Rub as directed except stir 2 tablespoons *maple syrup or maple-flavored syrup* into mustard mixture.

Nutrition facts per 3-ounce serving rubbed pork: 214 cal., 11 g total fat (4 g sat. fat), 77 mg chol., 126 mg sodium, 1 g carbo., 0 g fiber, 25 g pro. Daily Value: 7% iron.

◆ Red Wine Marinade

◆ Caramelized Onions

16 **Red Wine Marinade**

½ cup dry red wine
½ cup water
1 clove garlic, minced
1 teaspoon dried rosemary, crushed
½ teaspoon dried thyme, crushed
½ teaspoon salt
¼ teaspoon pepper
Beef or lamb, such as flank steak,
beef tenderloin, leg of lamb, or
lamb chops (up to 2 pounds)

In a clean, sealable plastic bag combine wine, water, garlic, rosemary, thyme, salt, and pepper. Add meat; seal bag. Place bag inside a bowl. Marinate in refrigerator, turning bag occasionally, for 4 to 24 hours. (To serve remaining marinade as a sauce with the meat, bring to a full boil, stirring often.) Grill or broil meat. Makes 1 cup marinade.

Nutrition facts per 3-ounce serving marinated beef: 189 cal., 9 g total fat (3 g sat. fat), 70 mg chol., 142 mg sodium, 0 g carbo., 0 g fiber, 24 g pro. Daily Value: 22% iron.

17 **Fennel White Wine Marinade:**
Prepare marinade as directed except substitute *dry white wine* for red wine and substitute 1 teaspoon *fennel seed*, crushed, for the rosemary and thyme.

Use to marinate poultry (up to 2 pounds). Makes 1 cup.

Nutrition facts per 3-ounce serving marinated chicken: 207 cal., 11 g total fat (3 g sat. fat), 91 mg chol., 157 mg sodium, 0 g carbo., 0 g fiber, 23 g pro. Daily Value: 16% vit. A, 0% vit. C, 1% calcium, 9% iron.

18 **Caramelized Onions**
THESE CARAMEL-FLAVORED ONIONS ARE A PERFECT COMPANION TO BURGERS.

2 tablespoons margarine or butter
2 large white or red onions, cut into
¾-inch chunks (2 cups)
4 teaspoons brown sugar

In a medium skillet heat margarine or butter over medium-low heat till melted. Add onion. Cover and cook on medium-low heat till onion is tender, about 13 to 15 minutes. Uncover; add sugar. Cook and stir over medium-high heat till onion is golden brown, stirring constantly, about 4 to 5 minutes. Serve hot over burgers, prime rib, or beef steaks. Makes about ⅓ cup.

Nutrition facts per tablespoon: 112 cal., 6 g total fat (1 g sat. fat), 0 mg chol., 71 mg sodium, 15 g carbo., 2 g fiber, 1 g pro. Daily Value: 7% vit. A, 8% vit. C, 2% calcium, 2% iron.

19 **Sweet Red Pepper Spread**
ROASTED RED SWEET PEPPERS MAKE A ROBUST TOPPER FOR FRENCH BREAD OR WHOLE-GRAIN CRACKERS.

2 medium red sweet peppers or 1
7-ounce jar roasted sweet peppers, drained
2 tablespoons tomato paste

◆ Sweet Red Pepper Spread

1 teaspoon sugar
1 teaspoon snipped fresh thyme or
¼ teaspoon dried thyme, crushed
¼ teaspoon salt
⅛ teaspoon garlic powder
Dash ground red pepper

To roast fresh peppers, cut in quarters lengthwise; remove seeds and stems. Line a baking sheet with foil. Place peppers, skin side up, on baking sheet, pressing to lie flat. Bake in a 425° oven for 20 minutes or till dark and blistered. Remove from oven and place in a clean paper bag. Close bag and let stand about 10 minutes. When cool enough to handle, peel the dark skins from peppers; discard skins.

Place roasted peppers in a blender container or food processor bowl. Cover; blend or process till chopped fine. Add the tomato paste, sugar, thyme, salt, garlic powder, and ground red pepper. Cover; blend till nearly smooth. Spread on bread or crackers. To store, cover and refrigerate for up to 1 week. Makes about ¾ cup.

Nutrition facts per tablespoon: 5 cal., 0 g total fat (0 g sat. fat), 0 mg chol., 35 mg sodium, 1 g carbo., 0 g fiber, 0 g pro. Daily Value: 7% vit. A, 27% vit. C.

Better Butters

GO AHEAD—SLATHER THEM ON. THIS MIX OF BUTTERS AND SPREADS ADDS PANACHE TO BREADS, CRACKERS, OR STEAMED VEGETABLES.

◆Chocolate-Cashew Spread

20 Chocolate-Cashew Spread

2 ounces semisweet chocolate, cut up
1 cup roasted unsalted cashews or
toasted blanched almonds
¼ cup butter, cut up

In a small heavy saucepan melt chocolate over low heat, stirring constantly till chocolate begins to melt. Immediately remove the chocolate from heat; stir till smooth. Cool slightly.

Place nuts in a food processor bowl or blender container. Cover and process or

blend till nuts are very finely chopped, stopping and scraping the sides as necessary. Add butter; process or blend till nearly smooth. Transfer mixture to a bowl; stir in melted chocolate. Serve at room temperature to spread on croissants, muffins, or biscuits. Makes 1 cup.

Nutrition facts per tablespoon: 90 cal., 8 g total fat (3 g sat. fat), 8 mg chol., 80 mg sodium, 4 g carbo., 0 g fiber, 1 g pro.

21 Orange-Ginger Butter

TRY THIS GINGER-FLAVORED BUTTER ON ASPARAGUS, SNOW PEAS, OR GREEN BEANS.

½ cup orange marmalade
½ cup butter or margarine, softened
1 tablespoon balsamic vinegar or
cider vinegar
1 tablespoon finely chopped crystallized
ginger

In a small saucepan heat and stir orange marmalade just till melted. In a medium bowl beat butter or margarine till fluffy. Beat in melted marmalade, vinegar, and ginger. Cover; chill at least 1 hour before serving. Serve with cooked vegetables. Makes about 1 cup.

22 Zesty Pepper Butter: Prepare as directed except substitute *hot pepper jelly* for the marmalade; omit the ginger. Serve with corn on the cob, carrots, or sugar snap peas. Makes about 1 cup.

Nutrition facts per tablespoon: 80 cal., 6 g total fat (4 g sat. fat), 16 mg chol., 61 mg sodium, 8 g carbo., 0 g fiber, 0 g pro.

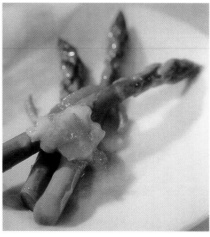

◆ Orange-Ginger Butter

◆ Spiced Peach Spread

◆ Hazelnut Butter

23 *Spiced Peach Spread*

SERVE THIS FLAVORFUL FRUIT SPREAD ON
MUFFINS, TOAST, OR CROISSANTS.

1 cup snipped dried peaches
½ cup water
¼ cup sugar
½ teaspoon apple pie spice or
pumpkin pie spice

In a small saucepan combine dried
peaches, water, sugar, and spice. Bring to
boiling over medium heat; reduce heat.
Simmer, covered, for 20 minutes or till
peaches are very soft. Place in a food
processor bowl or blender container.
Cover; process or blend till nearly
smooth. To store, cover and refrigerate
for up to 1 week. Makes 1 cup.

Nutrition facts per tablespoon: 42
cal., 0 g total fat (0 g sat. fat), 0 mg
chol., 1 mg sodium, 11 g carbo., 1 g
fiber, 0 g pro.

24 *Hazelnut Butter*

AN EASY AND DELICIOUS WAY TO DRESS
UP STEAMED VEGETABLES.

½ cup chopped toasted hazelnuts
½ cup butter or margarine, softened
1 teaspoon honey

In a small mixing bowl stir together
hazelnuts, butter or margarine, and
honey. If not serving immediately, cover
and chill. Bring to room temperature
before serving. Toss with cooked vegetables, such as baby carrots, asparagus, or
peas. Makes 1 cup.

Nutrition facts per tablespoon: 38
cal., 4 g total fat (2 g sat. fat), 8 mg
chol., 30 mg sodium, 1 g carbo., 0 g
fiber, 1 g pro.

◆ Roasted Garlic

25 **Roasted Garlic**

To serve as a bread spread, prepare one head of garlic per person.

1 medium head garlic
2 teaspoons olive oil

Peel away the dry outer layers of skin from the head of garlic. Leave skins of the cloves intact. Cut off the pointed top portion (about ¼ inch) with a knife, leaving the bulb intact but exposing the individual cloves.

Place the garlic head, cut side up, in a small baking dish. Drizzle with olive oil. Bake, covered, in a 400° oven for 25 to 35 minutes or till the cloves feel soft when pressed.

To serve, press garlic paste from individual cloves and spread on French bread. Makes about 1 tablespoon paste.

Nutrition facts per tablespoon: 128 cal., 9 g total fat (1 g sat. fat), 0 mg chol., 6 mg sodium, 11 g carbo., 1 g fiber, 2 g pro.

Salad Sensations

Let one or all of these salad toppers spiff up your lettuce bowl.

◆ Creamy Pesto Salad Dressing

◆ Spicy Broccoli Spread

26 *Spicy Broccoli Spread*
A MEDITERRANEAN-INSPIRED TOPPER
FOR CRACKERS OR BREADS.

2 cups broccoli flowerets
⅓ cup chopped onion
1 small clove garlic, chopped
¼ teaspoon crushed red pepper
2 tablespoons olive oil
2 tablespoons grated Parmesan cheese

In a small saucepan cook broccoli, covered, in a small amount of boiling salted water about 12 minutes or till tender. Drain well.

In a small skillet cook onion, garlic, and red pepper in hot oil till onion is soft, about 10 minutes. Combine broccoli, onion mixture, and Parmesan cheese in a food processor bowl. Cover; blend till smooth. Transfer to a small serving bowl. Serve at room temperature or cover and chill for up to 24 hours. If chilled, let stand at room temperature 30 minutes before serving. Serve with toasted bread or assorted crackers. Makes about ¾ cup.

◆ Crispy Herbed Croutons

Nutrition facts per tablespoon: 36 cal., 3 g total fat (1 g sat. fat), 1 mg chol., 27 mg sodium, 2 g carbo., 1 g fiber, 1 g pro. Daily Value: 6% vit. A, 21% vit. C, 2% calcium.

27 *Creamy Pesto Salad Dressing*
½ cup mayonnaise or salad dressing
¼ cup refrigerated purchased pesto
Buttermilk (about ⅓ cup)

In a small bowl stir together the mayonnaise or salad dressing and pesto. Add enough buttermilk till of desired consistency. Cover and store dressing in the refrigerator for up to 1 week. Serve atop mixed greens, fresh spinach, or stir into vegetable salads, such as potato. Makes about 1 cup.

Nutrition facts per tablespoon: 79 cal., 8 g total fat (1 g sat. fat), 5 mg chol., 74 mg sodium, 1 g carbo., 0 g fiber, 1 g pro.

28 *Crispy Herbed Croutons*
2 tablespoons olive oil
¾ teaspoon dried dillweed or Italian seasoning, crushed
⅛ teaspoon onion powder
4 slices whole wheat, white, or rye bread, cut into cubes

In a bowl stir together oil, dillweed or Italian seasoning, and onion powder. Add bread cubes; stir till coated. Spread bread cubes in a single layer in a shallow baking pan. Bake in a 300° oven for 10 minutes. Stir; bake 10 minutes more or till lightly browned. Cool. Serve atop salad greens. To store, place in an airtight container and refrigerate for up to 1 month. Bring to room temperature before serving. Makes 2 cups.

Nutrition facts per ¼ cup serving: 71 cal., 4 g total fat (1 g sat. fat), 0 mg chol., 89 mg sodium, 8 g carbo., 1 g fiber, 2 g pro.

◆ Marinated Greek Style Olives

29 *Marinated Greek-Style Olives*

1 6-ounce can pitted ripe black olives,
drained and rinsed
¼ cup lemon juice
2 slices lemon
2 whole garlic cloves
1 teaspoon dried oregano, crushed
¾ cup olive oil

In an airtight container combine the olives, lemon juice, lemon slices, garlic, and oregano; let olives stand, covered, at room temperature for two days, stirring occasionally. Pour the olive oil over the olives till completely covered. Cover container with an airtight lid. Refrigerate the olive mixture for 2 days; remove lemon slices. Bring to room temperature before serving. Or, if desired, return to refrigerator; chill, covered, up to 2 weeks. Drain olives before serving. Makes 1⅓ cups.

30 **Marinated Coriander Olives:**
Prepare Marinated Greek-Style Olives as directed except substitute 1 teaspoon *peppercorns* for the whole garlic cloves and 1 teaspoon *coriander seed* for the dried oregano.

Nutrition facts per 2 tablespoons olives: 76 cal., 9 g total fat (1 g sat. fat), 0 mg chol., 115 mg sodium, 1 g carbo., 1 g fiber, 1 g pro.

31 *Crunchy Lemon-Pepper Nuts*

2 tablespoons margarine or butter, melted
2 teaspoons soy sauce
1 teaspoon lemon juice
1 teaspoon lemon-pepper seasoning
2 cups unsalted nuts (such as pecan or walnut halves, whole almonds, or cashews)

In a medium bowl combine the melted margarine or butter, soy sauce, lemon juice, and lemon-pepper seasoning. Add nuts; stir till coated. Spread nuts in a 9x9x2-inch baking pan. Bake in a 325° oven about 15 minutes or till lightly toasted, stirring twice. Remove from oven. Cool. Store in an airtight container, refrigerated, for up to 1 month. Bring to room temperature before serving. Serve atop fruit or a salad. Makes 2 cups.

32 **Crunchy Five-Spice Nuts:**
Prepare nuts as directed above except substitute *sesame oil* for the lemon juice and *five-spice powder* for the lemon-pepper seasoning.

Nutrition facts per 2 tablespoons: 111 cal., 9 g fat, 0 mg chol., 63 mg sodium, 6 g carbo., 1 g fiber, 3 g pro.

◆ Crunchy Lemon-Pepper Nuts

33 *Fruited Vinaigrette*

⅓ cup salad oil
¼ cup orange marmalade
3 tablespoons water
3 tablespoons white wine vinegar
1 teaspoon Dijon-style mustard
¼ teaspoon dried basil, crushed

In a screw-top jar combine all of the ingredients. Cover; shake to combine. Store, covered, in the refrigerator for up to 2 weeks. Shake before serving. Makes 1 cup.

Nutrition facts per tablespoon: 61 cal., 5 g total fat, 0 mg chol., 10 mg sodium, 4 g carbo., 0 g pro.

34 *Berry-Kiwi Salsa*

SERVE THIS FRUIT SALSA WITH SEAFOOD, FISH, CHICKEN, OR BAKED PITA CHIPS (SEE RECIPE, PAGE 76).

½ cup coarsely chopped strawberries
½ cup peeled and chopped kiwi fruit
(1 to 2 fruit)

◆ Fruited Vinaigrette

¼ cup thinly sliced green onion
¼ cup chopped yellow or green sweet
pepper
1 tablespoon lime or lemon juice
2 teaspoons snipped fresh cilantro, parsley,
or basil
1 teaspoon sugar
Dash ground red pepper

In a medium bowl stir together the strawberries; kiwi fruit; green onion; sweet pepper; lime or lemon juice; cilantro, parsley, or basil; sugar; and red pepper. Cover and chill salsa for up to 6 hours. Makes about 1¼ cups.

35 Peach and Kiwi Salsa: Prepare salsa as directed except substitute ½ cup chopped *peach or nectarine* for the chopped *strawberries* and ¼ cup chopped *red onion* for the green onion. Makes 1¼ cups.

Nutrition facts per tablespoon: 6 cal., 0 g total fat, 0 mg chol., 0 mg sodium, 1 g carbo., 0 g fiber, 0 g pro.

Salsas and Dippers

SALSAS ARE HOT! BUT THEY'RE NOT FOR CHIPS ONLY. TRY THEM WITH CHICKEN, FISH, AND SEAFOOD TOO.

◆ Berry Kiwi Salsa with Baked Pita Chips

36 Orange-Avocado Salsa: Prepare Berry-Kiwi Salsa as directed except substitute one 8-ounce can *mandarin orange sections,* drained, for the strawberries; 1 small *avocado,* halved, seeded, and peeled, for the kiwi fruit; and *orange juice* for the lime or lemon juice. Add ¼ cup toasted slivered almonds before serving. Makes about 2 cups.

Nutrition facts per tablespoon: 19 cal., 1 g total fat, 0 mg chol., 1 mg sodium, 2 g carbo., 0 g pro.

◆ Pineapple Salsa

37 *Pineapple Salsa*

1 cup chunky salsa
½ cup chopped fresh pineapple or
one 8-ounce can crushed pineapple
(juice pack), drained
¼ teaspoon grated fresh gingerroot or
dash ground ginger

In a bowl combine salsa, pineapple, and ginger. Cover; chill till serving time. Bring to room temperature to serve. Serve with shrimp, tortilla chips, or pita chips. Makes 1½ cups.

38 Fresh Vegetable Salsa: Prepare salsa as directed except omit pineapple and ginger. Stir ½ cup chopped *yellow summer squash or zucchini* and 1 teaspoon snipped *fresh mint* into the salsa. Makes 1½ cups.

Nutrition facts per tablespoon of Pineapple or Fresh Vegetable Salsa: 8 cal., 0 g total fat, 0 mg chol., 66 mg sodium, 2 g carbo., 0 g pro.

39 *Black Bean Corn Salsa*

⅔ cup corn relish
½ of a 15-ounce can black beans,
drained and rinsed (about ¾ cup)
¼ cup thinly sliced radishes
1½ teaspoons lime juice
¼ teaspoon ground cumin

In a bowl stir together relish, beans, radishes, lime juice, and cumin. Let stand, covered, for 30 minutes. Serve with Baked Tortilla Strips (see recipe, right) or tortilla chips. Makes 1⅔ cups.

Nutrition facts per tablespoon: 15 cal., 0 g total fat (0 g sat. fat), 0 mg chol., 47 mg sodium, 3 g carbo., 0 g fiber, 1 g pro.

40 *Baked Pita Chips*

4 large pita bread rounds
Nonstick spray coating or olive oil-flavor spray coating
½ to ¾ teaspoon onion powder, garlic powder, or seasoned pepper

Split pita bread rounds in half horizontally. Lightly spray the cut side of each pita bread half with nonstick coating. Sprinkle lightly with onion or garlic powder or pepper. Cut each half into 6 wedges. Spread wedges in a single layer on a baking sheet. (You'll need to bake chips in batches.) Bake in a 350° oven for 10 to 12 minutes or till crisp. Serve with salsa. To store, place chips in an airtight container for up to 1 week. Makes 8 servings (6 chips per serving).

Nutrition facts per serving: 55 cal., 0 g total fat (0 g sat. fat), 0 mg chol., 108 mg sodium, 10 g carbo., 0 g fiber, 2 g pro.

◆ Black Bean Corn Salsa with Baked Tortilla Strips

41 Baked Tortilla Strips: Prepare as directed above except substitute eight 7-inch *corn tortillas* for the pita rounds. Cut whole tortillas into 1-inch-wide strips. Bake as above.

Nutrition facts per serving: 57 cal., 1 g total fat (0 g sat. fat), 0 mg chol., 40 mg sodium, 12 g carbo., 0 g fiber, 1 g pro.

42 *Strawberry-Rhubarb Sauce*

1½ cups fresh or frozen chopped rhubarb
½ cup sugar
2 tablespoons water
½ teaspoon ground cardamom or ground cinnamon
1 tablespoon cold water
1½ teaspoons cornstarch
1½ cups sliced strawberries

Super Ice Cream Sauces

WHO CAN RESIST ICE CREAM? CAP A BOWLFUL WITH ONE OF OUR VELVETY RICH SAUCES.

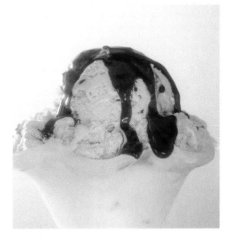

◆ Bittersweet Chocolate Sauce

◆ Strawberry-Rhubarb Sauce

In a 2-quart saucepan combine rhubarb, sugar, the 2 tablespoons water, and cardamom or cinnamon. Bring to boiling; reduce heat. Cover and simmer about 5 minutes or till the fruit is tender. Stir together the 1 tablespoon water and cornstarch. Add to the rhubarb mixture. Cook and stir over medium-heat till thickened and bubbly. Cook and stir for 2 minutes more. Stir in strawberries. Serve warm over ice cream. Makes 2 cups.

Nutrition facts per 2 tablespoons: 30 cal., 0 g total fat (0 g sat. fat), 0 mg chol., 1 mg sodium, 8 g carbo., 1 g fiber, 0 g pro.

43 *Bittersweet Chocolate Sauce*

4 ounces bittersweet chocolate or semisweet chocolate, cut up
2 tablespoons margarine or butter
¾ cup milk
½ cup sugar
2 tablespoons corn syrup

In a heavy, medium saucepan melt chocolate and margarine or butter over low heat till melted, stirring frequently. Add milk, sugar, and corn syrup. Bring to a gentle boil over medium heat. Boil gently, stirring frequently, for 8 minutes or till mixture is thickened. Remove from heat. Cool slightly. Serve warm. To store, cover and refrigerate for up to 1 week. Makes 1 cup.

44 Liqueur-Flavored Chocolate Sauce: Prepare the Bittersweet Chocolate Sauce as directed except stir 2 to 4 tablespoons desired *liqueur* (such as hazelnut, amaretto, or ginger) into the thickened sauce.

Nutrition facts per 2 tablespoons Bittersweet or Liqueur-Flavored Chocolate Sauce: 178 cal., 8 g total fat (4 g sat. fat), 2 mg chol., 49 mg sodium, 27 g carbo., 1 g fiber, 2 g pro.

45 Chocolate Peanut Butter Topping: Prepare Bittersweet Chocolate Sauce as directed except stir ⅓ cup *peanut butter* into the warm sauce. Stir in enough *milk* (about 1 tablespoon) till of desired consistency. Makes 1½ cups.

Nutrition facts per 2 tablespoons: 154 cal., 9 g total fat (3 g sat. fat), 1 mg chol., 67 mg sodium, 19 g carbo., 1 g fiber, 3 g pro.

◆ Luscious Apricot Sauce

46 *Luscious Apricot Sauce*

¾ cup snipped dried apricots
¼ teaspoon finely shredded orange peel
1¼ cups orange juice
¼ cup sugar
½ teaspoon cornstarch

In a saucepan combine dried apricots, orange peel, and juice. Bring to boiling; reduce heat. Cover and simmer about 5 minutes or till apricots are soft. Combine sugar and cornstarch. Add to saucepan. Bring to boiling; reduce heat. Cook and stir till bubbly. Cook for 2 minutes more. Serve over ice cream. Makes 1⅓ cups.

47 Amaretto Apricot Sauce: Prepare apricot sauce as directed above except reduce the orange juice to 1 cup. Stir in 3 tablespoons *amaretto* just before serving. Serve over ice cream. Makes 1⅓ cups.

Nutrition facts per 2 tablespoons sauce: 60 cal., 0 g total fat, 0 mg chol., 2 mg sodium, 14 g carbo., 1 g fiber, 0 g pro.

48 *Caramel-Scotch Sauce*

BE SURE TO WARM THE WHIPPING CREAM BEFORE ADDING IT TO THE CARAMELIZED SUGAR IN THE SKILLET.

1 cup sugar
½ cup whipping cream, warmed*
2 tablespoons butter or margarine, cut up
1 teaspoon vanilla

Place sugar in a heavy medium skillet. Cook over medium-high heat, without stirring, just till the sugar begins to melt and bubble, shaking the skillet occasionally to heat evenly. Reduce the heat to medium-low; cook about 5 minutes more or till the sugar is melted and golden, stirring occasionally with a wooden spoon after sugar begins to melt. Remove the skillet from heat.

Carefully and gradually stir the warmed whipping cream into the syrup (mixture will harden). Return to heat. Cook over medium heat, stirring constantly, till the caramel dissolves, about 2 to 3 minutes. Remove skillet from heat. Cool sauce slightly. Stir in the butter or margarine and vanilla. Pour the sauce into a heat-proof pitcher or container. Serve warm over ice cream. Makes about 1 cup.

Nutrition facts per 2 tablespoons: 168 cal., 8 g total fat (5 g sat. fat), 28 mg chol., 35 mg sodium, 25 g carbo., 0 g fiber, 0 g pro.

49 Orange Caramel Sauce: Prepare the caramel sauce as directed except substitute *orange juice** for the whipping cream. Continue boiling sauce till syrupy (about 3 to 4 minutes). Stir in butter or margarine and the vanilla. Serve warm over ice cream. Makes ¾ cup.

◆ Caramel Scotch Sauce

*To warm whipping cream or orange juice, place in a microwave-safe glass measure and heat in a microwave oven on 100% power (high) for 30 seconds or till warm.

Nutrition facts per 2 tablespoons: 164 cal., 4 g total fat (2 g sat. fat), 10 mg chol., 39 mg sodium, 34 g carbo., 0 g fiber, 0 g pro.

50 Praline Pecan Caramel-Scotch Sauce: Prepare Caramel-Scotch Sauce as directed. For pralines, place ¾ cup *sugar* in a heavy, large skillet. Cook over medium-high heat, without stirring, till the sugar begins to melt and bubble, shaking the skillet occasionally. Reduce the heat to medium-low; cook about 5 minutes more or till sugar is melted and golden, stirring occasionally with a wooden spoon after sugar begins to melt. Add 1 cup toasted *pecan pieces*. Stir till coated. Spread nuts on buttered foil. Cool; break apart. Stir desired amount of nuts into Caramel-Scotch Sauce just before serving. Makes about 1½ cups.

Nutrition facts per 2 tablespoons sauce: 276 cal., 14 g total fat (6 g sat. fat), 28 mg chol., 35 mg sodium, 39 g carbo., 2 g pro.

Prize Tested Recipes

Rhubarb-Raspberry Pie

USING A TRIO OF FRUIT FLAVORS, MAE
DISCOVERED A DELICIOUS COMBINATION
FOR THIS WINNING PIE

1¾ cups sugar
6 tablespoons all-purpose flour*
4 cups chopped fresh rhubarb or frozen
rhubarb*
1 cup raspberries
1 medium cooking apple, peeled and
shredded
Pastry for a double-crust pie

In a large mixing bowl stir together
the sugar and flour. Stir in rhubarb,
raspberries, and apple. Transfer to a pastry-lined 9-inch pie plate. Trim pastry
even with the rim of the pie plate. Cut
slits in the top crust. Place top crust over
fruit filling. Seal and flute the edge.
Cover edges with foil; bake in a 375°
oven for 25 minutes. Remove foil; bake
20 to 25 minutes more or till top is
golden and fruit is tender. Cool on a
wire rack. Makes 8 servings.

*Note: If using frozen rhubarb, use
½ cup flour instead of 6 tablespoons;
toss the chopped rhubarb with the sugar
and flour mixture. Let the mixture stand
about 30 minutes or till the fruit is partially thawed but still icy. Stir well.
Gently fold in the raspberries and apple.
Transfer rhubarb mixture to the pastry-
lined pie plate. Continue as directed
except bake pie for 50 minutes. Remove

◆ Rhubarb-Raspberry Pie

foil from edges and bake 10 to 20 minutes more or till the top is golden and
the fruit is tender.

Nutrition facts per serving: 476 cal.,
18 g total fat (4 g sat. fat), 0 mg chol.,
137 mg sodium, 77 g carbo., 3 g fiber,
4 g pro. Daily Value: 0% vit. A, 14%
vit. C, 5% calcium, 13% iron.
$200 WINNER
Mae M. Clark
Coeur d'Alene, Idaho

◆ Cheese and Vegetable Chowder

Cheese and Vegetable Chowder

HOW EASY! ADD A FEW INGREDIENTS TO A POTATO MIX AND IN 30 MINUTES, SERVE A HEARTY SOUP.

4 cups water
3 cups shredded cabbage
1 cup finely chopped Canadian-style bacon (4½ ounces)
2 large carrots, thinly sliced (1⅓ cups)
1 5.25- to 5.5-ounce package dry au gratin potato mix
1 cup milk
1 teaspoon cornstarch
1 cup frozen cut green beans

In a 4-quart Dutch oven combine the water, cabbage, Canadian-style bacon, carrots, and the dry potatoes with sauce mix. Bring to boiling; reduce heat. Simmer, covered, for 15 minutes. Combine the milk and cornstarch; add to soup along with frozen beans. Simmer, covered, for 10 to 15 minutes more or till beans are tender. Makes 4 to 6 main-dish servings.

Nutrition facts per serving: 292 cal., 5 g total fat (1 g sat. fat), 20 mg chol., 1,378 mg sodium, 48 g carbo., 4 g fiber, 15 g pro. Daily Value: 198% vit. A, 72% vit. C, 20% calcium, 12% iron.
$200 WINNER
Kim Ramm,
Lansing, Michigan

Curry-Cajun Spiced Chicken

SIMPLY MIX ALL OF THE INGREDIENTS TOGETHER, POUR OVER CHICKEN, AND BAKE FOR A QUICK DINNER.

◆ Curry Cajun Spiced Chicken

⅓ cup honey
3 tablespoons water
3 tablespoons prepared mustard
2 tablespoons margarine or butter, melted
2 to 3 teaspoons Cajun seasoning
2 to 3 teaspoons curry powder
1 teaspoon lemon juice
1 clove garlic, minced
6 skinless, boneless chicken breast halves (about 1½ pounds)
Hot cooked rice

In a 3-quart rectangular baking dish combine honey, water, mustard, melted margarine or butter, Cajun seasoning, curry powder, lemon juice, and garlic; mix well. Add chicken breast halves, turning to coat. Arrange in a single layer. Bake, uncovered, in a 350° oven about 30 minutes or till chicken is tender and no longer pink. Serve chicken and pan drippings with hot cooked rice. Makes 6 main-dish servings.

Nutrition facts per serving with ½ cup rice: 438 cal., 11 g total fat (2 g sat. fat), 89 mg chol., 389 mg sodium, 47 g carbo., 1 g fiber, 35 g pro. Daily Value: 12% vit. A, 2% vit. C, 4% calcium, 19% iron.
$100 WINNER
Audrey Green,
Pembroke Pines, Florida

◆ Rhubarb-Pineapple Crumble

Rhubarb-Pineapple Crumble

IRRESISTIBLE! GINGER IN THE RICH
SUGAR-CRUMB TOP COMPLEMENTS THE
LUSCIOUS FRUIT FILLING.

*7 cups fresh or frozen rhubarb,
cut into 1-inch pieces
1 8-ounce can crushed pineapple, drained
1 cup packed brown sugar
2 tablespoons cornstarch*

*2 teaspoons finely shredded lemon peel
⅔ cup all-purpose flour
¼ cup packed brown sugar
1 tablespoon granulated sugar
1 tablespoon chopped crystallized ginger
Dash salt
⅓ cup butter
Vanilla ice cream (optional)*

Thaw frozen rhubarb completely, if using, draining well. In a large bowl combine fresh or thawed rhubarb, pineapple, and the 1 cup brown sugar. Let stand 1 hour. Drain mixture, reserving juices. If necessary, add water to reserved juices to equal ⅔ cup. Place juices in a small saucepan. Stir in cornstarch. Cook and stir over medium heat till thickened and bubbly. Remove from heat. Stir into rhubarb-and-pineapple mixture; stir in lemon peel. Place mixture in a 2-quart square baking dish.

In another bowl combine flour, the ¼ cup brown sugar, granulated sugar, ginger, and salt. Cut in butter with a pastry blender till mixture is crumbly. Spoon over top of fruit. Bake in a 350° oven about 1 hour or till light brown and bubbly. Serve warm with ice cream, if desired. Makes 6 to 8 servings.

Nutrition facts per serving: 352 cal., 11 g total fat (6 g sat. fat), 27 mg chol., 144 mg sodium, 64 g carbo., 3 g fiber, 3 g pro. Daily Value: 10% vit. A, 27% vit. C, 14% calcium, 14% iron.

$100 WINNER
Ms. Carmela M. Meely,
Walnut Creek, California

May

Recipes to Save Your Day

Little Ways to Make Life Easier

Prize Tested Recipes

Paella Salad, Coconut Macaroon Cheesecake, Piña Colada Sherbet, Almond Chicken Pasta Salad

Recipes to Save Your Day

Ever had to cook up something inspired at a moment's notice and felt like dialing 911?
Relax, and try our tasty solutions to life's little cooking challenges.

By Julia Malloy

"I don't have the time or money to entertain friends. What can I do?"

SOLUTION

Invite them for an easy, affordable Tex-Mex brunch.

Scrambled Eggs Fajitas

SET THE EGGS AND WARM TORTILLAS ON THE BUFFET TABLE TO LET GUESTS HELP THEMSELVES. THEY CAN SHAPE TORTILLAS INTO A CONE TO HOLD THE EGG FILLING OR ROLL THEM ENCHILADA STYLE.

12 6-inch flour tortillas
12 eggs
⅔ cup milk, light cream, or half-and-half
¼ teaspoon salt
¼ teaspoon pepper
1 tablespoon cooking oil

1 11-ounce can whole kernel corn with sweet peppers, drained
½ cup thinly sliced green onion
1 cup shredded reduced-fat or regular Monterey Jack cheese with jalapeño peppers
Salsa

Wrap tortillas in a stack in foil; heat in a 350° oven for 10 minutes to soften. (Or, wrap tortillas in microwave-safe paper towels; heat in a microwave oven on high about 1 minute or till softened.)

Meanwhile, in a large bowl beat together eggs, milk or light cream, salt, and pepper.

To scramble eggs, in a very large skillet heat oil over medium heat. Add egg mixture. Cook, without stirring, till mixture begins to set on bottom and around edge. Add corn and ¼ cup of the green onion.

Using a large spatula, lift and fold partially cooked eggs so the uncooked portion flows underneath. Add cheese. Cook over medium heat till cooked but still glossy and moist. Remove from heat. Sprinkle with remaining green onion.

To serve, spoon eggs into a serving container and place tortillas in a tortilla warmer or basket. Let guests serve themselves from the buffet table. Serve with salsa. Makes 6 main-dish servings.

Nutrition facts per serving: 515 cal., 23 g total fat (7 g sat. fat), 441 mg chol., 917 mg sodium, 53 g carbo., 1 g fiber, 26 g pro. Daily Value: 27% vit. A, 25% vit. C, 15% calcium, 30% iron.

Cost per serving: $1.15

TEX-MEX BRUNCH

Feed a hungry crew for less than $2.00 a serving with this easy buffet-style brunch. The secret to saving money lies in the ingredients you use. For example, this menu has no costly meats or seasonings. For a fresh fruit serve-along, choose fruits that are in season or on special.

To ease preparation, stir up the egg filling and bake the buns the night before. Before your guests arrive in the morning, prepare the drink base, reheat the buns, and cut up the fruit. Wait until everyone arrives to scramble the eggs.

◆ Mock Margarita Punch, Scrambled Eggs Fajitas, Orange Spice Buns

Orange Spice Buns

SHAPE AND BAKE THESE CINNAMONY BUNS FROM FROZEN BREAD DOUGH THE NIGHT BEFORE. THE NEXT MORNING, REHEAT THE BUNS AND DRIZZLE WITH ORANGE GLAZE.

1 16-ounce loaf frozen sweet bread dough
1 tablespoon margarine or butter, melted
2 tablespoons sugar
1 teaspoon ground cinnamon
1 recipe Orange Glaze
(see recipe, below)

Thaw dough according to package directions. On a lightly floured surface, pat or roll dough into a 12x6-inch rectangle. (If dough is difficult to roll, let it rest for 10 minutes for easier handling.) Cut crosswise into twelve 6x1-inch strips. With your fingers, stretch each strip to 10 inches long. To shape into rosettes, tie each rope into a loose knot, leaving 1 long end. Tuck the end under the roll (see photograph, above). Place 2 inches apart on a lightly greased baking sheet. Cover with a clean towel and let rise in a warm place till double (about 30 minutes).

Brush rosettes with margarine or butter. Combine sugar and cinnamon; sprinkle over dough. Bake, uncovered, in a 375° oven for 10 to 12 minutes or till golden. Cool on a wire rack. Drizzle with Orange Glaze. Makes 12.

Orange Glaze: In a small bowl stir together 1 cup sifted *powdered sugar* and enough *orange juice* (1 to 2 tablespoons) to make an icing of drizzling consistency. If orange color is desired, stir in a few drops of *yellow and red food coloring*.

To shape each bun into a rosette, tie each rope into a loose knot, leaving one long end. Tuck the end under the roll.

Nutrition facts per bun: 69 cal., 1 g total fat (0 g sat. fat), 0 mg chol., 13 mg sodium, 13 g carbo., 0 g fiber, 1 g pro. Daily Value: 0% vit. A, 0% vit. C, 1% calcium, 3% iron.

Cost per serving: $.20

Mock Margarita Punch

FOR THE LOOK OF REAL MARGARITAS, MOISTEN AND DIP THE RIMS OF THE GLASSES INTO CRYSTAL OR COARSE SUGAR BEFORE POURING THIS FRUITY PUNCH.

1 cup orange juice
¾ cup unsweetened grapefruit juice
1 6-ounce can (⅔ cup) frozen limeade concentrate, thawed
2 cups sparkling water or lemon-lime carbonated beverage
Ice cubes
Orange, lemon, or lime slices (optional)

In a pitcher stir together orange juice, grapefruit juice, and limeade concentrate. Just before serving, stir in sparkling water. Add ice cubes and citrus slices, if desired. Makes 6 (6-ounce) servings.

Nutrition facts per serving: 84 cal., 0 g total fat (0 g sat. fat), 0 mg chol., 3 mg sodium, 21 g carbo., 0 g fiber, 0 g pro. Daily Value: 0% vit. A, 47% vit. C, 1% calcium, 0% iron.

Cost per serving: $.26

"How can I make yesterday's leftovers taste great today?"

SOLUTION

DAY 1
Roast Pork with Thyme-Mushroom Sauce
Save half for another meal.

DAY 2
Creamy Mostaccioli with Snap Peas
Your family will never recognize the leftovers.

Roast Pork with Thyme-Mushroom Sauce

PORK COOKS TO JUICY PERFECTION WHILE YOU DO OTHER THINGS. REMEMBER TO SAVE SOME OF THE ROAST TO MAKE CREAMY MOSTACCIOLI.

2 tablespoons dry white wine
1 tablespoon peppercorn mustard or Dijon-style mustard
1½ teaspoons snipped fresh thyme or ½ teaspoon dried thyme, crushed
¼ teaspoon salt
¼ teaspoon pepper
1 2- to 3-pound boneless pork rib-end roast (Chef's Prime)
1 pound tiny new potatoes, halved

◆ Roast Pork with Thyme Mushroom Sauce

8 ounces baby carrots
1 medium red onion, cut into wedges
1 tablespoon olive oil
1 tablespoon balsamic or white wine vinegar
½ teaspoon salt
1 cup Thyme-Mushroom Sauce
(see recipe, page 88)

For mustard coating, in a bowl mix wine, mustard, thyme, the ¼ teaspoon salt, and pepper. Brush onto roast. Place roast, fat side up, on a rack in a shallow roasting pan. Insert a meat thermometer. Roast in a 325° oven for 1 to 2 hours or till the temperature reaches 160°, brushing occasionally with mustard sauce.

Meanwhile, cook potatoes and carrots in boiling salted water about 10 minutes or till almost tender; drain. Toss potatoes, carrots, and onion wedges with the olive oil, vinegar, and the ½ teaspoon salt; add to the roasting pan the last 15 minutes of roasting.

Slice two-thirds of the roast; serve with the roasted vegetables and 1 cup of the Thyme-Mushroom Sauce. (Cover and chill remaining roast and sauce for up to 3 days to use with Creamy Mostaccioli with Snap Peas). Makes 4 servings.

Nutrition facts per serving: 425 cal., 16 g total fat (4 g sat. fat), 69 mg chol., 764 mg sodium, 40 g carbo., 4 g fiber, 28 g pro. Daily Value: 135% vit. A, 31% vit. C, 12% calcium, 24% iron.

◆ Creamy Mostaccioli with Snap Peas

Thyme-Mushroom Sauce

THIS SAUCE APPEARS FIRST AS A GRAVY FOR ROAST PORK, THEN AS A SAUCE FOR PASTA.

*6 ounces halved or cut-up fresh mushrooms
(porcini, morel, cèpes, oyster,
chanterelle, shiitake, or white)
½ cup chopped onion
2 cloves garlic, minced
1½ teaspoons snipped fresh thyme or
½ teaspoon dried thyme, crushed
½ teaspoon salt
¼ teaspoon pepper
2 tablespoons margarine or butter
1 12-ounce can (1½ cups)
evaporated skim milk
4 teaspoons cornstarch
¼ cup dry white wine*

In a large skillet cook mushrooms, onion, garlic, thyme, salt, and pepper in hot margarine or butter till tender.

Stir together milk and cornstarch; stir into skillet. Cook and stir till thickened and bubbly. Add wine; cook and stir for

2 minutes more. Use 1 cup as a sauce for Roast Pork with Thyme-Mushroom Sauce and remaining 1⅔ cups to toss with Creamy Mostaccioli with Snap Peas. Cover and chill any leftover sauce for up to 3 days. Makes about 2⅔ cups.

Nutrition facts per ¼-cup serving: 48 cal., 2 g total fat (0 g sat. fat), 1 mg chol., 172 mg sodium, 5 g carbo., 0 g fiber, 3 g pro. Daily Value: 3% vit. A, 0% vit. C, 6% calcium, 0% iron.

Creamy Mostaccioli with Snap Peas

WHIP UP THIS PASTA MAIN DISH IN JUST 15 MINUTES USING THE LEFTOVERS FROM ROAST PORK WITH THYME-MUSHROOM SAUCE.

*8 ounces mostaccioli or corkscrew
macaroni
2 cups fresh sugar snap peas,
halved crosswise
8 ounces cooked pork (if using left-overs
from Roast Pork with
Thyme-Mushroom Sauce, page 86,
use the reserved portion
of the pork roast)
1⅔ cups Thyme-Mushroom Sauce
(see recipe, left)
1 large tomato, seeded and chopped
Shredded smoked mozzarella or
Parmesan cheese (optional)*

In a Dutch oven or large saucepan cook the pasta in boiling salted water according to package directions. Add the peas the last 2 minutes of cooking. Drain.

◆ Citrus Marinated Flank Steak, Grilled Spring Vegetables

Meanwhile, cut pork into matchstick-size strips. In a medium saucepan heat Thyme-Mushroom Sauce, adding water if the sauce seems too thick. Add meat; heat through. Gently stir in tomato. Remove from heat.

To serve, turn pasta mixture into a serving bowl; top pasta and snap peas with mushroom sauce. If desired, sprinkle with cheese. Makes 4 main-dish servings.

Nutrition facts per serving: 476 cal., 11 g total fat (3 g sat. fat), 40 mg chol., 456 mg sodium, 63 g carbo., 3 g fiber, 28 g pro. Daily Value: 16% vit. A, 89% vit. C, 23% calcium, 34% iron.

Skip-the-Stress Dinner

You'll feel like a guest at your own dinner party because so much of this menu can be made ahead. The night before, marinate the steak, shake together the salad dressing, prepare the salad greens, precook the vegetables, and freeze the ice. Before dinner, grill the meat and vegetables and toss the salad.

Score meat on both sides by making diagonal cuts at 1-inch intervals on surface. Place in a plastic bag set in a shallow dish; add marinade and orange slices. Seal bag; turn to coat. Marinate in the refrigerator for 6 to 24 hours, turning bag occasionally.

Remove steak from bag, reserving marinade. Grill on an uncovered grill directly over medium coals to desired doneness, allowing 18 to 22 minutes for medium. Turn and brush with the reserved marinade halfway through the grilling time.

To serve, slice meat diagonally across grain into thin slices. Sprinkle with pepper. Makes 4 to 6 servings.

Nutrition facts per serving: 224 cal., 12 g total fat (4 g sat. fat), 53 mg chol., 161 mg sodium, 7 g carbo., 1 g fiber, 22 g pro. Daily Value: 1% vit. A, 54% vit. C, 2% calcium, 16% iron.

"Help! My boss is coming to dinner. What can I serve that won't stress me out?"

SOLUTION

Keep dinner simple and make it ahead.

Citrus-Marinated Flank Steak

◆ ◆ ◆

Grilled Spring Vegetables

◆ ◆ ◆

Spiced Greens with Feta and Walnuts

Rhubarb-Strawberry Ice

◆ ◆ ◆

Sparkling Water
Red or White Zinfandel

Citrus-Marinated Flank Steak

SCORING AND MARINATING FLANK STEAK MAKES IT TENDER AND TASTY.

*1 1- to 1½-pound beef flank steak,
cut about ¾ inch thick
1 cup Citrus-Spice Marinade
(see recipe, page 90)
1 medium orange, sliced
Crushed peppercorns*

Grilled Spring Vegetables

SAVE ON TIME AND ON DISHES. GRILL A SIDE DISH OF TENDER, COLORFUL VEGETABLES USING THIS HANDY CHART.

1 to 1½ tablespoons snipped fresh
cilantro or parsley
⅓ cup Citrus-Spice Marinade
(see recipe, below)
1 to 1½ pounds fresh vegetables, such as
sweet onions, sweet peppers, eggplant, baby
carrots, fennel, zucchini or yellow squash,
leeks, or new potatoes

Stir cilantro or parsley into Citrus-Spice Marinade. Prepare and grill vegetables according to the chart at right, brushing occasionally with the marinade. (If the vegetables are smaller than the grill rack, you may need to thread them onto metal skewers.) Season the vegetables with salt and pepper. Makes 4 to 6 side-dish servings.

Nutrition facts per serving: 66 cal., 3 g total fat (0 g sat. fat), 0 mg chol., 82 mg sodium, 10 g carbo., 2 g fiber, 2 g pro. Daily Value: 52% vit. A, 61% vit. C, 3% calcium, 7% iron.

Citrus-Spice Marinade

THIS SAUCE DOES TRIPLE DUTY—AS A MARINADE FOR CITRUS-MARINATED FLANK STEAK, AS A BRUSH-ON FOR GRILLED SPRING VEGETABLES, AND AS PART OF THE SALAD DRESSING FOR SPICED GREENS WITH FETA AND WALNUTS.

1 cup orange juice
⅓ cup lemon juice
¼ cup cooking oil

TIMINGS FOR GRILLED VEGETABLES

VEGETABLE	PREPARATION	PRECOOKING TIME	GRILLING TIME
Baby carrots	Cut off carrot tops. Wash and peel.	3 to 5 minutes	3 to 5 minutes
Eggplant	Cut off top and blossom ends. Cut crosswise into 1-inch-thick slices.	Do not precook.	8 minutes
Fennel	Snip off feathery leaves. Cut off stems. After precooking, cut into 6 to 8 wedges.	Precook whole bulbs for 10 minutes.	8 minutes
Leeks	Cut off green tops; trim bulb roots and remove 1 or 2 layers of white skin. After precooking, halve lengthwise.	10 minutes or till tender	5 minutes
New potatoes	Halve potatoes.	10 minutes or till almost tender	10 to 12 minutes
Sweet onions	Peel and halve.	Do not precook.	8 to 10 minutes
Sweet peppers	Remove stem. Quarter peppers. Remove seeds and membranes. Cut peppers into 1-inch-wide strips.	Do not precook.	8 to 10 minutes
Zucchini or yellow squash	Cut off ends. Quarter lengthwise into long strips.	Do not precook.	5 to 6 minutes

3 tablespoons Worcestershire sauce
3 cloves garlic, minced
1 teaspoon ground cumin
¾ teaspoon onion powder
½ teaspoon salt
½ teaspoon pepper

In a screw-top jar combine orange and lemon juice, cooking oil, Worcestershire sauce, garlic, cumin, onion powder, salt, and pepper. Cover and shake well to mix. Use as directed in Citrus-Marinated Flank Steak, Grilled Spring Vegetables, and Spiced Greens with Feta and Walnuts. Makes about 2 cups.

Spiced Greens with Feta and Walnuts

FOR A SPEEDIER SALAD, BUY A PACKAGE OF TORN MIXED GREENS RATHER THAN PREPARING THE GREENS YOURSELF.

⅔ cup Citrus-Spice Marinade
(see recipe, left)
⅓ cup salad oil
2 to 3 teaspoons sugar
½ teaspoon ground cinnamon
6 cups torn mixed greens
½ cup crumbled feta or blue cheese
⅓ cup toasted broken walnuts

For dressing, in a screw-top jar combine marinade, salad oil, sugar, and cinnamon; cover and shake well to mix. Chill till serving time.

Before serving, in a salad bowl toss together greens, feta or blue cheese, and walnuts. Shake dressing to mix; add to salad. Toss gently to coat. Serves 4 to 6.

Nutrition facts per serving: 229 cal., 19 g total fat (6 g sat. fat), 28 mg chol., 401 mg sodium, 10 g carbo., 2 g fiber, 7 g pro. Daily Value: 20% vit. A, 35% vit. C, 19% calcium, 12% iron.

Rhubarb-Strawberry Ice

INSTEAD OF FREEZING THE ICE IN A PAN, YOU CAN TRANSFER THE RHUBARB MIXTURE TO A 1- OR 2-QUART ICE-CREAM FREEZER AND FREEZE AS THE MANUFACTURER DIRECTS.

4 cups cut-up fresh rhubarb or
one 16-ounce package frozen unsweetened
sliced rhubarb, slightly thawed
1¼ cups cranberry juice cocktail or
unsweetened cherry juice
1 cup sugar
2 cups sliced fresh strawberries
Champagne or ginger ale (optional)
Fresh mint leaves (optional)

◆ Rhubarb-Strawberry Ice

In a medium saucepan stir together rhubarb, ½ cup of the juice, and sugar. Bring to boiling; reduce heat. Cover and simmer for 5 to 8 minutes or till rhubarb is tender and sugar is dissolved. Remove from heat. Add remaining ¾ cup juice and strawberries. Cool mixture to room temperature.

In a blender container or food processor bowl cover and blend or process rhubarb mixture, half at a time, till smooth. Transfer the mixture to a 9x9x2-inch nonmetal freezer container. Cover and freeze for 4 to 5 hours or till almost firm. Chill a large bowl in the refrigerator or freezer.

Break frozen mixture into small chunks. In the chilled bowl beat chunks with an electric mixer on medium speed till smooth but not melted. Return mixture to freezer container. Cover; freeze for at least 6 hours or till firm.

To serve, use a small ice cream scoop or melon baller to scrape the surface of ice and shape into balls. Spoon 4 or 5 small scoops of the ice into dessert dishes. If desired, pour champagne or ginger ale around ice; garnish with fresh mint. Serve immediately. Makes about 2 quarts (12 servings).

Nutrition facts per serving: 91 cal., 0 g total fat (0 g sat. fat), 0 mg chol., 3 mg sodium, 23 g carbo., 1 g fiber, 1 g pro. Daily Value: 0% vit. A, 44% vit. C, 3% calcium, 1% iron.

◆ Lemon Curd Pastry with Mixed Berries

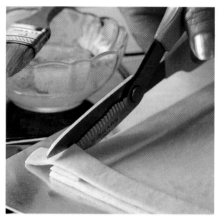

Place the 4 pastry strips atop the edges of the pastry rectangle, trimming to fit.

"I need a quick dessert that looks like I spent hours in the kitchen."

Lemon Curd Pastry with Mixed Berries
Hats off to frozen puff pastry.

Lemon-Curd Pastry with Mixed Berries

LEMON CURD IS A TANGY-SWEET ENGLISH SPREAD. LOOK FOR A BOTTLED VERSION IN THE JAM OR SPECIALTY FOODS SECTION OF THE SUPERMARKET OR A GOURMET FOOD SHOP. YOU CAN SUBSTITUTE LEMON PUDDING, ALTHOUGH THE FLAVOR WILL BE MILDER.

½ of a 17¼-ounce package (1 sheet) frozen puff pastry
1 slightly beaten egg white
1 teaspoon water
Coarse sugar or granulated sugar
⅔ cup lemon curd (at room temperature)
⅔ cup dairy sour cream
¼ teaspoon ground ginger
1 to 2 drops almond extract
3 cups desired fresh berries, such as raspberries, blackberries, blueberries, and/or quartered strawberries
¼ cup toasted sliced almonds
2 tablespoons honey
Powdered sugar (optional)

Let folded pastry thaw at room temperature for 20 minutes. On a lightly floured surface, unfold pastry and roll into a 15x10-inch rectangle. Cut from edges of rectangle 2 lengthwise ¾-inch-wide strips and 2 crosswise ¾-inch-wide strips. Set aside the 4 pastry strips.

Place the pastry rectangle on an ungreased baking sheet. Combine egg white and water; brush onto the rectangle. Place the 4 pastry strips atop edges of rectangle, trimming to fit (see photograph, above). Brush strips with egg white mixture; sprinkle with coarse sugar. Prick the bottom of the pastry several times with the tines of a fork.

Bake in a 375° oven for 20 to 25 minutes or till light brown. Remove from oven. Cool on a wire rack.

For filling, in a medium bowl stir curd till smooth. Stir together sour cream, ginger, and almond extract; fold into lemon curd.

Spread filling atop cooled pastry. Cover and chill till serving time, up to 4 hours.

Before serving, top with desired berries and sliced almonds. Drizzle with honey. Sprinkle with powdered sugar. Makes 8 servings.

Nutrition facts per serving: 379 cal., 23 g total fat (5 g sat. fat), 67 mg chol., 208 mg sodium, 41 g carbo., 4 g fiber, 6 g pro. Daily Value: 14% vit. A, 25% vit. C, 5% calcium, 4% iron.

With long-tined fork or skewers, poke holes in the top of each cake layer.

"What no-bake dessert can I put together and serve on the spot?"

SOLUTION

Tiramisu Cake

They'll never know you bought the angel food cake.

Tiramisu Cake

TIRAMISU (TEE RAH MEE SU), MEANING "PICK ME UP," IS A TRIFLE-LIKE DESSERT FROM THE TUSCAN REGION OF ITALY.

1 8-ounce container mascarpone cheese* or
1 8-ounce package cream cheese, softened
½ cup sifted powdered sugar
3 tablespoons coffee liqueur
2 cups whipping cream
¼ cup sifted powdered sugar
2 tablespoons coffee liqueur
1 8- to 10-inch round angel food cake
¾ cup strong black coffee
¼ cup coffee liqueur

◆ Tiramisu Cake

1 recipe Mocha Fudge Sauce (optional)
(see recipe, right)

Chill a medium bowl and beaters of an electric mixer.

For filling, in a large bowl combine mascarpone or cream cheese, the ½ cup powdered sugar, and the 3 tablespoons liqueur; beat with an electric mixer on medium speed till blended and smooth.

In the chilled bowl combine whipping cream, the ¼ cup powdered sugar, and the 2 tablespoons liqueur; beat till stiff peaks form. Fold ½ cup of the whipped cream mixture into mascarpone mixture.

Use a serrated knife to cut angel food cake horizontally into 3 layers. Place 1 cake layer on a serving platter. With a long-tined fork or skewers, poke holes in tops of layers (see photograph, above). In a small bowl combine coffee and the ¼ cup liqueur; drizzle over each layer. Spread the first layer with half of the mascarpone filling. Add a second layer and remaining filling. Add third cake layer. Frost with the remaining whipped mixture. If desired, cover and chill for up to 2 hours.

Before serving, if desired, drizzle top and sides with Mocha Fudge Sauce. Slice into wedges to serve. If desired, drizzle fudge sauce onto dessert plates before adding cake slices. Makes 16 servings.

*Note: Mascarpone is a rich Italian cream cheese often served with fruit for dessert. You can buy it at the cheese counter in your supermarket or at an Italian specialty shop.

Mocha Fudge Sauce: In a small saucepan heat ¼ cup *fudge ice cream topping* just till warm. Stir in *coffee liqueur* (1 to 2 tablespoons) to make of drizzling consistency.

Nutrition facts per serving: 354 cal., 19 g fat (11 g sat. fat), 59 mg chol., 170 mg sodium, 40 g carbo., 0 g fiber, 8 g pro. Daily Value: 13% vit. A, 0% vit. C, 5% calcium, 3% iron.

◆ May Flower Cookies

"What fun school treat can the kids help me make?"

May Flower Cookies
Color and shape a spring bouquet from purchased cookie dough.

May Flower Cookies

A ROLL OF REFRIGERATED SUGAR COOKIE DOUGH GROWS INTO A GARDEN OF FANCIFUL SPRING BLOSSOMS, FUN FOR KIDS TO MAKE AND TAKE TO SCHOOL.

1 20-ounce roll refrigerated sugar cookie dough
½ cup almond paste
Food coloring
Colored sugars, coarse sugar, or edible glitter

Divide sugar cookie dough among 4 small mixing bowls. Add 2 tablespoons almond paste and desired food coloring to each bowl of cookie dough.

Using clean beaters for each dough, beat with a handheld electric mixer on medium speed till color is well mixed. Break off small pieces of different colors of dough and shape them into the following kinds of flowers, or create your own flower shapes.

For daisy- or pansy-style flowers, shape dough into ¼- to ½-inch balls. Flatten the balls to make petals. If desired, overlap petals. Place 1 ball in the center.

For daisy- or pansy-style flowers, shape colored dough into ¼- to ½-inch balls. Use the balls for the flower centers and petals. Or, flatten the balls to make petals. If desired, overlap the petals around the center (see photograph, above).

For tulips, roll colored dough into 2½-inch-long logs. Place 5 logs side by side; pinch the logs together at one end to make the flower stem base. Curl out the tips at the other end to make opening petals (see photograph, above).

If desired, sprinkle the flowers with colored sugars, coarse sugar, or edible glitter. Place flowers 2 inches apart on ungreased cookie sheets. For 2½- to 3-inch cookies, bake in a 375° oven for 8 to 10 minutes or till the edges are light brown. Carefully transfer cookies to a wire rack to cool. Makes about 24 (2½- to 3-inch) cookies.

Nutrition facts per cookie: 133 cal., 6 g total fat (1 g sat. fat), 7 mg chol., 99 mg sodium, 18 g carbo., 0 g fiber, 2 g pro. Daily Value: 0% vit. A, 0% vit. C, 2% calcium, 3% iron.

"It's my turn to take treats tomorrow and I don't feel like running to the store. Any suggestions?"

Create this luscious coffee cake from ingredients you keep on hand in your pantry.

Ribbon-of-Fruit Teacake

A LAYER OF FRUIT PIE FILLING SWIRLS THROUGH THIS STREUSEL QUICK BREAD.

2¼ cups all-purpose flour
¾ cup sugar
¾ cup margarine or butter
½ teaspoon baking powder
½ teaspoon baking soda
¼ teaspoon ground nutmeg
⅛ teaspoon salt
1 beaten egg
⅔ cup sour milk or buttermilk*
1 teaspoon vanilla
1¼ cups canned fruit pie filling, such as cherry, apricot, raisin, strawberry, peach, blueberry, or blackberry
1 recipe Vanilla Icing (see recipe, right)

Grease and flour an 11-inch fluted tart pan with a removable bottom or a 2-quart rectangular baking dish.

In a large bowl stir together flour and sugar. Cut in margarine or butter till

◆ Ribbon of Fruit Tea Cake

mixture resembles coarse crumbs. Reserve ½ cup for topping.

For batter, into remaining flour mixture stir baking powder, baking soda, nutmeg, and salt. Make a well in the center. In a small bowl combine egg, sour milk, and vanilla; add all at once to flour mixture. Stir just till moistened. Reserve 1 cup batter.

Spread remaining batter onto bottom and 1 inch up sides of prepared pan. Carefully spread the desired pie filling on top. Spoon reserved batter into small mounds atop filling. Sprinkle with the topping.

Bake in a 350° oven till golden, allowing 45 minutes for the tart pan or 40 minutes for the baking dish. Cover edges with foil after 30 minutes, if necessary, to prevent overbrowning.

Cool in the pan on a wire rack for 15 minutes. For tart pan, remove sides and bottom. Drizzle with Vanilla Icing. Serve warm or cool. Cut into wedges or squares. Makes 8 servings.

*Note: To make sour milk, add 1 teaspoon lemon juice to ⅔ cup milk. Let stand for 5 minutes.

Vanilla Icing: Combine ½ cup sifted *powdered sugar*, ½ teaspoon *vanilla*, and *milk* (1 to 2 teaspoons) to make an icing of drizzling consistency.

Nutrition facts per serving: 442 cal., 19 g total fat (4 g sat. fat), 28 mg chol., 310 mg sodium, 64 g carbo., 1 g fiber, 5 g pro. Daily Value: 24% vit. A, 1% vit. C, 3% calcium, 11% iron.

◆ Tarragon Rice Salad

"I need a great idea to tote to our neighborhood potluck."

Take along an extraordinary salad or a platter of vegetables with a sensational dip.

Tarragon Rice Salad

THE HERB VINAIGRETTE MAKES THIS A SAFE SALAD TO TOTE ON WARM DAYS.

1 cup water or vegetable broth
½ cup regular brown rice
⅓ cup salad oil
¼ cup white wine vinegar
2 tablespoons water
4 teaspoons snipped fresh tarragon or
1 teaspoon dried tarragon, crushed
½ teaspoon salt
⅛ teaspoon pepper
1 medium cucumber, chopped (1¼ cups)
½ cup snipped fresh parsley

◆ Creamy Artichoke Dip

½ cup thinly sliced green onion
1 cup halved pea pods, steamed and chilled
⅓ cup halved and thinly sliced radishes
1 head butterhead lettuce
Sliced honeydew and cantaloupe (optional)

In a saucepan bring the 1 cup water or broth to boiling; add uncooked brown rice. Reduce heat. Cover and cook for 30 to 35 minutes or till tender. Cool.

For dressing, in a screw-top jar combine oil, vinegar, the 2 tablespoons water, tarragon, salt, and pepper; cover and shake well to mix.

In a large bowl combine rice, cucumber, parsley, and green onion. Add dressing to rice mixture; toss to coat. Cover and chill overnight.

Stir in pea pods and radishes. Using a slotted spoon, spoon salad into lettuce cups. If desired, arrange sliced melon around lettuce cups; garnish with fresh tarragon. Makes 6 to 8 servings.

Nutrition facts per serving: 189 cal., 13 g fat (2 g sat. fat), 0 mg chol., 188 mg sodium, 17 g carbo., 2 g fiber, 3 g pro. Daily Value: 8% vit. A, 45% vit. C, 3% calcium, 10% iron.

Creamy Artichoke Dip

TO TAKE THIS DIP TO YOUR NEXT GATHERING, PACK THE DIP AND DIPPERS IN SEPARATE CONTAINERS ON ICE. ASSEMBLE THE VEGETABLE PLATTER AT THE PARTY.

2 large artichokes
2 tablespoons water
½ cup shredded smoked mozzarella,
edam, gouda, or cheddar cheese (2 ounces)
1 8-ounce carton dairy sour cream or
low-fat dairy sour cream
2 teaspoons capers, drained
2 teaspoons snipped fresh basil or
½ teaspoon dried basil, crushed
Assorted vegetable dippers, such as
Belgian endive leaves, steamed pea pods,
cauliflower flowerets, red or yellow
cherry tomatoes, cut-up radishes, or
peeled baby carrots

Wash artichokes; trim stems. Place in a microwave-safe casserole with water. Cook, covered, on 100% power (high) 7 to 9 minutes or till a leaf pulls out easily. Drain. Discard small outer leaves of 1 cooled artichoke. Pull off large leaves; cover and chill leaves till serving time. Pull out the tender leaves from the center as a single clump. Remove the fuzzy choke by scooping it out with a spoon; discard the choke. Finely chop the heart.

In a blender container or food processor combine cheese, sour cream, capers, and basil. Cover and blend or process till smooth, stopping occasionally to scrape down sides. Stir in the artichoke heart. Cover and chill till serving time.

To serve, remove center leaves, choke, and heart from remaining artichoke. Spoon dip into center, spreading outer leaves. If desired, garnish with additional capers and a Belgian endive leaf. Arrange artichoke leaves and other vegetables around dip. Makes 1½ cups dip.

Nutrition facts per tablespoon dip: 62 cal., 5 g total fat (3 g sat. fat), 11 mg chol., 57 mg sodium, 3 g carbo., 1 g fiber, 2 g pro. Daily Value: 5% vit. A, 3% vit. C, 5% calcium, 1% iron.

"We need dinner fast, but how can we have fresh flavor too?"

SOLUTION

This fabulous fish dish goes together quickly and cooks in 10 minutes, thanks to your microwave oven.

Halibut with Garden-Style Marinara Sauce

GO FISH! SERVE THIS HEALTHFUL ENTRÉE WITH COUSCOUS, A GRAINLIKE PASTA. LOOK FOR COUSCOUS NEAR THE RICE OR PASTA SECTION OF YOUR SUPERMARKET.

2 fresh or frozen cod, halibut, salmon, or
shark steaks, cut 1 inch thick
(about 1 pound)
½ teaspoon lemon-pepper seasoning
1 small zucchini and/or yellow summer
squash
½ of a small onion, sliced and separated
into rings
1 clove garlic, minced
2 tablespoons water
1½ teaspoons snipped fresh oregano or
½ teaspoon dried oregano, crushed
1 8-ounce can stewed tomatoes
2 teaspoons cornstarch
Dash bottled hot pepper sauce
Hot cooked couscous (optional)

Thaw fish, if frozen. Place steaks in a 2-quart square microwave-safe baking

◆ Halibut with Garden-Style Marinara Sauce

dish. Cover with microwave-safe plastic wrap; turn back one corner to vent. Cook on 100% power (high) for 4 to 8 minutes or till fish flakes easily, turning and sprinkling with ¼ teaspoon of the lemon-pepper seasoning after 1 minute. Let fish stand, covered, while preparing the sauce.

For sauce, cut squash in half lengthwise; cut into thin slices. (You should have 1 cup.) In a 1-quart microwave-safe casserole combine squash, onion, garlic, water, oregano, and remaining lemon-pepper. Cook, covered, on high about 3 minutes or till nearly tender.

Stir together tomatoes, cornstarch, and pepper sauce; add to vegetable mixture. Cook, covered, on high for 1 to 3 minutes more or till thickened and bubbly, stirring every 30 seconds. Cook on high for 1 minute more. To serve, spoon vegetables and sauce atop fish. If desired, serve with hot cooked couscous. Makes 4 servings.

Nutrition facts per serving: 115 cal., 1 g total fat (0 g sat. fat), 43 mg chol., 343 mg sodium, 8 g carbo., 1 g fiber, 19 g pro. Daily Value: 4% vit. A, 17% vit. C, 3% calcium, 7% iron.

Prize Tested Recipes

◆ Paella Salad

◆ Piña Colada Sherbet

Paella Salad

THIS SEAFOOD AND SAUSAGE SALAD IS
PATTERNED AFTER PAELLA (PAH AY YUH),
A SPANISH FAVORITE.

12 ounces fresh or frozen shrimp in shells
½ teaspoon salt
1 6-ounce package long grain and wild
rice mix
1 cup frozen peas, thawed and drained
4 ounces fully cooked smoked sausage,
sliced into bite-size pieces
1 2-ounce jar sliced pimiento, drained
1 0.75-ounce envelope garlic and herbs dry
salad dressing mix

1 6-ounce can crabmeat, drained, cartilage
removed, and broken into chunks
Lettuce leaves (optional)
Tomato slices (optional)

Thaw shrimp, if frozen. Peel and
devein. In a large saucepan, bring 3 cups
water and the salt to a boil. Add shrimp.
Simmer, uncovered, for 1 to 3 minutes
or till shrimp turn pink, stirring occasionally. Drain. Rinse the shrimp under
cold running water to cool. Drain and
set aside.

Meanwhile, prepare rice mix in a
medium saucepan according to package
directions. Set rice aside to cool.

In a large bowl, combine the cooked
shrimp, cooled rice, thawed peas,
sausage, and pimiento. Mix well. Prepare
dressing according to package directions.
Pour half of the dressing (about ½ cup)
over salad mixture; toss to coat. (Use
remaining dressing for another meal.)
Add crabmeat to salad and toss gently.
Cover and chill thoroughly. To serve, if
desired, line 6 dinner plates with lettuce
leaves. Spoon rice mixture atop lettuce
and garnish with sliced tomatoes, if
desired. Makes 6 main-dish servings.

Nutrition facts per serving: 371 cal.,
21 g total fat (4 g sat. fat), 104 mg chol.,
1,189 mg sodium, 26 g carbo., 4 g fiber,
20 g pro. Daily Value: 9% vit. A, 29%
vit. C, 4% calcium, 19% iron.

$200 WINNER
Margaret Goodman
New York, New York

Piña Colada Sherbet

Kristina captured the wonderful flavor of a tropical cocktail in this refreshing sherbet.

1 15- or 16-ounce can cream of coconut
1 15¼-ounce can crushed pineapple
1 cup orange juice
¼ cup light rum

In a blender container or food processor bowl combine cream of coconut, undrained pineapple, orange juice, and rum. (If using a food processor, process only half of the ingredients at a time.) Cover; blend or process till nearly smooth. Pour into a 9x5x3-inch loaf dish or a 13x9x2-inch baking dish. Cover; freeze several hours or till firm. Break sherbet into pieces. Place sherbet, half at a time, in a blender container or food processor bowl. Cover; blend or process till fluffy. (Or, if desired, place in a chilled bowl and beat with an electric mixer till fluffy.) Return pineapple mixture to pan. Cover and freeze at least 4 hours or till firm. Makes 5 cups.

Nutrition facts per ⅓-cup serving: 245 cal., 19 g total fat (5 g sat. fat), 0 mg chol., 10 mg sodium, 15 g carbo., 0 g fiber, 0 g pro. Daily Value: 1% vit. A, 33% vit. C.

$100 WINNER
Kristina Karkkainen
Holland, Michigan

Coconut Macaroon Cheesecake

When baked, the topping on this cheesecake tastes like a light meringue cookie.

◆ Coconut Macaroon Cheesecake

1 cup flaked coconut, toasted
½ cup ground pecans
2 tablespoons margarine or butter, melted
3 8-ounce packages cream cheese, softened
½ cup sugar
½ teaspoon vanilla
¼ teaspoon almond extract
3 eggs
1 egg white
½ teaspoon vanilla
⅓ cup sugar
⅔ cup flaked coconut, toasted

In a small bowl mix the 1 cup toasted coconut, the ground pecans, and melted margarine or butter. Press into bottom of a 9-inch springform pan. Set aside.

In a large mixer bowl beat cream cheese with an electric mixer on low speed; gradually add the ½ cup sugar, first ½ teaspoon vanilla, and the almond extract. Beat till fluffy. Add the 3 whole eggs; beat on low speed just till combined. Pour into crust-lined pan. Bake in a 350° oven for 35 minutes. (Cheesecake will not be completely done.)

Meanwhile, in a small bowl beat egg white and remaining vanilla with an electric mixer till soft peaks form (tips curl); gradually beat in ⅓ cup sugar till stiff peaks form. Fold in ⅔ cup toasted coconut. Carefully spread atop partially baked cheesecake. Return to oven and bake 20 minutes more. Cool on rack for 15 minutes. Loosen sides of cheesecake from pan. Cool 30 minutes; remove sides of pan. Cool completely. Cover; chill at least 4 hours before serving. To serve, garnish with fruit and toasted coconut, if desired. Serves 12 to 16.

Nutrition facts per serving: 374 cal., 30 g total fat (14 g sat. fat), 121 mg chol., 230 mg sodium, 21 g carbo., 0 g fiber, 7 g pro. Daily Value: 28% vit. A, 0% vit. C, 4% calcium.

$200 WINNER
Maria Manning,
Yuma, Arizona

● Almond Chicken Pasta Salad

Almond Chicken Pasta Salad

THE GINGER, HONEY, AND LIME DRESS-
ING GIVES THIS PASTA SALAD THE
WINNING EDGE.

4 cups cooked, cubed chicken
2 medium apples, cored and coarsely
chopped (2 cups)
8 ounces corkscrew or bow tie pasta,
cooked and drained

1 8½-ounce can pineapple chunks,
drained
½ cup halved seedless grapes
⅓ cup bias-sliced celery (about 1 stalk)
¼ cup thinly sliced green onion
¾ cup mayonnaise or salad dressing
⅓ cup low-fat plain yogurt
1 tablespoon sesame seed
1 teaspoon finely shredded lime peel
3 tablespoons lime juice
1 tablespoon honey
2 teaspoons grated fresh gingerroot
¼ teaspoon salt
Lettuce leaves (optional)
½ cup toasted sliced almonds
Lime slices (optional)
Avocado slices (optional)
Diced red sweet pepper (optional)

In a large bowl toss together the
cooked chicken, apples, cooked pasta,
pineapple, grapes, celery, and onion. For
dressing, in a small bowl combine the
mayonnaise or salad dressing, yogurt,
sesame seed, lime peel, lime juice, honey,
gingerroot, and salt. Pour over the pasta
mixture; toss gently to combine. Cover
and chill. To serve, if necessary, add several tablespoons of milk to moisten. Toss
gently. Serve on lettuce-lined plates. Top
with almonds. If desired, garnish with
lime slices, avocado, and red sweet pepper. Makes 10 main-dish servings.

Nutrition facts per serving: 475 cal.,
23 g total fat (4 g sat. fat), 66 mg chol.,
262 mg sodium, 39 g carbo., 2 g fiber,
28 g pro. Daily Value: 3% vit. A, 12%
vit. C, 5% calcium, 18% iron.

$100 WINNER
Judy Acheson,
Calico Rock, Arkansas

June

Simply Summer

Tempting Recipes for Picnics and Potlucks

Prize Tested Recipes

Sour Cream and Berry Pie, Zesty Steak Carbonnade,
Peachy Cream Cheese Pie, Sweet and Spicy BBQ Ribs

Simply Summer

Sunny days are meant to be enjoyed with good friends and family—swimming at the beach, churning homemade ice cream, and sharing picnic and potluck dinners. To pack your basket, choose from our 15 summer sensations.

By Lisa Holderness

BBQ Chicken with Sesame-Chili Sauce

IF GRILLING AWAY FROM HOME, MAKE THE SAUCE AHEAD AND PLACE IN A STORAGE CONTAINER. TRANSFER THE RINSED AND DRIED CHICKEN PIECES TO A SEALED PLASTIC BAG AND PACK THE CHICKEN AND SAUCE ON ICE IN A COOLER.

1 8½-ounce jar plum sauce or ¾ cup sweet-and-sour sauce
⅓ cup hoisin sauce
¼ cup soy sauce
3 tablespoons honey
3 tablespoons water
1 tablespoon sesame seed
2 cloves garlic, minced
2 teaspoons grated gingerroot or ½ teaspoon ground ginger
1½ teaspoons Oriental chili sauce or several dashes bottled hot pepper sauce
½ teaspoon five-spice powder
2 2½- to 3-pound broiler-fryer chickens, quartered or cut up

For Sesame-Chili Sauce, in a small saucepan combine all of the ingredients except chicken. Cook over medium heat till bubbly, stirring frequently. Reduce heat. Cover and simmer for 5 minutes. Set aside.

Rinse chicken; pat dry with paper towels. If desired, remove skin from chicken and discard. If using quartered chickens, break wing, hip, and drumstick joints so the bird will lie flat during cooking. Twist wing tips under backs.

Place chicken, skin side down, on an uncovered grill directly over medium coals. Grill for 20 minutes. Turn; grill 15 to 25 minutes more or till tender and no longer pink. Brush the chicken with sauce frequently during the last 10 minutes of grilling.

◆ BBQ Chicken with Sesame Chili Sauce and Ginger Peanut Pasta Salad

Transfer chicken to a serving platter. Heat any remaining sauce either on the grill or stove top; pass with chicken. Makes 12 servings.

Make-ahead tip: The Sesame-Chili Sauce can be made up to 5 days ahead and stored, covered, in the refrigerator.

Nutrition facts per serving (skin on): 302 cal., 12 g total fat (3 g sat. fat), 90 mg chol., 477 mg sodium, 13 g carbo., 0 g fiber, 33 g pro. Daily Value: 4% vit. A, 1% vit. C, 2% calcium, 11% iron.

Ginger-Peanut Pasta Salad

TO TURN THIS PEPPY PASTA SALAD INTO A MAIN DISH, TOSS IN COOKED SHRIMP OR BITE-SIZE STRIPS OF CHICKEN.

*8 ounces corkscrew macaroni or
fine noodles, broken up
20 fresh pea pods, tips and strings
removed (about 1 cup)
1 medium kohlrabi, peeled and
cut up, or 1 small cucumber,
quartered lengthwise and sliced
2 medium carrots, cut into long
thin strips (about 1 cup)*

*1 medium yellow and/or green sweet
pepper, cut into thin strips
¾ cup thinly sliced radishes
½ cup bias-sliced green onions
3 tablespoons snipped fresh
cilantro or parsley
1 recipe Ginger Salad Dressing
(see recipe, page 104)
⅓ cup chopped peanuts*

Cook macaroni according to package directions. During the last 30 seconds of cooking time, add the pea pods. Drain pasta and pea pods. Rinse with cold water and drain thoroughly.

continued on page 104

continued from page 103

In a large serving bowl combine the macaroni and pea pods, kohlrabi or cucumber, carrots, sweet pepper, radishes, green onions, and cilantro or parsley. Add the Ginger Salad Dressing and toss gently to coat. Cover and chill for 2 to 8 hours.

To serve, toss the salad again and sprinkle with peanuts. Makes 12 side-dish servings.

Ginger Salad Dressing: In a screw-top jar combine ¼ cup *salad oil*, 3 tablespoons *rice vinegar*, 2 tablespoons *sugar*, 2 tablespoons *soy sauce*, 1 teaspoon grated *gingerroot*, and 1 teaspoon *chili oil* or several dashes *bottled hot pepper sauce*. Cover and shake to combine. If desired, chill for up to 3 days. Shake dressing before using.

Nutrition facts per serving: 165 cal., 7 g total fat (1 g sat. fat), 0 mg chol., 197 mg sodium, 21 g carbo., 1 g fiber, 4 g pro. Daily Value: 35% vit. A, 40% vit. C, 1% calcium, 8% iron.

Pork Medallions with Summer Salsa

FOR OUTDOOR GATHERINGS, TOTE THE MARINATING PORK ON ICE IN A COOLER, ALONG WITH A CONTAINER OF THE SUMMER SALSA.

8 boneless pork loin chops, cut 1¼ to 1½ inches thick (America's Cut)
¼ cup lime juice
¼ cup Worcestershire sauce
¼ cup coarse-grain brown mustard or Dijon-style mustard
3 tablespoons vinegar
2 tablespoons water
1½ teaspoons ground cumin
¼ teaspoon salt
⅛ teaspoon pepper
1 recipe Summer Salsa (see recipe, page 105)

Place the pork loin chops in a clean, heavy plastic bag. Set the bag in a large bowl. Combine the remaining ingredients except salsa and pour over the pork in bag; seal the bag. Chill for 4 to 24 hours, turning occasionally.

Remove the pork from the bag, reserving marinade. Grill* pork on an uncovered grill directly over medium coals for 20 to 30 minutes or till 160° (juices run clear and meat is slightly pink in center), turning once halfway through cooking and brushing with marinade.

◆ Pork Medallions with Summer Salsa

Serve with Summer Salsa. Makes 8 main-dish servings.

*To broil: Place pork on the unheated rack of a broiler pan. Broil 4 to 5 inches from the heat for 22 to 24 minutes or till 160° (juices run clear), turning once halfway through cooking and brushing with marinade.

Nutrition facts per serving: 248 cal., 12 g total fat (4 g sat. fat), 77 mg chol., 182 mg sodium, 11 g carbo., 1 g fiber, 25 g pro. Daily Value: 18% vit. A, 61% vit. C, 2% calcium, 11% iron.

Summer Salsa

LIME JUICE AND JALAPEÑO PEPPERS ADD ZING TO THIS JUICY APRICOT SALSA.

1½ cups chopped fresh apricots or
peeled peaches
¾ cup chopped red or green sweet pepper
¾ cup chopped, seeded cucumber
¼ cup sliced green onion
1 to 2 jalapeño peppers, seeded
and finely chopped
2 tablespoons honey
2 tablespoons lime juice
1 tablespoon snipped fresh cilantro or
parsley

In a medium mixing bowl combine all ingredients. Cover and chill for up to 4 hours, stirring once or twice. Serve with a slotted spoon. Makes about 2½ cups salsa.

Nutrition facts per 3-tablespoon serving: 36 cal., 0 g total fat (0 g sat. fat), 0 mg chol., 1 mg sodium, 9 g carbo., 1 g fiber, 1 g pro. Daily Value: 18% vit. A, 47% vit. C, 0% calcium, 2% iron.

◆ Grilled Burgers Italiano

In a large mixing bowl combine egg and the ¼ cup spaghetti sauce. Stir in bread crumbs, onion, basil or oregano, and garlic. Add beef and sausage; mix well. Shape meat mixture into eight ½-inch-thick patties.

Place sweet pepper slices on a piece of foil (about 18x12 inches) and drizzle with oil. Bring up long sides of foil and, leaving space for steam, seal tightly with a double fold. Fold short ends to seal and form a foil packet.

Grill the burgers and foil packet on an uncovered grill directly over medium coals for 10 to 12 minutes or till burgers are no longer pink and peppers are tender, turning burgers and foil packet once halfway through grilling time.

Top burgers with pepper strips and a half slice of cheese; cover and grill about 15 seconds more or till cheese is melted.

Meanwhile, heat remaining spaghetti sauce, either on the grill or stove top. To serve, place burgers in kaiser buns. Spoon spaghetti sauce atop burgers. Pass any remaining sauce. Makes 8 servings.

Nutrition facts per serving: 540 cal., 27 g total fat (10 g sat. fat), 106 mg chol., 995 mg sodium, 41 g carbo., 0 g fiber, 31 g pro. Daily Value: 24% vit. A, 66% vit. C, 19% calcium, 27% iron.

Roasted New Potato Salad

PERFECT FOR OUTDOOR GATHERINGS, THIS COLORFUL SALAD PACKS EASILY IN AN ICE-FILLED COOLER. PLUS, YOU CAN MAKE IT AHEAD AND CHILL IT FOR UP TO 24 HOURS.

1½ pounds whole tiny new potatoes, quartered
3 tablespoons olive oil or cooking oil
2 cloves garlic, minced

Grilled Burgers Italiano

SHAPE THESE HERB-SEASONED PATTIES AT HOME AND GRILL ALONG WITH THE BURGER TOPPINGS AT YOUR COOKOUT .

1 egg
¼ cup meatless spaghetti sauce
⅓ cup fine dry bread crumbs
⅓ cup chopped onion
3 tablespoons snipped fresh basil or oregano or 1 teaspoon dried basil or oregano leaves, crushed
2 cloves garlic, minced
1 pound lean ground beef
1 pound bulk Italian sausage
2 medium green, yellow, and/or red sweet peppers, cut into rings and halved
1 tablespoon olive oil or cooking oil
1 6-ounce package sliced mozzarella cheese, halved crosswise
1 cup meatless spaghetti sauce
8 kaiser rolls, split and toasted

4 teaspoons snipped fresh rosemary or
1¼ teaspoons dried rosemary, crushed
½ teaspoon salt
¼ teaspoon pepper
1 9¼-ounce can chunk white tuna (water
pack), drained and broken into chunks
1 6-ounce can pitted ripe olives
1 large green sweet pepper, cut
into bite-size pieces
12 tiny pear-shaped red and/or
yellow tomatoes, halved; or
cherry tomatoes, halved
1 recipe Herb Vinaigrette (see recipe,
below) or ¾ cup bottled
Italian salad dressing

◆ Roasted New Potato Salad, Herb Vinaigrette

Place potatoes in a 13x9x2-inch pan. Combine oil, garlic, rosemary, salt, and pepper. Drizzle over potatoes; toss gently to coat. Roast, uncovered, in a 450° oven for 35 to 40 minutes or till tender and brown on the edges, stirring every 10 minutes. Cool slightly.

Meanwhile, in a large bowl combine tuna, olives, green pepper, and tomatoes. Add the potatoes. Toss with the Herb Vinaigrette or bottled Italian salad dressing. Cover; chill for up to 24 hours. Serve in a lettuce-lined bowl; garnish with fresh rosemary sprigs, if desired. Makes 8 servings.

Nutrition facts per serving: 288 cal., 17 g total fat (3 g sat. fat), 14 mg chol., 544 mg sodium, 23 g carbo., 2 g fiber, 11 g pro. Daily Value: 3% vit. A, 42% vit. C, 18% iron.

Herb Vinaigrette

USE THIS FLAVORFUL DRESSING FOR THE ROASTED NEW POTATO SALAD OR ON YOUR FAVORITE TOSSED SALAD.

⅓ cup olive oil or salad oil
⅓ cup white wine vinegar
1 tablespoon snipped fresh thyme or basil or
1 teaspoon dried thyme or basil, crushed
1 teaspoon sugar
1 teaspoon coarse-grain brown mustard or
Dijon-style mustard
¼ teaspoon salt
¼ teaspoon pepper

In a screw-top jar combine oil, white wine vinegar, thyme or basil, sugar, mustard, salt, and pepper. Cover; shake well. Store in the refrigerator for up to 2 weeks. Shake dressing well before serving. Makes about ¾ cup.

Nutrition facts per tablespoon: 54 cal., 6 g total fat (1 g sat. fat), 0 mg chol., 6 mg sodium, 1 g carbo., 0 g fiber, 0 g pro. Daily Value: 0% vit. A, 0% vit. C, 0% calcium, 1% iron.

◆ Peach and Almond Crisp

Peach and Almond Crisp

GUARANTEED TO SATISFY ALL AGES, THIS CRUNCHY FRUIT DESSERT IS EXTRA DELICIOUS WITH A SCOOP OF ICE CREAM.

8 cups sliced peeled peaches or nectarines or frozen unsweetened peach slices
⅔ cup packed brown sugar
½ cup rolled oats
½ cup toasted sliced almonds
¾ cup all-purpose flour
3 tablespoons granulated sugar
½ cup margarine or butter, cut up
⅓ cup granulated sugar
½ teaspoon ground cinnamon
¼ teaspoon ground nutmeg
⅛ teaspoon ground ginger
¼ cup peach nectar or orange juice
Vanilla ice cream (optional)

Thaw frozen peach slices, if using. Do not drain.

For topping, in a medium bowl stir together the brown sugar, oats, almonds, ½ cup of the flour, and the 3 tablespoons granulated sugar. Using a pastry blender or 2 forks, cut in the margarine or butter till the mixture resembles coarse crumbs.

For filling, in a large mixing bowl stir together remaining flour, the ⅓ cup granulated sugar, cinnamon, nutmeg, and ginger. Add the peach or nectarine slices with their juices and peach nectar or orange juice. Toss gently to coat.

Transfer filling to an ungreased 3-quart rectangular baking dish. Sprinkle topping over the filling.

Bake in a 400° oven for 30 to 35 minutes or till fruit is tender and topping is golden. Serve warm or at room temperature with ice cream, if desired. To keep warm till serving time, see the Toting Hot Foods tip on page 115. Cover any leftover crisp; chill for up to 24 hours. Makes 12 servings.

Nutrition facts per serving: 258 cal., 11 g total fat (2 g sat. fat), 0 mg chol., 94 mg sodium, 40 g carbo., 3 g fiber, 3 g pro. Daily Value: 15% vit. A, 13% vit. C, 2% calcium, 6% iron.

Frosty Chocolate-Cherry Yogurt

TO KEEP THE FROZEN YOGURT COLD AFTER CHURNING (EVEN OUTDOORS), SEE "GET MORE FLAVOR FROM FROZEN YOGURT," ON PAGE 110.

2 16-ounce cartons (3½ cups) vanilla yogurt (no gelatin added)*
1 pound fresh dark sweet cherries, pitted (2½ cups), or 2½ cups frozen unsweetened pitted dark sweet cherries (13 ounces)
⅓ cup milk
⅓ cup light corn syrup
½ cup miniature semisweet chocolate pieces

In a blender container or food processor bowl combine yogurt, 1 cup of the cherries, milk, and corn syrup. Cover and blend or process till almost smooth. If using a food processor, process half at a time.

◆ Frosty Chocolate-Cherry Yogurt

Freeze mixture in a 2-quart ice cream maker according to manufacturer's directions till almost firm. Add remaining cherries and chocolate; continue to freeze as directed till firm. Makes 6 cups (12 servings).

***Note:** Yogurt without gelatin gives this dessert a better texture when frozen. The ingredient list on the carton will tell you if a refrigerated yogurt contains gelatin.

Nutrition facts per serving: 173 cal., 4 g total fat (2 g sat. fat), 5 mg chol., 63 mg sodium, 30 g carbo., 1 g fiber, 5 g pro. Daily Value: 1% vit. A, 4% vit. C, 10% calcium.

◆ Sunset Fruit Compote

Sunset Fruit Compote

2 cups water
1 cup fresh mint leaves
⅓ cup honey
1 6-ounce can frozen lemonade concentrate
10 cups assorted fresh fruit such as blackberries, raspberries, halved strawberries, sliced peaches, sliced carambola (star fruit), peeled kiwi fruit wedges, and melon balls

In a medium saucepan combine water, mint, and honey. Bring mixture to boiling. Reduce heat; cover and simmer for 10 minutes. Strain into a medium mixing bowl, discarding mint leaves. Stir in lemonade concentrate. If desired, cover and chill for up to 24 hours.

Place fruit in a large serving bowl. Pour lemonade mixture over fruit. Cover and chill till needed, up to 8 hours. If toting, transfer to a storage container and keep on ice in a cooler till serving time. Toss before serving. Sprinkle with small mint leaves, if desired. Makes 12 to 15 servings.

Nutrition facts per serving: 104 cal., 0 g total fat, 0 mg chol., 3 mg sodium, 26 g carbo., 3 g fiber, 1 g pro. Daily Value: 5% vit. A, 72% vit. C.

Raspberry Citrus Bars

A TAKEOFF ON ALL-TIME FAVORITE LEMON BARS, THESE COOKIES MAKE A TEMPTING SNACK OR DESSERT FOR LARGE GET-TOGETHERS.

1 cup butter, softened
¾ cup sifted powdered sugar
2 cups all-purpose flour

◆ Raspberry Citrus Bars

4 eggs
1½ cups granulated sugar
⅓ cup lemon juice
2 tablespoons finely shredded orange peel
¼ cup all-purpose flour
1 teaspoon baking powder
1½ cups fresh raspberries and/or blueberries
Powdered sugar

For the crust, beat butter with an electric mixer on medium speed for 30 seconds to soften. Add the ¾ cup powdered sugar. Beat till combined. Add the 2 cups flour; beat till combined. Press mixture onto the bottom of a greased 13x9x2-inch baking pan. Bake in a 350° oven for 20 minutes or till golden.

Meanwhile, for filling, in a large mixing bowl combine eggs, granulated sugar, lemon juice, orange peel, the ¼ cup flour, and baking powder. Beat for 2 minutes with an electric mixer till combined. Sprinkle berries over crust. Pour filling over berries, arranging berries evenly with a spoon.

Bake in a 350° oven for 30 to 35 minutes or till light brown and filling is set. Cool thoroughly in the pan on a wire rack. Cut into triangles and/or bars. Just before serving, sprinkle with powdered sugar. To store, cover and chill for up to 2 days. Makes about 30 bars.

Make-ahead tip: Place cut bars into a storage container or freezer bag and freeze for up to 3 months. Thaw, covered, in the refrigerator for 24 hours or till no longer frozen.

Nutrition facts per serving: 149 cal., 7 g total fat (4 g sat. fat), 45 mg chol., 83 mg sodium, 21 g carbo., 1 g fiber, 2 g pro. Daily Value: 7% vit A, 5% vit C, 1% calcium, 3% iron.

Banana Split Cake

BANANA SPLIT LOVERS WILL FIND THIS CAKE, WITH STRAWBERRY, PINEAPPLE, AND HOT FUDGE FILLINGS, EVERY BIT AS SATISFYING AS THE REAL THING.

*1 recipe Homemade Banana Layer Cake
(see recipe, right) or one
2-layer-size banana cake mix
2 cups sweetened whipped cream* or
6 ounces frozen whipped dessert
topping, thawed
1 cup sliced fresh strawberries
1 8¼-ounce can crushed pineapple,
well drained
1 11- to 12-ounce jar fudge ice cream
topping
½ cup chopped peanuts*

Prepare the Homemade Banana Layer Cake or, if using banana cake mix, prepare according to package directions for a two-layer cake.

For fillings, divide whipped cream or dessert topping in half. Fold berries into half of the whipped cream. Fold drained pineapple into the other half of the whipped cream. In a small saucepan heat and stir fudge ice cream topping over low heat just till warm (not hot).

To assemble, using a serrated knife, split each cake layer in half horizontally. Place bottom of one split layer on a serving plate. Top with the strawberry-cream mixture, spreading to edge of the cake layer. Place another split cake layer atop. Spread with half of the warm fudge topping, letting it drizzle down the sides. Sprinkle with half of the nuts.

Top with another split cake layer. Spread with the pineapple-cream mixture. Top with remaining split cake layer. Spread remaining warm fudge top-

ping atop cake, letting some of it drip down the sides of the cake. Sprinkle top of the cake with the remaining chopped nuts. Serve immediately or cover loosely with plastic wrap, placing a few toothpicks in top of the cake so the wrap doesn't stick to the topping, and chill for up to 2 hours. If desired, garnish with banana slices. Makes 12 servings.

*Note: For 2 cups sweetened whipped cream, in a chilled mixing bowl combine 1 cup whipping cream and 1 tablespoon sugar. Beat with chilled beaters of an electric mixer on low to medium speed just till soft peaks form (tips curl). Do not overbeat.

Make-ahead tip: To freeze baked cake layers, wrap layers individually in freezer wrap and freeze for up to 1 month. To serve, thaw wrapped cake layers at room temperature, then split and assemble.

Nutrition facts per serving: 509 cal., 25 g total fat (11 g sat. fat), 63 mg chol., 230 mg sodium, 68 g carbo., 2 g fiber, 8 g pro. Daily Value: 12% vit. A, 16% vit. C, 7% calcium, 11% iron.

Homemade Banana Layer Cake

USE THIS EASY ONE-BOWL CAKE FOR THE BANANA SPLIT CAKE OR FROST IT WITH ANY FROSTING RECIPE THAT WILL COVER A TWO-LAYER CAKE.

*2 cups all-purpose flour
1½ cups sugar
1½ teaspoons baking powder
¾ teaspoon baking soda
½ teaspoon salt
1 cup mashed ripe banana (3 medium)
½ cup buttermilk or sour milk*
½ cup shortening
2 eggs
1 teaspoon vanilla*

Grease and flour two 9x1½-inch round baking pans; set aside.

In a large mixing bowl combine flour, sugar, baking powder, baking soda, and salt. Add banana, buttermilk or sour milk, shortening, eggs, and vanilla. Beat with an electric mixer on low speed till combined. Beat on medium speed for 3 minutes. Pour into prepared pans.

Bake in a 350° oven 30 minutes or till a toothpick inserted near center comes out clean. Cool on wire racks for 10 minutes. Remove from pans; cool completely on racks. Serves 12.

*Note: To make ½ cup sour milk, combine ½ cup milk with 1½ teaspoons lemon juice or vinegar and let stand for 5 minutes before using.

Nutrition facts per serving: 294 cal., 11 g total fat (3 g sat. fat), 36 mg chol., 235 mg sodium, 47 g carbo., 1 g fiber, 4 g pro. Daily Value: 1% vit. A, 4% vit. C.

◆ Banana Split Cake

Garden Zucchini Pie

TAKE ADVANTAGE OF SUMMER'S BOUNTI-
FUL SUPPLY OF FRESH ZUCCHINI IN THIS
QUICHELIKE VEGETABLE PIE.

3 cups refrigerated loose-pack hash brown
potatoes or 5 medium potatoes
1 beaten egg
¼ cup finely chopped onion
¼ cup grated Parmesan cheese
2 medium zucchini, thinly sliced
(2½ cups)

1 clove garlic, minced
1 tablespoon margarine or butter
3 beaten eggs
¾ cup shredded cheddar or
Swiss cheese (3 ounces)
½ cup milk
2 teaspoons snipped fresh oregano or
½ teaspoon dried oregano, crushed
¼ teaspoon salt
¼ teaspoon pepper

If using whole potatoes, wash and peel. In a food processor fitted with a medium shredding disc, coarsely shred the potato. Or, shred potato with a grater. To prevent darkening, place shredded potato in a bowl of cold water immediately after shredding. Rinse potato shreds well and drain. Squeeze potato shreds to remove any excess water.

In a large mixing bowl combine the 1 egg, onion, and Parmesan cheese. Stir in potatoes. Transfer potato mixture to a 9-inch pie plate or a 10-inch quiche dish. Pat the mixture in the bottom and up the sides of the dish.

Bake, uncovered, in a 400° oven for 35 to 40 minutes or till golden. Cool slightly on a wire rack. Reduce oven temperature to 350°.

In a large skillet, cook zucchini and garlic in hot margarine or butter till zucchini is crisp-tender; cool slightly. Arrange zucchini mixture atop the crust.

In a small mixing bowl combine the remaining 3 eggs, cheddar or Swiss cheese, milk, oregano, salt, and pepper. Pour atop zucchini mixture in the crust.

Bake in the 350° oven for 25 to 30 minutes or till the filling appears set when gently shaken. Let stand for 10 minutes before serving. To keep warm till serving time, see the Toting Hot Foods tip at right. If desired, before serving, sprinkle with fresh oregano. Makes 8 side-dish servings.

◆ Garden Zucchini Pie

Toting Hot Foods

Keeping hot dishes hot at picnics and outdoor gatherings gives you better flavor and guards against food-borne illness.

Just before you leave home, take the hot foods from the oven. If desired, transfer hot food (such as baked beans, soups, or casseroles) to an electric slow crockery cooker for extra insulation. Wrap the covered dish, container, or crockery cooker in heavy foil, several layers of newspaper, or a heavy towel. Then, place in an insulated container to tote. The food should stay hot for up to 2 hours. If there is electricity at your picnic spot and you have a crockery cooker, your food will stay warm for hours on the low-heat setting (add additional liquid as needed).

Make-ahead tip: Cool unfilled crust after baking, cover with freezer wrap or foil, and freeze for up to 2 weeks. Thaw crust in the refrigerator overnight before preparing and adding zucchini filling.

Nutrition facts per serving: 191 cal., 9 g total fat (4 g sat. fat), 121 mg chol., 258 mg sodium, 19 g carbo., 1 g fiber, 10 g pro. Daily Value: 12% vit. A, 18% vit. C, 14% calcium, 12% iron.

◆ Curried Beans and Apples

In a 3- or 4-quart casserole combine onion, pork and beans, apples, catsup, brown sugar or molasses, mustard seed or mustard, curry powder, and Worcestershire sauce.

Bake, uncovered, in a 350° oven for 1 hour or to desired consistency, stirring frequently. Before serving, top with the crumbled bacon. For toting information, see the tip on page 115. Makes 12 side-dish servings.

Crockery cooker method: Prepare as directed except place the ingredients in a 3½- or 4-quart electric slow crockery cooker instead of the casserole. Cover and cook on the low-heat setting for 5 to 6 hours or on the high-heat setting for 2½ to 3 hours.

Make-ahead tip: Prepare the recipe as directed but, instead of baking, cover and chill the mixture for up to 24 hours. Bake as directed, allowing an extra 10 to 20 minutes because beans will be cold.

Nutrition facts per serving: 216 cal., 4 g total fat (1 g sat. fat), 13 mg chol., 842 mg sodium, 41 g carbo., 9 g fiber, 9 g pro. Daily Value: 4% vit. A, 13% vit. C, 8% calcium, 36% iron.

Curried Beans And Apples

YOU CAN BAKE AND TOTE THIS PICNIC FAVORITE IN A CROCKERY COOKER.

6 slices bacon
1 cup chopped onion
2 31-ounce cans pork and beans with tomato sauce
2 medium baking apples (such as Granny Smith or Rome Beauty), peeled, cored, and cut into bite-size pieces
½ cup catsup
¼ cup packed brown sugar or light molasses
4 teaspoons mustard seed or coarse-grain brown mustard
3½ to 4 teaspoons curry powder
2 teaspoons Worcestershire sauce

In a medium skillet cook bacon till crisp. Remove the bacon, reserving 2 tablespoons drippings. Drain and crumble bacon. Wrap and chill bacon. Cook onion in reserved bacon drippings over medium heat till onion is tender but not brown.

Tortellini and Garden Vegetable Bake

FOR A LOWER-FAT VERSION OF THIS CREAMY CASSEROLE, USE THE LIGHT CREAM CHEESE OPTION AND A PASTA OTHER THAN THE FILLED TORTELLINI.

10 ounces dried cheese-filled tortellini (2½ cups) or 6 ounces other pasta (2½ cups)
1 medium carrot, thinly sliced
1½ cups sugar snap peas, halved crosswise
1 pound skinless, boneless chicken breasts, cut into bite-size pieces
1 cup sliced fresh mushrooms
1 tablespoon margarine or butter
⅓ cup chicken broth
2 tablespoons snipped fresh oregano or 1½ teaspoons dried oregano, crushed
2 teaspoons all-purpose flour
¾ teaspoon garlic salt
½ teaspoon black pepper
1 cup milk
1 8-ounce package cream cheese or light cream cheese (Neufchâtel), cubed and softened
1 tablespoon lemon juice
1 cup quartered cherry tomatoes
1 small red or green sweet pepper, coarsely chopped
2 tablespoons grated Parmesan cheese

◆ Tortellini and Garden Vegetable Bake

Cook the tortellini or pasta in boiling salted water according to package directions, adding the carrot during the last 5 minutes of cooking and the sugar snap peas during the last 1 minute of cooking; drain.

Meanwhile, in a 12-inch skillet cook the chicken and mushrooms in hot margarine or butter about 5 minutes or till the chicken is no longer pink. Remove from skillet.

In a screw-top jar shake together chicken broth, oregano, flour, garlic salt, and black pepper till smooth. Add to skillet along with milk. Cook and stir till thickened and bubbly; add cream cheese. Cook and stir till cream cheese is smooth. Remove from heat. Stir in lemon juice. Add pasta mixture, chicken mixture, tomatoes, and sweet pepper. Toss to coat. Turn into an ungreased shallow 3-quart baking dish.

Bake, covered, in a 350° oven for 30 to 35 minutes or till heated through. Stir mixture and sprinkle with Parmesan cheese; let stand for 5 minutes before serving. For toting information, see tip, page 115. Makes 8 main-dish servings.

Make-ahead tip: Prepare as directed except, instead of baking, cover and chill for up to 24 hours. Bake, covered, in a 350° oven about 55 minutes or till hot.

Nutrition facts per serving: 370 cal., 18 g total fat (7 g sat. fat), 65 mg chol., 715 mg sodium, 28 g carbo., 2 g fiber, 23 g pro.

Prize Tested Recipes

◆ Sour Cream and Berry Pie

Sour Cream and Berry Pie

THE TANGINESS OF SOUR CREAM MAKES A PERFECT PARTNER TO THESE JUICY, SWEET BERRIES.

1 cup graham cracker crumbs
¼ cup finely chopped pecans or walnuts
2 tablespoons all-purpose flour
1 tablespoon sugar
⅓ cup margarine or butter, melted
½ cup sugar
3 tablespoons cornstarch
1 teaspoon unflavored gelatin
1⅓ cups milk
1½ cups dairy sour cream
1 tablespoon vanilla
3 cups blueberries, raspberries, and/or small whole strawberries
Fresh berries (optional)

For crust, in a small bowl combine the cracker crumbs, pecans or walnuts, flour, and the 1 tablespoon sugar. Stir in the melted margarine or butter. Toss to mix well. Press mixture onto the bottom

◆ Zesty Steak Carbonnade

and up sides of a 9-inch pie plate. Bake in a 375° oven for 8 minutes. Cool on a wire rack.

For filling, in a medium saucepan combine the ½ cup sugar, cornstarch, and gelatin; stir in milk. Cook and stir till thickened and bubbly; cook and stir for 2 minutes more. Place sour cream in a medium bowl. Gradually stir milk mixture into the sour cream; stir in vanilla. Cover and chill for 1 hour, stirring once or twice.

Stir berries into sour cream mixture. Turn filling into cooled crust. Cover and chill at least 6 hours or up to 24 hours. If desired, garnish with additional berries before serving. Makes 8 servings.

Nutrition facts per serving: 332 cal., 18 g total fat (6 g sat. fat), 20 mg chol., 189 mg sodium, 39 g carbo., 2 g fiber, 5 g pro. Daily Value: 17% vit. A, 13% vit. C, 9% calcium, 5% iron.

$200 WINNER
Susan Brinskele
Petaluma, California

Zesty Steak Carbonnade

CARBONNADE IS FRENCH FOR MEAT COOKED OVER HOT COALS, BUT MEXICAN FLAVORS DOMINATE HERE.

⅔ cup beer
½ cup chopped onion
⅓ cup salsa catsup or catsup
2 tablespoons sugar
1 tablespoon Worcestershire sauce
4 teaspoons lemon juice
½ teaspoon paprika
½ teaspoon chili powder
¼ teaspoon pepper
6 top loin steaks, cut 1 inch thick
(about 2 pounds)

In a small saucepan combine beer, onion, catsup, sugar, Worcestershire, lemon juice, paprika, chili powder, and pepper. Bring to boiling, reduce heat. Simmer, uncovered, 5 minutes. Cool.

Use a sharp knife to score steaks on both sides. Place steaks in a plastic bag set inside a deep bowl. Pour marinade over steaks. Seal bag and turn steaks to coat. Marinate in the refrigerator for at least 1 hour or up to 24 hours.

Remove steaks from bag; reserve marinade. Place steaks on the grill rack of an uncovered grill directly over medium-hot coals. Grill steaks, uncovered, for 8 to 12 minutes for rare doneness or 12 to 15 minutes for medium doneness; turning the meat halfway through grilling.

Meanwhile, place reserved marinade in a small saucepan; bring to a full boil. Cook and stir for 1 to 2 minutes. Serve with steaks. Makes 6 servings.

Nutrition facts per serving: 283 cal., 10 g total fat (4 g sat. fat), 101 mg chol., 282 mg sodium, 11 g carbo., 1 g fiber, 35 g pro. Daily Value: 4% vit. A, 15% vit. C, 1% calcium, 28% iron.

◆ Sweet and Spicy BBQ Ribs

$200 WINNER
Sharon Naylor,
East Hanover, New Jersey

Sweet and Spicy BBQ Ribs

THIS CURRY-SPICED SAUCE MAKES PORK OR BEEF RIBS FINGER-LICKING TASTY.

1½ cups catsup
¾ cup white wine vinegar
½ cup packed brown sugar
2 tablespoons curry powder
1 tablespoon Worcestershire sauce
1 teaspoon hickory-flavored salt
1 teaspoon pepper
2 to 3 cloves garlic, minced
3½ to 4 pounds pork loin back ribs

In a large bowl combine catsup, vinegar, brown sugar, curry powder, Worcestershire sauce, hickory-flavored salt, pepper, and garlic. Cover; let stand at room temperature 30 minutes or refrigerate for up to five days. In a covered grill arrange hot coals around a drip pan. Test for medium heat above the pan. Place ribs, fat side up, on grill rack over drip pan but not over coals. Lower grill hood. Grill for 1½ to 2 hours or till meat is very tender, basting generously with sauce the last 15 minutes of cooking. Makes 8 main-dish servings.

Nutrition facts per serving: 444 cal., 26 g total fat (10 g sat. fat), 104 mg chol., 977 mg sodium, 28 g carbo., 2 g fiber, 26 g pro. Daily Value: 19% vit. C, 20% iron.

$100 WINNER
Sharon Byrne
Red Bluff, California

◆ Peachy Cream Cheese Pie

1 cup frozen whipped dessert
topping, thawed
3 cups peeled, sliced peaches
⅓ cup orange marmalade

In a medium bowl stir together wafer crumbs, ground walnuts, and the 1 tablespoon sugar; add melted margarine or butter. Toss to mix well.

Spread mixture evenly into a 9-inch microwave-safe pie plate. Press onto bottom and up the sides of the pie plate. Micro-cook on 100% power (high) for 2 minutes or till set. (Or, if using an oven-safe 9-inch pie plate, bake in a 375° oven for 4 to 5 minutes or till edges are light brown.) Cool completely on a wire rack.

Meanwhile, in a medium bowl beat cream cheese, ¼ cup sugar, and orange juice concentrate with an electric mixer on medium speed till smooth. Fold in whipped topping. Spread over cooled crust. Cover surface with plastic wrap and chill at least 1 hour. Just before serving, arrange peach slices over filling. In a small saucepan, heat and stir the orange marmalade just till melted; brush onto peaches. If desired, garnish with raspberries. Makes 8 servings.

Nutrition facts per serving: 389 cal., 26 g total fat (10 g sat. fat), 22 mg chol., 235 mg sodium, 37 g carbo., 2 g fiber, 5 g pro. Daily Value: 23% vit. A, 20% vit. C, 3% calcium, 4% iron.

$100 WINNER
Gayle Nicholas Scott
Chesapeake, Virginia

Peachy Cream Cheese Pie

THIS NO-BAKE PIE IS PERFECT ON HOT SUMMER DAYS. YOU CAN MICRO-COOK THE CRUST.

¾ cup vanilla wafer crumbs
(about 17 cookies)
⅔ cup toasted ground walnuts
1 tablespoon sugar
5 tablespoons margarine or butter, melted
1 8-ounce package light cream cheese
(Neufchâtel), softened
¼ cup sugar
2 tablespoons frozen orange juice
concentrate, thawed

July

Cool and Carefree
Summer Favorites

Prize Tested Recipes

Zesty Mango Sauce, Fresh Corn Frittata with Cheese Sauce,
Creamy Corn Raita, Raspberry-Walnut Sauce

Cool and Carefree Summer Favorites

As cool as a wedge of juicy watermelon and as carefree as a tossed green salad, summer foods are meant to be fun, easy, and downright satisfying. Fun is the main ingredient in these delicious recipes. Ease plays a big role, too. You'll use just a few ingredients and only the simplest cooking steps. The result is a lively mix of breezy summer favorites that will surprise, delight, and refresh.

BY JULIA MALLOY AND KRISTI FULLER

So Long Sub

HOLLOW OUT THE BOTTOM HALF OF THE BREAD LOAF TO MAKE ROOM FOR THE FILLING. USE THE LEFTOVER BREAD TO MAKE CROUTONS FOR SALADS.

⅓ cup chopped fresh basil leaves
2 tablespoons olive oil
1 tablespoon balsamic vinegar or white wine vinegar
1 8-ounce or ½ of a 16-ounce loaf unsliced French bread
6 ounces thinly sliced mozzarella cheese
4 to 6 ounces thinly sliced lean pastrami
2 plum tomatoes, thinly sliced lengthwise
⅛ teaspoon cracked black pepper

In a small bowl combine basil, oil, and vinegar; set aside.

Slice bread in half lengthwise. Using a spoon, hollow out bottom half, leaving a ½-inch-thick shell. In the shell layer half of the cheese, the pastrami, and the tomatoes. Top with basil mixture; sprinkle with pepper. Top with remaining cheese and bread top. Wrap in a piece of heavy foil.

Heat on an uncovered grill directly over medium coals 20 to 25 minutes or till heated through, turning every 5 minutes. To serve, cut crosswise into 4 to 6 slices. Makes 4 to 6 main-dish servings.

Nutrition facts per serving: 436 cal., 24 g total fat (9 g sat. fat), 50 mg chol., 863 mg sodium, 33 g carbo., 1 g fiber, 21 g pro. Daily Value: 11% vit. A, 13% vit. C, 28% calcium, 18% iron.

Shrimp Kabobs on the Barbie, right ◆
So Long Sub, below ◆

Shrimp Kabobs on The Barbie

FOR A JUICY GO-ALONG, GRILL SOME FRESH PINEAPPLE WEDGES ALONGSIDE THE SHRIMP SKEWERS ON THE BARBECUE OR "BARBIE," AS THEY SAY DOWN UNDER.

1¼ pounds fresh or frozen large shrimp
in shells
1 cup bottled barbecue sauce
⅔ cup unsweetened pineapple juice
2 tablespoons cooking oil
4 teaspoons grated gingerroot or
1½ teaspoons ground ginger
¼ of a fresh pineapple, cut into wedges
1 medium papaya, peeled, seeded,
and sliced
3 medium kiwi fruit, peeled and
quartered lengthwise
Butterhead lettuce leaves

Thaw shrimp, if frozen. For sauce, in a medium bowl stir together barbecue sauce, pineapple juice, oil, and ginger. Set aside.

Peel and devein shrimp, leaving tails intact. Thread shrimp onto 6 long skewers; brush with sauce.

continued on page 124

continued from page 123

Grill on an uncovered grill directly over medium-hot coals for 10 to 12 minutes or till pink, turning and brushing often with sauce. (Or, arrange skewers on the unheated rack of a broiler pan. Broil 4 inches from heat for 8 to 10 minutes or till pink, turning and brushing often with sauce.) Add pineapple wedges the last 5 minutes of cooking; turn once. Remove pineapple when hot.

Serve kabobs and fruit atop lettuce. Heat remaining sauce to boiling; pass for dipping. Store remaining sauce in the refrigerator for up to 1 week. Makes 6 main-dish servings.

Nutrition facts per serving: 180 cal., 2 g total fat (0 g sat. fat), 116 mg chol., 478 mg sodium, 26 g carbo., 2 g fiber, 14 g pro. Daily Value: 12% vit. A, 172% vit. C, 6% calcium, 18% iron.

◆ Hot Tots and Brats

Hot Tots and Brats

WHY NOT GRILL YOUR WHOLE DINNER? WRAP THE POTATOES IN A FOIL PACKET TO COOK ALONGSIDE THE SAUSAGE AND PEPPERS.

½ cup Italian salad dressing
3 tablespoons Dijon-style mustard
1 pound whole tiny new red potatoes, quartered
1 medium onion, cut into wedges
Cracked black pepper
4 fresh bratwurst (12 ounces)
3 medium red, yellow, or green sweet peppers

For sauce, stir together Italian salad dressing and Dijon-style mustard. Set aside ¼ cup.

For foil packet, tear off a 36x18-inch piece of heavy foil. Fold in half to make a double thickness that measures 18x18 inches. Place potatoes and onion in the center of the foil. Drizzle with the remaining sauce. Sprinkle with black pepper. Bring up two opposite edges of foil; seal with a double fold. Fold ends to completely enclose the vegetables, leaving room for steam to build.

In a covered grill arrange preheated coals around a drip pan. Test for medium heat above the pan. Place the foil packet directly over the coals. Lower grill hood and grill for 25 minutes.

Turn over foil packet. Place the bratwurst over the drip pan; brush with some of the reserved sauce. Cover and grill for 15 minutes.

Meanwhile, quarter peppers lengthwise; remove seeds and membranes. Place peppers on the grill rack directly over coals. Turn over foil packet and bratwurst. Brush meat with remaining sauce. Cover and grill for 7 to 8 minutes, turning peppers once halfway through cooking. Grill till the peppers are crisp-tender, potatoes are tender, and bratwurst juices are clear. Makes 4 main-dish servings.

Nutrition facts per serving: 541 cal., 37 g total fat (10 g sat. fat), 51 mg chol., 999 mg sodium, 36 g carbo., 2 g fiber, 16 g pro. Daily Value: 41% vit. A, 183% vit. C, 5% calcium, 21% iron.

Can't-Be-Beet Beef Salad

THE SMALL SPECIALTY BEETS USED IN THIS SALAD MAY BE IN YOUR SUPERMARKET OR FARMER'S MARKET THIS SUMMER. IF YOU USE GOLD, WHITE, OR STRIPED BEETS, COOK THEM SEPARATELY FROM RED BEETS BECAUSE THE RED PIGMENT MAY DISCOLOR THEM.

¾ *pound small red, striped, gold, or white*
beets or regular red beets
⅓ *cup buttermilk*
⅓ *cup mayonnaise or salad dressing*
2 *teaspoons snipped fresh dill or*
½ *teaspoon dried dillweed*
1 *teaspoon honey or sugar*
1 *teaspoon prepared horseradish*
6 *cups torn mixed greens*
10 *ounces thinly sliced fully cooked beef*
½ *of a medium cucumber or yellow*
summer squash, halved
lengthwise and sliced
1 *cup enoki mushrooms*

For beets, cut off all but 1 inch of stems and roots; wash tops. In a medium saucepan cook fresh whole beets, covered, in boiling water till crisp-tender, allowing 15 to 20 minutes for small beets or 40 to 50 minutes for regular beets. (If using beets of several colors, cook red beets separately.) Drain; cool slightly. Slip skins off beets; slice beets. (You should have about 1½ cups.) Cover and chill till ready to use.

Meanwhile, for dressing, in a small bowl stir together buttermilk, mayonnaise or salad dressing, dill, honey or sugar, and horseradish.

◆ Can't-Be-Beet Beef Salad

To serve, arrange mixed greens on 4 dinner plates. Top with cooked beets, beef, cucumber or squash, and enoki mushrooms. Serve dressing with salads. Makes 4 main-dish servings.

Nutrition facts per serving: 313 cal., 19 g total fat (4 g sat. fat), 75 mg chol., 225 mg sodium, 11 g carbo., 3 g fiber, 25 g pro. Daily Value: 5% vit. A, 18% vit. C, 5% calcium, 22% iron.

◆ The New Layered Salad

Place mixed greens in the bottom of a 2½-quart clear salad bowl. Layer in the following order: garbanzo beans, tomatoes, sliced fennel or celery, colored peppers, turkey ham, and green onion.

For dressing, stir together mayonnaise or salad dressing, milk, snipped fennel tops or fennel seed, and white pepper. Spread the dressing over the top of the salad, sealing to the edge of the bowl. Cover tightly with clear plastic wrap. Chill for 4 to 24 hours.

Before serving, top salad with cheese; toss gently to mix. Makes 8 to 10 side-dish servings.

Nutrition facts per serving: 283 cal., 11 g total fat (2 g sat. fat), 30 mg chol., 345 mg sodium, 7 g carbo., 1 g fiber, 8 g pro. Daily Value: 8% vit. A, 35% vit. C, 8% calcium, 7% iron.

Teriyaki Chicken Noodle Salad

THE SEASONING FROM THE NOODLE PACKAGE IS THE ONLY FLAVORING NEEDED IN THE SALAD DRESSING. WHAT COULD BE EASIER?

¼ cup rice vinegar or white wine vinegar
2 tablespoons orange juice
2 tablespoons salad oil
Few dashes bottled hot pepper sauce
1 3-ounce package ramen-style noodles
with chicken or Oriental flavor
6 cups torn mixed greens
2 cups fresh vegetables, such as bean
sprouts, halved pea pods, julienne-cut
carrots, or sliced yellow summer squash,
zucchini, leeks, cucumber, green onions,
kohlrabi, and/or jicama

The New Layered Salad

YOU CAN MAKE THIS PRETTY, TIERED SALAD A DAY AHEAD BECAUSE THE SALAD DRESSING ON TOP SEALS IN FRESHNESS.

4 cups torn mixed greens
1 15-ounce can garbanzo beans, drained
1 cup red and/or yellow cherry tomatoes,
quartered or halved
1 cup thinly sliced fresh fennel
bulb or celery

1 cup chopped yellow and/or red sweet
peppers (1 large)
1 cup diced fully cooked turkey
ham (6 ounces)
¼ cup thinly sliced green onion
1 cup reduced-calorie mayonnaise dressing
or salad dressing
2 tablespoons milk
1 tablespoon snipped fresh fennel tops or
1 teaspoon fennel seed, crushed
⅛ teaspoon ground white or black pepper
¾ cup shredded reduced-fat or smoke-
flavored cheddar cheese

◆ Teriyaki Chicken Noodle Salad

2 oranges, peeled, thinly sliced, and halved
1 12-ounce package teriyaki-marinated chicken strips or skinless, boneless chicken breast halves, cut into thin strips
2 tablespoons cooking oil
Cracked black pepper

For dressing, in a screw-top jar combine vinegar, orange juice, the first 2 tablespoons oil, hot pepper sauce, and contents of the flavoring packet from the noodles. Cover and shake to mix.

In a large salad bowl combine greens, desired vegetables, and orange slices; toss gently to mix. Break noodles into pieces; add to salad. Cover and chill for up to 1 hour.

Meanwhile, in a wok or large skillet over medium-high heat, or in a special grilling wok set into medium-hot coals, stir-fry chicken strips in the remaining 2 tablespoons hot oil for 2 to 3 minutes or till tender. While chicken is cooking, pour the dressing over salad; toss gently to coat. Let stand about 5 minutes to soften noodles, tossing occasionally.

Add chicken and pan juices to salad; toss gently to mix. Sprinkle with black pepper. Serve immediately. Makes 4 main-dish servings.

Nutrition facts per serving: 351 cal., 17 g total fat (2 g sat. fat), 10 mg chol., 713 mg sodium, 29 g carbo., 3 g fiber, 22 g pro. Daily Value: 17% vit. A, 65% vit. C, 6% calcium, 15% iron.

Boston Bean Salad

THIS GENEROUS SALAD, WITH ITS MOLASSES VINAIGRETTE DRESSING, IS THE PERFECT DISH TO TOTE TO YOUR NEXT POTLUCK.

1 15-ounce can navy beans, rinsed and drained
1 15-ounce can red beans, rinsed and drained
1 15-ounce can black beans, rinsed and drained
2 stalks celery, sliced (1 cup)
½ cup thinly sliced green onion
½ cup vinegar
¼ cup molasses
¼ cup salad oil
1 tablespoon Dijon-style mustard
¼ teaspoon pepper
Lettuce leaves
2 cups torn curly endive
2 slices bacon, crisp-cooked, drained, and crumbled
Green onion strips (optional)

◆ Boston Bean Salad

In a large bowl combine beans, celery, and green onion.

For dressing, in a screw-top jar combine vinegar, molasses, oil, mustard, and pepper. Cover and shake well to mix. Pour dressing over bean mixture; stir to coat. Cover and chill for 4 to 24 hours, stirring occasionally.

To serve, line a salad bowl or platter with lettuce leaves. Stir curly endive and bacon into the bean mixture. Using a slotted spoon, transfer bean mixture to the salad bowl. If desired, garnish with green onion strips. Makes 10 to 12 side-dish servings.

Nutrition facts per serving: 195 cal., 7 g total fat (1 g sat. fat), 1 mg chol., 325 mg sodium, 29 g carbo., 7 g fiber, 10 g pro. Daily Value: 6% vit. A, 10% vit. C, 7% calcium, 19% iron.

◆ Feta Quesadilla

Feta Quesadilla

NO ROOM ON THE GRILL? NO PROBLEM.
YOU CAN MICROWAVE THESE TASTY APPE-
TIZERS IN MINUTES INSTEAD.

1 3-ounce package cream cheese, softened*
1 cup shredded Monterey Jack cheese
(4 ounces)*
⅓ cup crumbled feta cheese
2 teaspoons snipped fresh oregano or
½ teaspoon dried oregano, crushed
⅓ cup chopped pitted ripe olives
2 tablespoons diced pimiento
2 tablespoons thinly sliced green onion
4 6-inch flour tortillas

For filling, stir together the cream
cheese, Monterey Jack cheese, feta cheese
and oregano.

Spread filling onto one half of each
tortilla. Top with olives, pimiento, and
green onion. Fold plain side over filling;
press gently to seal edges.

Grill filled tortillas on an uncovered
grill directly over medium coals for 1 to
2 minutes on each side or till golden
brown and heated through. Or, place
2 of the quesadillas on a microwave-safe
platter. Micro-cook, uncovered, on
100% power (high) for 1 to 2 minutes
or till heated through. Repeat with
remaining quesadillas.

Cut each quesadilla into 3 wedges.
Makes 12 appetizers.

*Note: To save 3 grams of fat
per wedge, use light cream cheese
(Neufchâtel) and reduced-fat Monterey
Jack cheese.

Nutrition facts per wedge: 113 cal., 8
g total fat (5 g sat. fat), 22 mg chol., 210
mg sodium, 6 g carbo., 0 g fiber, 5 g
pro. Daily Value: 7% vit. A, 3% vit. C,
10% calcium, 3% iron.

Go Nutty Grilled Cheese

FOR AN APPETIZER, GRILL THIS CARAMEL-
TOPPED CHEESE SPREAD BEFORE GRILLING
THE ENTRÉE. OR, FOR A LUSCIOUS
DESSERT, SET IT OVER LOW COALS WHILE
YOU'RE DINING.

2 tablespoons caramel ice cream topping
2 tablespoons finely chopped
pecans or walnuts
2 teaspoons margarine or butter, melted
¼ teaspoon ground allspice
3 ounces baby Swiss, Gruyère, fontina, or
Havarti cheese, cut ¾ inch thick
Fresh fruit, such as strawberries, sliced
peaches, grapes, and/or apricots
French bread slices

Combine ice cream topping, nuts,
melted margarine or butter, and allspice.

Use a 6-inch cast-iron skillet or form a
6-inch-wide pan using a double thickness of heavy foil. (To make a foil pan,
fold an 18x12-inch piece of heavy foil in
half to make a double thickness that
measures 9x12 inches. Fold up about 1½
inches around the edges.)

Spread caramel mixture in pan. Place
cheese atop. Place skillet or foil pan on
grill rack directly over low coals. Lower
grill hood; grill 6 to 8 minutes or till
cheese is soft and warm, checking often
to make sure cheese does not completely
melt. (It shouldn't lose its shape or run.)

To serve, invert cheese onto a serving
platter. Spoon on any topping remaining
in pan. Serve with fresh fruit and French
bread. Makes 4 to 6 appetizer servings.

***Nutrition facts per serving with ¼
cup fruit and 1 slice French bread:*** 233
cal., 12 g total fat (5 g sat. fat), 23 mg
chol., 282 mg sodium, 23 g carbo., 1 g
fiber, 9 g pro. Daily Value: 10% vit. A,
35% vit. C, 20% calcium, 6% iron.

◆ Go Nutty Grilled Cheese and Tang o Mango Sipper

Tang-o Mango Sipper

A JAR OF SLICED MANGO SAVES YOU THE
WORK OF PITTING FRESH MANGOS FOR
THIS TANGY TROPICAL TEASER.

1 26-ounce jar mango slices, chilled
1 1-liter bottle ginger ale, chilled
Ice cubes
Lime slices, cilantro, mint sprigs, or
mango slices (optional)

If desired, reserve some mango slices
for a garnish. In a covered blender container blend remaining undrained
mango slices till smooth. Transfer to a
2-quart pitcher. Stir in ginger ale.

Place ice cubes in 6 or 7 tall glasses;
pour the juice mixture over ice. If

desired, garnish with lime, cilantro,
mint, or mango. Makes 6 or 7 (about
8-ounce) servings.

Nutrition facts per serving: 140 cal.,
0 g total fat (0 g sat. fat), 0 mg chol., 15
mg sodium, 36 g carbo., 2 g fiber, 1 g
pro. Daily Value: 33% vit. A, 39%
vit. C, 1% calcium, 3% iron.

◆ Margarita Pie

Margarita Pie

IF YOU'RE IN A HURRY, BYPASS THE FANCY CRUST AND FOLLOW THE PACKAGE DIRECTIONS FOR BAKING THE PLAIN REFRIGERATED PIECRUST.

*1 15-ounce package folded refrigerated unbaked piecrust (2 crusts),
at room temperature
1 teaspoon all-purpose flour
3 cups vanilla ice cream
⅓ cup frozen margarita mix
concentrate, thawed
2 tablespoons tequila (optional)
1½ cups lime sherbet
Whipped cream (optional)
Slivered lime peel (optional)
Edible flowers, such as strawberry
blossoms and leaves (optional)*

Trim one of the piecrusts to a 9-inch circle. Sprinkle one side with flour. Center the circle, flour side down, in the bottom of a 9-inch pie plate. Using a fluted round cutter, cut remaining piecrust into twenty 2-inch rounds. Brush edge of crust in pie plate with water. Arrange and overlap the 2-inch rounds around edge of pie crust to form a rim; press rounds to the edge of piecrust circle to seal. With fork, prick bottom and sides of piecrust.

Cover piecrust edge with foil. Bake in a 450° oven for 7 minutes. Remove foil; bake for 5 to 6 minutes more or till golden. Cool thoroughly on a wire rack.

In a medium bowl, stir vanilla ice cream just enough to soften. Stir in margarita mix. Return to freezer; freeze till nearly firm.

Stir tequila into lime sherbet to soften. Return to freezer; freeze till nearly firm.

To assemble pie, randomly drop spoonfuls of lime sherbet into ice cream mixture, folding with a spatula just to marble slightly. Do not overmix. If mixture seems soft, return to freezer and freeze till nearly firm. Gently transfer ice cream mixture to pie shell, spreading evenly. Cover; freeze 4 hours or till firm.

Before serving, let pie stand at room temperature about 20 minutes to soften slightly, if desired. To serve, cut into wedges. If desired, garnish with whipped cream, lime peel slivers, and edible flowers. Makes 8 servings.

Nutrition facts per serving: 417 cal., 21 g total fat (4 g sat. fat), 39 mg chol., 261 mg sodium, 52 g carbo., 0 g fiber, 4 g pro. Daily Value: 6% vit. A, 5% vit. C, 6% calcium, 0% iron.

Stir 'n' Swirl Ice Cream

CHOOSE ONE FLAVORING FROM THE VARIETY LISTED BELOW TO SWIRL INTO THE ICE CREAM OR COMBINE A COUPLE TO MAKE YOUR OWN DESIGNER DESSERT.

4 cups vanilla ice cream
Choose from:
1 cup flavored tiny marshmallows or canned fruit pie filling
½ cup peanut butter, fruit preserves, ice cream topping, toasted chopped nuts, toasted coconut, miniature semisweet chocolate pieces, chopped layered chocolate-mint candies, crushed gingersnaps, or chocolate wafers
¼ cup honey or raisins
2 tablespoons liqueur, such as coffee, hazelnut, orange, or almond liqueur
1 teaspoon ground cinnamon or finely shredded lemon, lime, or orange peel
½ to 1 teaspoon almond, anise, lemon, or mint extract

Place ice cream in a chilled large bowl. Stir ice cream to soften. Stir in 1 or more ingredients. (The photograph below shows from left to right: peanut butter and chocolate pieces, fudge topping and cinnamon, cherry pie filling, chopped layered chocolate-mint candies, and grape preserves.)

Pour ice cream into a 7x3x1½-inch loaf pan; cover and refreeze for at least 2 hours.

To serve, using an ice-cream scoop, scoop into serving dishes. Serves 4.

Nutrition facts per serving made with peanut butter and chocolate pieces: 276 cal., 18 g total fat (6 g sat. fat), 29 mg chol., 130 mg sodium, 26 g carbo., 1 g fiber, 7 g pro. Daily Value: 7% vit. A, 0% vit. C, 7% calcium, 4% iron.

The Ice Cream Shake-Up

You can use low-fat ice creams for the dessert recipes in this story. When you shop for frozen confections, you'll no longer see lower-fat versions labeled ice milk or frozen dessert. Instead, you'll see these products all labeled as ice cream, with the following descriptions. These descriptions indicate the amount of fat in each ½ cup serving:

Regular: 6 to 8 grams of fat

Reduced fat: 4 to 5 grams of fat

Light: 3 grams of fat

Low fat: less than 3 grams of fat

Fat free: 0 grams of fat

◆ Stir 'n' Swirl Ice Cream

Stars and Stripes Forever

FIND YOUR STAR-SHAPED COOKIE CUT-TERS TO CUT OUT THE PASTRY STARS FOR THIS DAZZLING DESSERT.

*½ of a 17¼-ounce package frozen
puff pastry (1 sheet)
2 cups sliced fresh strawberries
1½ cups fresh raspberries or blackberries
1 cup fresh blueberries
¼ cup sugar
Coarse sugar, red or blue sugar,
granulated sugar, or powdered sugar
½ cup whipping cream
¼ cup dairy sour cream
1 tablespoon sugar*

Thaw puff pastry according to package directions. Chill a medium mixing bowl and the beaters of an electric mixer. (A chilled bowl and beaters will help the cream to whip into peaks faster.)

In a large mixing bowl toss the berries and the ¼ cup sugar. Set aside.

On a lightly floured surface, unfold puff pastry. Using floured, star-shaped cutters of different sizes, cut pastry into stars (see photograph, above.) Arrange star pastries on an ungreased baking sheet. Bake in a 350° oven 15 minutes or till golden. Remove from baking sheet; cool slightly on a rack. Brush stars lightly with water; sprinkle with coarse or colored sugar or powdered sugar.

Meanwhile, in the chilled bowl combine whipping cream, sour cream, and the 1 tablespoon sugar. Beat with the chilled beaters of the electric mixer on low speed till soft peaks form.

To serve, arrange the berries and pastry stars on 6 serving plates. Pipe or spoon whipped cream onto plates. Makes 6 servings.

For Stars and Stripes Forever, use lightly floured, star-shaped cutters of different sizes to cut the pastry into stars.

Nutrition facts per serving: 362 cal., 23 g total fat (6 g sat. fat), 31 mg chol., 168 mg sodium, 39 g carbo., 3 g fiber, 3 g pro. Daily Value: 11% vit. A, 65% vit. C, 3% calcium, 2% iron.

Choose-a-Color Daiquiris

MAKE A BATCH OF EACH COLOR DAIQUIRI AHEAD AND HAVE THEM READY IN YOUR FREEZER IN PLASTIC PITCHERS. YOUR GUESTS CAN CHOOSE ONE FLAVOR OR LAYER ALL THREE IN A GLASS FOR A STRIPED SIPPER.

*1 6-ounce can frozen lemonade concentrate
½ of a 6-ounce can frozen limeade
concentrate (⅓ cup)
1 juice can light rum (⅔ cup)
¼ to ⅓ cup powdered sugar
3 cups ice cubes
Lime or lemon wedges (optional)*

White Daiquiris: In a blender container combine lemonade and limeade concentrates, rum, and powdered sugar; cover and blend till smooth. With blender running, add ice cubes, a few at a time, through lid opening, blending till slushy. Pour into 6 chilled glasses. If desired, top with a lime or lemon wedge. Makes 6 (5-ounce) servings.

Nutrition facts per serving: 163 cal., 0 g total fat (0 g sat. fat), 0 mg chol., 3 mg sodium, 26 g carbo., 1 g fiber, 0 g pro. Daily Value: 0% vit. A, 17% vit. C, 0% calcium, 0% iron.

Red Daiquiris: Prepare as for White Daiquiris, except use one 6-ounce can *frozen lemonade or limeade concentrate.* Add 2 cups *frozen unsweetened strawberries or lightly sweetened red raspberries* to the blender with the concentrate. If desired, garnish with fresh strawberries. Makes 6 (6-ounce) servings.

Nutrition facts per serving: 153 cal., 0 g total fat (0 g sat. fat), 0 mg chol., 4 mg sodium, 23 g carbo., 2 g fiber, 0 g pro. Daily Value: 0% vit. A, 48% vit. C, 0% calcium, 3% iron.

Blue Daiquiris: Prepare as for White Daiquiris, except add ¼ cup *blue curaçao liqueur* along with the frozen lemonade and limeade concentrates, light rum, and powdered sugar. If desired, garnish each serving with *star fruit slices.* Makes 6 (6-ounce) servings.

Nutrition facts per serving: 205 cal., 0 g total fat (0 g sat. fat), 0 mg chol., 3 mg sodium, 29 g carbo., 1 g fiber, 0 g pro. Daily Value: 0% vit. A, 17% vit. C, 0% calcium, 3% iron.

Nonalcoholic Daiquiris: Prepare as for White Daiquiris, except omit the sugar and substitute ¾ cup *unsweetened pineapple juice* for the rum. If desired, garnish each serving with a *fresh pineapple spear.* Makes 6 (4- to 5-ounce) servings.

Nutrition facts per serving: 117 cal., 0 g total fat (0 g sat. fat), 0 mg chol., 4 mg sodium, 30 g carbo., 1 g fiber, 0 g pro. Daily Value: 0% vit. A, 28% vit. C, 0% calcium, 1% iron.

◆ Star and Stripes Forever

◆ Just Like Fried Ice Cream

Just Like Fried Ice Cream

HERE'S A DESSERT THAT'S PERFECT NO MATTER WHAT FLAVOR ICE CREAM YOU USE. FOR A STRIPED ICE-CREAM BALL, TRY ROLLING NEAPOLITAN ICE CREAM IN THE CRUNCHY COATING. SERVE YOUR ICE CREAM DESSERT WITH SUMMER-FRESH FRUIT, SUCH AS RASPBERRIES OR SLICED PEACHES.

2 cups any flavor ice cream
1¼ cups almond cluster multigrain cereal,
coarsely crushed

2 teaspoons margarine or butter, melted
4 teaspoons honey
¼ teaspoon ground cinnamon

Using a large ice-cream scoop, make four ½-cup scoops of ice cream. Place in a shallow pan. Cover and store in the freezer till firm.

For coating, in a small mixing bowl toss together the crushed cereal and melted margarine or butter. Quickly roll the frozen ice-cream balls in the cereal mixture. Return the coated ice-cream balls to the pan. Cover and freeze till ready to serve.

To serve, stir together honey and cinnamon. Place 1 ice-cream ball on each serving plate. Drizzle 1 teaspoon of the honey mixture over each serving. Makes 4 servings.

Note: For a crispy ice cream treat on a cone, try serving these cereal-coated ice cream balls in a sugar cone and skip the honey glaze. Or, add your own toppings and turn them into a super sundae.

Nutrition facts per serving: 212 cal., 8 g total fat (5 g sat. fat), 19 mg chol., 146 mg sodium, 34 g carbo., 0 g fiber, 3 g pro. Daily Value: 7% vit. A, 18% vit. C, 6% calcium, 5% iron.

Prize Tested Recipes

Fresh Corn Frittata with Cheese Sauce

ENJOY THIS FRESH-VEGETABLE-FILLED EGG DISH FOR A SPECIAL BREAKFAST OR BRUNCH.

2 tablespoons olive oil
1 cup cut fresh corn (2 ears) or frozen whole kernel corn
½ cup chopped zucchini
⅓ cup thinly sliced green onions
¾ cup chopped plum tomatoes
8 beaten eggs
1 tablespoon snipped fresh mint or 1 teaspoon dried mint, crushed
1 12-ounce squeezable bottle process cheese sauce

In a 10-inch skillet with flared sides heat olive oil. Add corn, zucchini, and green onions. Cook and stir for 3 minutes. Add tomatoes; reduce heat. Simmer, uncovered, for 5 minutes or till corn and zucchini are crisp-tender, stirring occasionally. Add eggs and mint. Cook over medium heat. As eggs set, run a spatula around the edge of the skillet, lifting the egg mixture to allow the uncooked portion to flow underneath. When eggs are set but still shiny, remove from heat. Carefully slide onto a plate or platter; invert back into skillet. Cook 2 minutes more. Meanwhile, heat the cheese sauce according to package directions. To serve, cut frittata into wedges. Serve with warm cheese sauce. Makes 4 main-dish servings.

◆ Fresh Corn Frittata with Cheese Sauce

Nutrition facts per serving with 2 tablespoons sauce: 364 cal., 24 g total fat (8 g sat. fat), 441 mg chol., 607 mg sodium, 18 g carbo., 2 g fiber, 16 g pro. Daily Value: 27% vit. A, 21% vit. C, 9% calcium, 15% iron.

$200 WINNER
Hyacinth Rizzo
Snyder, New York

◆ Zesty Mango Sauce

occasionally. Serve sauce over grilled fish or seafood; garnish with reserved red onion slices. Makes 3¼ cups sauce.

Nutrition facts per ½ cup sauce: 53 cal., 0 g total fat (0 g sat. fat), 0 mg chol., 141 mg sodium, 13 g carbo., 2 g fiber, 1 g pro. Daily Value: 14% vit. A, 38% vit. C, 0% calcium, 2% iron.

$200 WINNER
Mildred Bickley
Bristol, Virginia

Zesty Mango Sauce

THIS SPICY SAUCE, WITH MANGO, PINEAPPLE, AND TOMATO, COMPLEMENTS SEAFOOD DELICIOUSLY.

1 ripe mango, halved, seeded, peeled, and cut up
¼ cup lemon juice
1 small red onion
1½ cups coarsely chopped fresh pineapple or one 20-ounce can pineapple tidbits (juice pack)
1 medium tomato, chopped
1 teaspoon instant chicken bouillon granules
1 teaspoon chili powder
¼ teaspoon bottled hot pepper sauce

In a blender container or food processor bowl combine mango and lemon juice; cover and blend or process till smooth. Cut several thin slices from onion; reserve for garnish. Chop remaining red onion.

In a large skillet combine the mango mixture, chopped onion, pineapple, tomato, bouillon granules, chili powder, and hot pepper sauce. Bring to boiling; reduce heat. Simmer, uncovered, for 4 to 5 minutes or till onion is tender, stirring

Creamy Corn Raita

RAITA IS A TRADITIONAL INDIAN SALAD THAT COMBINES YOGURT WITH FRESH VEGETABLES.

2 cups cooked fresh or frozen whole kernel corn, drained and cooled
½ cup low-fat or nonfat plain yogurt
2 tablespoons dairy sour cream
¼ teaspoon salt
1½ teaspoons cooking oil
¼ teaspoon cumin seed
¼ teaspoon mustard seed
1 fresh serrano chili pepper, seeded and finely chopped
Leaf lettuce (optional)
Chopped red or green sweet pepper (optional)

In a medium bowl combine cooled corn, yogurt, sour cream, and salt. In a small saucepan combine oil, cumin seed, mustard seed, and chili pepper. Place over low heat and cook about 5 minutes or just till mustard seeds begin to "dance." (Do not overheat or seeds will pop out of the pan.)

◆ Creamy Corn Raita

Stir mustard seed mixture into the corn mixture. Serve immediately or cover and chill up to 4 hours. Serve on lettuce leaves. Sprinkle with chopped red or green pepper, if desired. Makes 4 side-dish servings.

Nutrition facts per serving: 134 cal., 5 g total fat (2 g sat. fat), 5 mg chol., 171 mg sodium, 22 g carbo., 3 g fiber, 4 g pro. Daily Value: 4% vit. A, 17% vit. C, 5% calcium, 4% iron.

$100 WINNER
Laxmi Hiremath
Martinez, California

Raspberry-Walnut Sauce

This luscious fruit sauce, spiked with blackberry brandy, makes poultry extra special.

1 tablespoon margarine or butter
1 tablespoon sugar
⅓ cup orange juice
¼ cup chicken or beef broth
2 tablespoons blackberry brandy or orange juice
1 cup fresh raspberries
½ cup seedless raspberry preserves
¼ teaspoon ground ginger
⅛ teaspoon ground allspice
¼ cup coarsely chopped walnuts

In a heavy skillet melt margarine or butter. Add sugar and cook and stir over medium-high heat till golden. Slowly stir in orange juice, broth, and brandy. Bring mixture to boiling. Cook, uncovered, over medium-high heat till mixture is reduced to ¼ cup (about 5 minutes). Stir in ¼ cup of the berries, preserves, ginger, and allspice. Simmer, uncovered, for 10 minutes, stirring occasionally. Remove from heat; stir in nuts and remaining berries. Serve sauce with roasted or grilled poultry. Makes 1⅓ cups.

Nutrition facts per ⅓ cup sauce: 243 cal., 8 g total fat (2 g sat. fat), 8 mg chol., 84 mg sodium, 40 g carbo., 2 g fiber, 3 g pro. Daily Value: 4% vit. A, 33% vit. C, 5% iron.

$100 WINNER
Anne Hanson
Scottsdale, Arizona

◆ Raspberry Walnut Sauce

August

Sunset Suppers

*30-Minute Recipes for Easygoing Summer
Evenings*

Prize Tested Recipes

*Basil-Tomato Tart, Peach-Praline Cobbler, Peaches 'n' Cream Roll,
Curried Tomato Soup*

Sunset Suppers

One of summer's little pleasures is lingering over a great meal out on the porch or deck, watching and feeling another great day come to an end. The pleasure is all the greater when your cooking shows off the fruits of your labor. Not a gardener? Then brag about your farmer's market finds! And, when friends and family gush over dinner, smile smugly as the sun sets knowing that your meal cooked in less than 30 minutes (but don't bother telling).

BY JOY TAYLOR

Star-Bright Chicken and Fruit Salad

WHEN TIME IS AT A PREMIUM, USE PURCHASED CROUTONS IN PLACE OF THE HOMEMADE ONES AND SKIP THE CUCUMBER STARS.

3 thin slices French bread
Nonstick spray coating
¼ teaspoon ground ginger
¼ of a cucumber, thinly sliced
3 skinless, boneless chicken breast halves
(about 9 ounces)
1 recipe Blueberry Vinaigrette
(see recipe, right)
1 10-ounce bag (about 8 cups) torn
mixed greens for salads
(European mix or Mesclun)

½ of a small cantaloupe, peeled and
cut into thin wedges
1 cup fresh blueberries

Using a star-shaped miniature cookie cutter, cut bread slices into stars. (Reserve trimmings for another use, such as bread crumbs.) Spray one side of stars with nonstick coating; sprinkle with ground ginger. Using the same cutter, cut stars from cucumber slices; set aside.

Rinse chicken; pat dry. Place chicken on the unheated rack of a broiler pan. Set aside ¼ cup of the Blueberry Vinaigrette. Brush chicken with some of the remaining vinaigrette. Broil chicken 4 inches from the heat for 10 to 12 minutes or till tender and no longer pink, turning once and brushing with vinaigrette once or twice. During the last 1 to 2 minutes of broiling time, place bread stars, ginger side up, on same pan; broil till golden.

Line three plates with mixed greens. Thinly slice the chicken; arrange chicken slices, cucumber stars, and cantaloupe on plates. Sprinkle berries over each salad; drizzle with the reserved ¼ cup vinaigrette and top with star croutons. Makes 3 main-dish servings.

Nutrition facts per serving with vinaigrette: 435 cal., 23 g total fat (4 g sat. fat), 45 mg chol., 271 mg sodium, 40 g carbo., 6 g fiber, 22 g pro. Daily Value: 84% vit. A, 147% vit. C, 25% iron.

Blueberry Vinaigrette

YOU CAN PURCHASE BLUEBERRY VINEGAR OR EASILY MAKE YOUR OWN.

⅓ cup salad oil
⅓ cup Blueberry Vinegar
1 tablespoon sugar
1 tablespoon grated gingerroot
⅛ teaspoon salt

In a screw-top jar combine all ingredients. Cover and shake well. Store in the refrigerator for up to 2 weeks. Shake before using. Makes ⅔ cup dressing.

Blueberry Vinegar: Place 1 cup blueberries in a hot, clean glass jar. Heat 2 cups white wine vinegar; pour into jar. Cover loosely. Let stand in a cool dark place one week. Strain to remove berries. Store vinegar in the refrigerator.

Nutrition facts per tablespoon vinaigrette: 70 cal., 7 g fat (1 g sat. fat.), 0 mg chol., 27 mg sodium, 2 g carbo.

◆ Star Bright Chicken and Fruit Salad

Peppercorn Beef with Grilled Vegetables

IF YOU HANKER FOR AN ALL-AMERICAN STEAK DINNER, THIS MEAL WILL SATISFY. WHEN YOU'RE READY TO EAT, GRILL THE MARINATED MEAT IN 30 MINUTES OR LESS, DEPENDING ON HOW YOU LIKE YOUR STEAK.

⅓ cup olive oil and vinegar
salad dressing
⅓ cup dry red wine
¼ cup snipped garlic chives or ¼ cup
snipped chives plus 2 cloves
garlic, minced
1 teaspoon cracked multicolored or
black peppercorns
4 beef tenderloin steaks (about 1½
pounds) or 1 to 1½ pounds
boneless beef sirloin steak,
cut 1 to 1¼ inches thick
1 recipe Vegetable Kabobs
(see recipe, page 143) (optional)

For marinade, combine salad dressing, wine, chives, minced garlic (if using), and pepper. Place beef in a plastic bag set into a bowl. Pour marinade over beef in bag; close bag. Marinate in the refrigerator for 8 to 12 hours (no longer).

Drain beef, reserving marinade. Grill steak on the grill rack of an uncovered grill directly over medium coals for 16 to 30 minutes or till desired doneness, turning once and brushing with reserved marinade halfway through cooking time. Discard marinade. If desired, during the last 10 to 12 minutes of grilling time, arrange kabobs over coals and cook till done. Makes 4 servings.

Nutrition facts per serving: 342 cal., 21 g total fat (5 g sat. fat), 96 mg chol., 365 mg sodium, 2 g carbo., 33 g pro. Daily Value: 29% iron.

Vegetable Kabobs

8 tiny new potatoes, quartered
2 tablespoons water
8 baby yellow sunburst squash
4 miniature sweet peppers or
1 red sweet pepper, quartered
2 small red onions, each cut
into 6 wedges
1 small zucchini, halved lengthwise
and sliced
¼ cup clear olive oil and vinegar
salad dressing*
2 teaspoons snipped fresh rosemary

Place potatoes and water in a 2-quart microwave-safe casserole. Micro-cook, covered, on 100% power (high) for 5 minutes. Gently stir in squash, sweet peppers, and onion wedges. Cover; cook 4 to 6 minutes or till nearly tender. Drain. Cool slightly.

Alternately skewer precooked vegetables and uncooked zucchini onto eight 10-inch skewers. Combine salad dressing and fresh rosemary; brush over kabobs. Grill over medium coals for 10 to 12 minutes or till browned and tender, brushing with dressing and turning occasionally. Remove from skewers to serve. Makes 4 servings.

*Use a clear-colored dressing so the vegetables don't discolor.

Nutrition facts per serving: 162 cal., 8 g total fat (1 g sat. fat), 0 mg chol., 217 mg sodium, 22 g carbo., 2 g fiber, 3 g pro. Daily Value: 23% vit. A, 82% vit. C.

◆ Peppercorn Beef with Grilled Vegetables

◆ Grilled Cheese and Veggie Sandwich

Grilled Cheese and Veggie Sandwich

LOOK IN THE PRODUCE SECTION FOR BROCCOLI COLESLAW MIX—IT'S A BLEND OF CHOPPED BROCCOLI, CARROT, AND RED CABBAGE.

3 tablespoons margarine or butter, softened
8 large slices sourdough bread
(about ¾ inch thick)
2 to 4 tablespoons honey mustard
1½ cups broccoli coleslaw mix
½ cup bean sprouts, snipped
6 ounces sliced Havarti cheese with
dill or plain Havarti

Spread margarine or butter over one side of each slice of bread. Turn bread over and generously brush four of the slices with honey mustard. Stir together the broccoli mix and bean sprouts. Spoon vegetables over the mustard side of four bread slices; top each with cheese and a second piece of bread (margarine side out). On a griddle or in a large skillet cook sandwiches, two at a time, over medium heat about 2 minutes or till lightly browned. Turn; cook about 2 minutes more or till golden and cheese is melted. Makes 4 large sandwiches.

Nutrition information per half sandwich: 301 cal., 14 g total fat (1 g sat. fat), 26 mg chol., 529 mg sodium, 33 g carbo., 1 g fiber, 10 g pro.

◆ Tuna with Light Pepper Mayonnaise

Tuna with Light Pepper Mayonnaise

4 6-ounce fresh or frozen tuna steaks,
cut 1 inch thick
1 small onion, cut up
2 tablespoons lemon juice
2 tablespoons olive oil
½ teaspoon lemon-pepper seasoning
Romaine leaves

1 recipe Light Pepper Mayonnaise
Snipped fresh cilantro (optional)

Thaw fish, if frozen. For marinade, in a blender container or food processor bowl combine onion, lemon juice, oil, and lemon-pepper seasoning. Blend till smooth. Place fish in a shallow dish. Pour marinade over fish; turn to coat.

Cover; marinate at room temperature 30 minutes, turning fish occasionally.

Remove fish from marinade. Grill tuna on the greased rack of an uncovered grill directly over medium coals for 8 to 12 minutes or just till it begins to flake, turning once. Serve on romaine leaves. Spoon Light Pepper Mayonnaise over fish; sprinkle with cilantro. Serves 4.

COOKING WITH HERBS

When your summer herb garden calls it quits, dried herbs can substitute for the fresh herb. Use the following substitution levels for various herbs. Taste your dish after adding a dried herb, and add more as desired.

Strong-flavored herbs such as thyme, marjoram, sage, rosemary, tarragon, and dillweed: Substitute ½ teaspoon dried herb for each tablespoon of the fresh herb.

Mild-flavored herbs such as basil, oregano, mint, and savory: Use about 1 teaspoon dried herb for each tablespoon of the fresh herb.

◆ Tropical Turkey

Light Pepper Mayonnaise: Stir together ¼ cup *reduced-calorie mayonnaise or salad dressing;* ¼ cup *reduced-calorie dairy sour cream;* 1 or 2 *red or green jalapeño peppers,* seeded and finely chopped; 2 tablespoons *milk;* ½ teaspoon grated *lemon peel;* 1 teaspoon *lemon juice;* ⅛ teaspoon *salt;* and ⅛ teaspoon *pepper.* Cover; chill mayonnaise till needed.

Nutrition facts per serving: 413 cal., 22 g total fat (5 g sat. fat), 73 mg chol., 408 mg sodium, 6 g carbo., 45 g pro. Daily Value: 118% vit. A.

Tropical Turkey

1 carrot, cut into julienne strips
2 tablespoons margarine or butter
1 cup sugar snap peas, halved crosswise
3 tablespoons white wine
Worcestershire sauce
¼ teaspoon cracked black pepper
1 pound turkey tenderloin steaks or turkey breast steaks (¼ to ½ inch thick)
1 8-ounce can pineapple tidbits (juice pack)
1 tablespoon snipped fresh mint
1 teaspoon sugar
½ teaspoon instant chicken bouillon granules
Hot cooked couscous

In a 10-inch skillet cook and stir the carrot in margarine over medium heat 2 minutes. Add snap peas; cook and stir 2 minutes more. Remove from skillet.

Sprinkle 2 tablespoons of the Worcestershire sauce and the cracked pepper over the turkey. In the same skillet cook the turkey for 5 to 6 minutes per side or till no longer pink. (Add additional margarine, if necessary.) Add the remaining Worcestershire sauce, undrained pineapple, mint, sugar, and bouillon granules to skillet. Bring to a gentle boil; reduce heat. Return carrots and snap peas to skillet; heat through. Serve with couscous. Makes 4 servings.

Nutrition facts per serving: 232 cal., 8 g total fat (2 g sat. fat), 50 mg chol., 329 mg sodium, 17 g carbo., 2 g fiber, 23 g pro. Daily Values: 50% vit. A, 48% vit C., 16% iron.

◆ Smoky Vegetable Pizza

each bread shell. Top each with remaining shredded Gouda, feta, basil, and rosemary. Transfer two bread shells to a large piece of double thickness foil. Grill, covered, over medium coals about 8 minutes or till hot and cheese is melted. Repeat with remaining two bread shells. (Or, arrange pizzas on a large foil-lined baking sheet and bake in a 425° oven about 10 minutes or till heated through.) Makes 4 main-dish servings or 8 appetizer servings.

Nutrition facts per main-dish serving: 505 cal., 21 g total fat (7 g sat. fat), 52 mg chol., 1,170 mg sodium, 60 g carbo., 4 g fiber, 24 g pro. Daily Value: 13% vit. A, 29% vit. C, 35% calcium, 20% iron.

Smoky Vegetable Pizza

1 6-ounce jar marinated artichoke hearts
1 small red onion, cut into wedges
½ of a small eggplant, thinly sliced
(8 ounces)
2 8-ounce packages (4 total) 6-inch Italian
bread shells (Boboli)
4 ounces smoked Gouda or mozzarella
cheese, shredded
2 to 3 plum tomatoes, sliced
2 green onions, thinly sliced
¼ cup crumbled feta cheese with tomato
and basil or plain feta
1 tablespoon snipped fresh basil
1 tablespoon snipped fresh rosemary

Drain artichoke hearts, reserving marinade. Halve artichoke hearts; set aside.

Thread onion wedges on skewers. Brush onion and eggplant with some of the reserved artichoke marinade. Grill onion and eggplant on the grill rack of an uncovered grill directly over medium coals about 5 minutes or till just tender, turning once. Cool slightly. Remove onion from skewers. (Or, omit skewers and bake the vegetables on a foil-lined baking sheet in a 425° oven for 10 to 12 minutes without turning.)

Brush bread shells with some of the reserved marinade. Sprinkle about ¼ cup shredded cheese over each bread shell. Arrange artichoke hearts, onion wedges, eggplant, and sliced tomatoes on bread shells, mixing and matching vegetables as desired. Sprinkle green onion over

Summer Tomato Sauce with Beans

4 large ripe tomatoes, peeled, seeded,
and coarsely chopped
1 large onion, sliced and separated
into rings
3 tablespoons olive oil
1 orange or red sweet pepper, cut into strips
1 green sweet pepper, cut into strips
2 tablespoons chopped fresh oregano
½ teaspoon salt
¼ teaspoon ground red pepper
1 15-ounce can small white beans,
rinsed and drained
1 tablespoon tomato paste
1 teaspoon sugar
2 tablespoons white wine vinegar
Hot cooked spaghetti squash* or pasta
Grated Parmesan cheese

Place chopped tomatoes in a colander to drain. Meanwhile, in a 3-quart saucepan cook the onion in hot olive oil over medium heat till almost tender.

◆ Summer Tomato Sauce with Beans

Add the sweet pepper strips, oregano, salt, and pepper. Cook and stir about 5 minutes or till peppers are crisp-tender. Stir in the tomatoes, beans, tomato paste, and sugar; heat through. Do not boil. Stir in vinegar. To serve, spoon sauce over spaghetti squash or pasta; top each serving with cheese. Makes 4½ cups sauce (4 main-dish servings).

*To cook spaghetti squash: Halve one 2½-pound spaghetti squash lengthwise; remove seeds. Place halves, cut side down, in a microwave-safe dish with ¼ cup water. Micro-cook, covered, on high for 15 to 20 minutes or till tender, rearranging once. Scrape squash from shell with a fork.

Nutrition facts per serving with spaghetti squash: 266 cal., 13 g total fat (2 g sat. fat), 4 mg chol., 552 mg sodium, 37 g carbo., 10 g fiber, 11 g pro. Daily Value: 27% vit. A, 135% vit. C, 11% calcium, 18% iron.

◆ Garden Chicken on a Bun

Garden Chicken on a Bun

1 12-ounce package (4) frozen breaded
fully-cooked chicken patties
1 small kohlrabi, cut into match-
stick pieces
1 cup sliced fresh mushrooms
1 small onion, sliced and separated
into rings
1 stalk celery, thinly sliced
1 tablespoon snipped fresh rosemary
1 tablespoon olive oil
2 large ripe tomatoes, chopped
2 teaspoons minced garlic
4 kaiser rolls, toasted, if desired
2 tablespoons mayonnaise or salad dressing
Lettuce leaves

Bake chicken patties according to
package directions. Meanwhile, in a 10-
inch skillet cook kohlrabi, mushrooms,
onion, celery, rosemary, and ½ teaspoon
salt in hot oil over medium heat 10 minutes. Stir in tomatoes and garlic.
Simmer, uncovered, 5 minutes more.
Spread bottom of buns with mayonnaise
or salad dressing; place lettuce and chick-
en patty on each. Spoon sauce over. Add
bun top. Makes 4 servings.

Nutrition facts per serving: 538 cal.,
28 g total fat (3 g sat. fat), 49 mg chol.,
928 mg sodium, 50 g carbo.,
3 g fiber, 23 g pro. Daily Value: 8% vit.
A, 69% vit. C, 25% iron.

Mediterranean Omelet
AN EASY LATE-EVENING MEAL FOR TWO.

⅓ of a 6-ounce package frozen, peeled,
cooked tiny shrimp (⅔ cup)
4 pitted ripe olives, thinly sliced
1 small tomato, seeded and chopped
(½ cup)
2 tablespoons toasted pinenuts or
slivered almonds
1 tablespoon snipped fresh basil
2 teaspoons capers, drained
3 eggs
3 tablespoons water
⅛ teaspoon salt
1 tablespoon margarine or butter
2 ounces sliced provolone cheese
Sliced green onion and chopped
tomato (optional)

Run cold water over shrimp in colander to thaw. Drain; pat dry. Stir together shrimp, olives, tomato, nuts, basil,
and capers. Beat the eggs, water, salt,
and ⅛ teaspoon pepper with a fork till
combined.

In a nonstick 10-inch skillet with
flared sides, melt margarine. Tilt pan to
coat sides. Cook eggs in skillet over
medium heat without stirring. As eggs
set, run a spatula around the edge, letting uncooked portion flow underneath.
When eggs are set, but still shiny,
remove from heat. Top with cheese;
spoon shrimp mixture onto one-half of
the omelet. Fold omelet in half; heat
through over low heat. Cut omelet in
half; transfer to plates. Sprinkle with
onion and tomato. Makes 2 servings.

Nutrition facts per serving: 366 cal.,
28 g total fat (9 g sat. fat), 395 mg chol.,
700 mg sodium, 6 g carbo., 1 g fiber, 26
g pro. Daily Value: 33% vit. A, 23% calcium, 22% iron.

◆ Mediterranean Omelet

Pork Medallions with Summer Pasta

⅛ cup dried mushrooms (such as
shiitake or porcini)
¼ cup dried tomatoes (not oil packed)
6 ounces bow tie pasta
2 cups green beans cut into 1-inch pieces
1 medium yellow summer squash, sliced
(1¼ cups)
1 cup half-and-half or milk
¾ cup chicken broth
1 green onion, sliced
1 tablespoon cornstarch
½ teaspoon lemon-pepper seasoning
¼ teaspoon salt
1 pound boneless pork loin roast, cut
crosswise into 4 steaks
1 tablespoon olive oil

Soak mushrooms and tomatoes in enough boiling water to cover for 5 minutes. Drain and snip, discarding mushroom stems; set aside.

Cook the pasta according to package directions, except add the beans to the boiling water at the beginning of the pasta cooking time, and add the squash

◆ Pork Medallions with Summer Pasta

to the boiling water for the last 2 minutes of the cooking time. Drain; cover to keep warm.

Meanwhile, stir together the half-and-half, broth, onion, cornstarch, lemon-pepper seasoning, and salt; set aside. Season pork lightly with additional salt and lemon-pepper seasoning. In a 10-inch skillet cook pork in hot oil over medium heat for 5 minutes per side or till only a little pink remains in center of meat. Remove from skillet. Cover; keep warm. Drain fat from skillet. Pour cornstarch mixture into skillet. Cook and stir

till thickened and bubbly, scraping up any brown bits from bottom of skillet. Reduce heat; cook for 2 minutes more. Stir in mushrooms and tomatoes. To serve, divide pasta and vegetables among four plates. Arrange pork on each plate; spoon sauce over all. Makes 4 servings.

Nutrition facts per serving: 453 cal., 20 g total fat (8 g sat. fat), 110 mg chol., 659 mg sodium, 43 g carbo., 2 g fiber, 26 g pro. Daily Value: 14% vit. A, 16% vit. C, 23% iron.

Prize Tested Recipes

Basil-Tomato Tart

BE READY. YOUR FRIENDS WILL REQUEST THE RECIPE FOR THIS GARDEN-FRESH APPETIZER OR ENTRÉE.

½ of a 15-ounce package folded
refrigerated unbaked piecrust (1 crust)
1½ cups shredded mozzarella
cheese (6 ounces)
5 Roma or 4 medium tomatoes
1 cup loosely packed fresh basil leaves
4 cloves garlic
½ cup mayonnaise or salad dressing
¼ cup grated Parmesan cheese
⅛ teaspoon ground white pepper
Fresh basil leaves (optional)

Unfold piecrust according to package directions. Place in a 9-inch quiche dish or glass pie plate. Flute edge; press with the tines of a fork, if desired. Prebake according to package directions. Remove from oven. Sprinkle with ½ cup of the mozzarella cheese. Cool on a wire rack.

Cut tomatoes into wedges; drain on paper towels. Arrange tomato wedges atop melted cheese in the baked pie shell. In a food processor bowl combine basil and garlic; cover and process till coarsely chopped. Sprinkle mixture over tomatoes.

In a medium mixing bowl combine remaining mozzarella cheese, mayonnaise, Parmesan cheese, and pepper. Spoon cheese mixture over basil mixture, spreading to evenly cover the top.

◆ Basil Tomato Tart

Bake in a 375° oven for 35 to 40 minutes or till top is golden and bubbly. Serve warm. If desired, sprinkle with basil leaves. Makes 8 appetizer or 4 main-dish servings.

Nutrition facts per appetizer serving: 312 cal., 24 g total fat (5 g sat. fat), 27 mg chol., 341 mg sodium, 18 g carbo., 1 g fiber, 8 g pro. Daily Values: 9% vit. A, 29% vit. C, 16% calcium, 3% iron.

$200 WINNER
Kathleen M. Bonerb
Glen, New Hampshire

Peach-Praline Cobbler

SPLASH A LITTLE CREAM ONTO THE NUTTY BISCUIT SPIRALS AND STEAMY PEACH FILLING.

◆ Peach Praline Cobbler

◆ Curried Tomato Soup

8 cups sliced, peeled, fresh or
frozen peaches (thawed)
1 cup sugar
1 cup water
2 tablespoons cornstarch
1 teaspoon ground cinnamon
¾ cup packed brown sugar
¼ cup margarine or butter, melted
1½ cups chopped pecans
2 cups self-rising flour*
2 teaspoons sugar
½ cup shortening
¾ cup buttermilk
Light cream (optional)

In a Dutch oven combine peaches, 1 cup sugar, water, cornstarch, and cinnamon. Cook and stir till thickened and bubbly. Transfer to a 3-quart rectangular baking dish.

Meanwhile, for the filling, stir together brown sugar and melted margarine or butter. Add pecans; toss to coat. Set filling aside.

For dough, in a large mixing bowl stir together self-rising flour and the 2 teaspoons sugar. Cut in shortening till mixture resembles coarse crumbs. Make a well in the center; add buttermilk. Stir just till dough clings together.

Turn dough out onto a lightly floured surface. Knead gently for 10 to 12 strokes. Roll to a 12x8-inch rectangle; spread with pecan filling. Roll up from one of the long sides. Cut into twelve 1-inch-thick slices. Place slices, cut side down, atop hot peaches. Bake, uncovered, in a 400° oven for 25 to 30 minutes or till biscuits are golden. Serve

warm with half-and-half or light cream, if desired. Makes 12 servings.

*Note: As an option for the self-rising flour, you can use 2 cups *all-purpose flour*, 2 teaspoons *baking powder*, ½ teaspoon *baking soda*, and ½ teaspoon *salt*.

Nutrition facts per serving: 466 cal., 22 g total fat (3 g sat. fat), 1 mg chol., 332 mg sodium, 67 g carbo., 6 g fiber, 5 g pro. Daily Values: 12% vit. A, 16% vit. C.

$200 WINNER
Carrie Smart
Rochelle, Illinois

Curried Tomato Soup

THIS SOUP IS EQUALLY GOOD SERVED CHILLED ON HOT SUMMER DAYS OR WARM ON COOL DAYS.

1 medium onion, chopped (½ cup)
1 small clove garlic, minced
2 teaspoons olive oil
¾ teaspoon curry powder
1½ pounds tomatoes, halved, cored, and seeded
1½ cups chicken broth
½ teaspoon dried fines herbes, crushed
¼ teaspoon salt
⅛ to ¼ teaspoon pepper
continued on page 152

continued from page 151

In a saucepan cook onion and garlic in hot oil till tender. Add curry powder; cook and stir for 1 minute more. Add tomatoes, broth, fines herbes, salt, and pepper. Bring to boiling; reduce heat. Cover and simmer for 10 minutes. Cool slightly.

In a food processor or blender container cover and process cooled mixture, half at a time, till smooth. If desired, press through a sieve. Serve hot or chilled. If desired, top with yogurt, fresh thyme, and quartered cherry tomatoes. Makes 6 side-dish servings.

Nutrition facts per serving: 61 cal., 2 g total fat (0 g sat. fat), 0 mg chol., 296 mg sodium, 9 g carbo., 1 g fiber, 3 g pro. Daily Values: 8% vit. A, 44% vit. C, 1% calcium, 6% iron.

$100 WINNER
Pat Hockett,
Alva Oklahoma

◆ Peaches 'n' Cream Roll

Peaches 'n' Cream Roll

THE SECRET TO AN EASY-TO-ROLL SPONGE CAKE IS USING PANCAKE MIX IN THE BATTER.

3 eggs
¼ teaspoon salt
¼ teaspoon vanilla
¾ cup granulated sugar
¾ cup packaged complete buttermilk pancake mix
1 tablespoon light or dark rum
4 large peaches, peeled, pitted, and chopped (4 cups), or one 16-ounce package frozen unsweetened peach slices, thawed, drained, and chopped
1 cup whipping cream
½ cup granulated sugar

Grease and flour a 15x10x1-inch jelly-roll pan; set aside. In a large mixing bowl beat eggs, salt, and vanilla with an electric mixer on high speed for about 4 minutes or till thick. Gradually add the ¾ cup granulated sugar; beat on medium speed for 4 to 5 minutes or till light and fluffy. Add pancake mix; beat on low speed just till combined. Spread batter in prepared pan. Bake in a 400° oven for 8 to 10 minutes or till golden and cake springs back when lightly touched near center. Immediately loosen edges of cake from pan and turn cake out onto a towel sprinkled with powdered sugar. Roll up towel and cake, jelly-roll style, starting from one of the short sides. Cool on a wire rack.

Meanwhile, add rum to peaches; set aside. Beat together whipping cream and ½ cup granulated sugar till stiff peaks form. Unroll cake; remove towel. Spread cake with half of the whipped cream; top with drained peaches. Spread with remaining cream. Roll up cake. Place, seam side down, on a serving platter. If desired, sprinkle with powdered sugar. Cover and chill till serving time, for up to 2 hours. Makes 10 servings.

Nutrition facts per serving: 280 cal., 11 g total fat (6 g sat. fat), 97 mg chol., 233 mg sodium, 44 g carbo., 1 g fiber, 4 g pro. Daily Values: 17% vit. A, 7% vit. C, 6% calcium, 4% iron.

$100 WINNER
Lisa Waldorf
Alpharetta, Georgia

September

Super Sandwiches from
Coast to Coast

Prize Tested Recipes

Apricot-Date Loaves with Rosemary, Feta-Mint Rice,
Two-Grain Vegetable Casserole, Pepper Twists

Super Sandwiches

BY KRISTI FULLER

Nothing can take the place of a classic tuna salad sandwich or BLT. But when you want to veer off the beaten sandwich path, look no further. Here you'll find the hottest sandwiches being served all across the country.

Oriental Grilled Fish

*4 fresh or frozen, skinless, boneless
fish fillets or steaks (such as salmon,
haddock, or halibut), cut
½ inch thick (about 1 pound total)
¼ cup orange juice
2 tablespoons reduced-sodium soy sauce
1 teaspoon ground ginger
1 teaspoon sesame oil
4 Kaiser rolls, split and toasted
1 recipe Soy-Ginger Mayonnaise
(see right)
Shredded spinach leaves
8 to 12 pea pods, cooked*

Thaw fish, if frozen. In a large shallow dish combine juice, soy sauce, ginger, and oil. Add fish; turn to coat. Let fish stand, covered, for 30 minutes, turning occasionally.

Brush grill rack with cooking oil. Place fish on grill rack. Grill, uncovered, directly over medium-hot coals for 4 to 6 minutes per ½ inch or till fish flakes easily, turning once.

Spread rolls with Soy-Ginger Mayonnaise. Place shredded spinach on roll bottoms; top with fish, pea pods, and roll tops. Makes 4 servings.

Soy-Ginger Mayonnaise: In a bowl stir together ¼ cup *reduced-calorie mayonnaise dressing*, 1 tablespoon *orange marmalade*, 2 teaspoons *reduced-sodium soy sauce*, and ¼ teaspoon *ground ginger*. Cover; chill. Makes ¼ cup.

Nutrition facts per serving with 1 tablespoon Soy-Ginger Mayonnaise: 347 cal., 9 g total fat (2 g sat. fat), 43 mg chol., 859 mg sodium, 39 g carbo., 1 g fiber, 25 g pro.

◆ Oriental Grilled Fish

◆ Panini

Panini

8 slices sourdough bread
2 tablespoons olive oil
6 ounces thinly sliced fully cooked
lower-sodium ham
4 slices fontina cheese (4 ounces)
4 canned roasted sweet pepper
halves, drained
8 large fresh basil leaves
Pepper

Brush both sides of each bread slice with oil. Top half of the bread slices, oil side down, with ham, cheese, a roasted pepper half, 2 basil leaves, and a dash black pepper. Top with a bread slice, oil side up.

Place 2 sandwiches at a time on a pre-heated waffle or pancake baker. Close lid. Bake for 2 to 3 minutes or just till cheese melts. Repeat with remaining sandwiches. (Or, cook in a skillet over medium heat for 6 to 8 minutes or till light brown, turning once.) Makes 4 servings.

Nutrition facts per serving: 372 cal., 19 g total fat (7 g sat. fat), 46 mg chol., 1,013 mg sodium, 28 g carbo., 0 g fiber, 21 g pro.

◆ Grilled Vegetables on Focaccia

Nutrition facts per serving with Herb Focaccia: 563 cal., 29 g total fat (6 g sat. fat), 57 mg chol., 436 mg sodium, 63 g carbo., 2 g fiber, 14 g pro. Daily Value: 27% vit. A, 91% vit. C, 24% iron.

Grilled Vegetables On Focaccia

IF YOU DON'T HAVE TIME TO MAKE FOCACCIA (SEE RECIPE, RIGHT), LOOK FOR IT IN ITALIAN BAKERIES OR YOUR SUPERMARKET.

3 tablespoons salad oil
3 tablespoons balsamic or wine vinegar
1 teaspoon dried oregano, crushed
2 large red sweet peppers
1 medium eggplant, cut crosswise into ½-inch slices
2 medium zucchini, halved crosswise and sliced
1 recipe Herb Focaccia (see recipe, right) or purchased focaccia (about a 12-inch round)
4 ounces soft goat cheese (chèvre)

In a small bowl combine oil, vinegar, and oregano. Set aside. Cut peppers in quarters. Remove stem and seeds. Arrange all vegetables on grill rack directly over medium-hot coals; brush with oil mixture. Grill, uncovered, till slightly charred, allowing 8 to 10 minutes for peppers and eggplant, and 5 to 6 minutes for zucchini. Turn occasionally.

Cut each 9-inch Herb Focaccia into 2 layers. (Or, if using a 12- or 13-inch focaccia, cut in half. Cut halves into 2 layers to form 4 layers total.) Brush cut sides with oil mixture. Spread goat cheese over bottom layers of focaccia; top with eggplant, red pepper, zucchini, and top halves of focaccia. To serve, cut into wedges. Makes 6 to 8 servings.

Herb Focaccia

1 16-ounce package hot roll mix
1 egg
2 tablespoons olive oil
⅓ cup finely chopped onion
½ teaspoon dried rosemary, crushed
3 tablespoons olive oil or cooking oil

Lightly grease two 9x1½-inch round baking pans or a 12- or 13-inch pizza pan. Set aside.

Prepare hot roll mix according to package directions for basic dough, using the 1 egg and substituting the 2 tablespoons olive oil for margarine. Knead dough; allow to rest as directed. If using round baking pans, divide dough in half; roll into two 9-inch rounds. If using a pizza pan, roll dough into a 12-inch round. Place in prepared pan(s).

In a skillet cook onion and rosemary in 3 tablespoons oil till onion is tender but not brown. With fingertips, press indentations every inch or so in dough round(s). Top dough evenly with onion mixture. Cover; let rise in a warm place till nearly double (30 to 40 minutes).

Bake in a 375° oven for 15 to 20 minutes or till golden. Transfer to a rack. Cool. Makes 6 to 8 servings.

Nutrition facts per serving: 413 cal., 17 g total fat (3 g sat. fat), 40 mg chol., 322 mg sodium, 56 g carbo., 0 g fiber, 10 g pro. Daily Value: 1% vit. C, 5% calcium, 18% iron.

◆ Muffuletta

Muffuletta

1 16-ounce jar pickled mixed vegetables
(1½ cups)
¼ cup chopped pimiento-stuffed green
olives and/or pitted ripe olives, drained
1 clove garlic, minced
1 tablespoon olive oil or salad oil
1 9-inch round loaf unsliced Italian bread
6 ounces thinly sliced lower-sodium
fully cooked ham
4 ounces sliced provolone cheese
4 ounces thinly sliced salami

Drain vegetables, reserving 2 table-spoons liquid. Chop vegetables. Combine vegetables, reserved liquid, olives, garlic, and oil.

Slice bread in half horizontally. On bottom half layer ham, cheese, and salami. Top with vegetable mixture. Sprinkle with black pepper. Cover with bread top. Secure with wooden picks. To serve, cut into wedges. Serves 6 to 8.

Nutrition facts per serving: 476 cal., 21 g total fat (7 g sat. fat), 43 mg chol., 1,776 mg sodium, 49 g carbo., 1 g fiber, 23 g pro. Daily Value: 13% vit. C, 17% calcium, 19% iron.

Note: To reduce sodium by 200 mg per serving, omit pickled vegetables; substitute 1½ cups chopped assorted *fresh vegetables, such as broccoli, carrot, celery, and sweet peppers.* Add 2 tablespoons *lemon juice* in place of reserved liquid and add an additional 1 tablespoon *oil.*

◆ Italian Beef

Italian Beef

CHILL THE ROAST BEEF AT LEAST 2 HOURS BEFORE SERVING SO IT'S EASIER TO SLICE.

1 3-pound boneless beef round rump roast
1 14½-ounce can beef broth
½ cup water
6 cloves garlic, minced
2 teaspoons dried oregano, crushed
½ to 1 teaspoon crushed red pepper
¼ teaspoon black pepper
3 green sweet peppers, seeded and
cut into strips
8 hoagie buns, split

Place roast, fat side up, on a rack in a shallow roasting pan. Roast, uncovered, in a 325° oven 1½ to 2 hours or to 145° (do not overcook or meat will be tough).

Transfer roast to a platter. Skim fat from the pan juices. (Transfer juices to a covered container; chill.) Cool roast for 30 minutes. Cover; chill.

Using a very sharp knife, electric knife, or meat slicer, thinly slice the chilled roast across the grain. To serve, in a 3-quart saucepan combine reserved meat juices, beef broth, water, garlic, oregano, and red and black peppers. Bring broth mixture to boiling; reduce heat. Add sliced meat and pepper strips. Simmer, uncovered, 5 to 10 minutes or till peppers are tender. Remove from heat. Keep warm.

Meanwhile, warm buns in a 350° oven for 5 to 10 minutes. Spoon beef, peppers, and juices onto buns. Pass remaining juices. Makes 8 servings.

Nutrition facts per serving: 638 cal., 13 g total fat (4 g sat. fat), 83 mg chol., 930 mg sodium, 80 g carbo., 5 g fiber, 47 g pro. Daily Value: 68% vit. C, 6% calcium, 41% iron.

Roast Pork Sandwich With Apple Mustard

½ cup apple butter
1 tablespoon coarse-grain mustard
8 slices marbled rye bread

◆ Roast Pork Sandwich with Apple Mustard

1½ cups preshredded coleslaw mix or
shredded cabbage
8 ounces thinly sliced cooked pork
4 ounces thinly sliced Swiss cheese
1 medium apple, cored and sliced
into thin wedges

In a small bowl combine apple butter and mustard. Toast bread, if desired. Spread one side of bread slices with apple butter mixture. Top half of the bread slices with coleslaw mix, pork, cheese, apples, and the remaining bread with apple butter side down. Makes 4 servings.

Nutrition facts per serving: 495 cal., 17 g total fat (8 g sat. fat), 63 mg chol., 593 mg sodium, 54 g carbo., 1 g fiber, 30 g pro.

Lahvosh Roll

LAHVOSH, A CRISP, CRACKERLIKE BREAD, IS SOFTENED BEFORE USING. CHECK YOUR SUPERMARKET FOR THE PRESOFT-ENED VARIETY TO SAVE A STEP.

1 15-inch sesame seed Armenian cracker
bread (lahvosh) or two 10-inch tortillas
4 ounces soft-style cream cheese with
chives and onion

◆ Lahvosh Roll

¼ cup chopped, drained marinated
artichoke hearts
2 tablespoons diced pimiento
1 teaspoon dried oregano, crushed
6 ounces thinly sliced prosciutto or
fully cooked ham
4 ounces sliced provolone cheese
1 large romaine lettuce leaf, rib removed

To soften lahvosh, dampen both sides by holding it briefly under gently running cold water. Place the bread, sesame side down, between 2 damp clean kitchen towels. Let stand about 1 hour or till soft.

In a bowl stir together cream cheese, artichoke, pimiento, and oregano. Remove top towel from lahvosh. Spread cream cheese filling onto lahvosh to edges. Arrange prosciutto or ham over cream cheese. Spread cheese slices in the center. Place lettuce leaf along one side of the cheese. Roll from lettuce edge, using the towel to lift and roll the bread. (Or, if using tortillas, spread cream cheese mixture onto the tortillas. Divide remaining ingredients between the tortillas. Roll up tortillas.) Cover and chill, seam side down, for 2 to 24 hours. Cut roll into 1-inch-thick slices. Serves 6.

Nutrition facts per serving: 327 cal., 20 g total fat (7 g sat. fat), 33 mg chol., 879 mg sodium, 21 g carbo., 16 g pro. Daily Value: 11% vit. A, 10% vit. C, 13% calcium, 6% iron.

♦ Foot-Long Turkey Hero on Tomato-Basil Bread

Spread top bread half with 2 tablespoons mayonnaise. Place atop sandwich. Makes 6 servings.

Tomato Mayonnaise: In a blender container combine ½ cup *mayonnaise or salad dressing;* 6 *dried tomato halves (oil pack),* drained and cut into quarters; 1 teaspoon *lemon juice;* and ½ teaspoon *dried basil,* crushed. Cover; blend till combined. Transfer to a small container. Cover; refrigerate till needed or for up to 2 weeks. Makes ½ cup.

Nutrition facts per serving: 468 cal., 22 g total fat (7 g sat. fat), 57 mg chol., 712 mg sodium, 43 g carbo., 4 g fiber, 26 g pro. Daily Value: 16% vit. A, 15% vit. C, 18% calcium.

Tomato-Basil Bread

2 to 2½ cups all-purpose flour
2 packages active dry yeast
1 teaspoon dried basil, crushed
1¾ cups milk
½ cup snipped dried tomatoes
¼ cup packed brown sugar
3 tablespoons margarine or butter
2 teaspoons salt
2 cups whole wheat flour
½ cup yellow cornmeal
1 slightly beaten egg white
1 tablespoon water

In a mixing bowl stir together 1½ cups of the all-purpose flour, the yeast, and basil. In a saucepan heat the milk, dried tomatoes, brown sugar, margarine or butter, and salt till warm (120° to 130°) and margarine almost melts. Add to flour mixture.

Beat the flour mixture with an electric mixer on low to medium speed 30 seconds. Beat on high for 3 minutes. Stir in whole wheat flour, ½ cup cornmeal, and

Foot-Long Turkey Hero

1 pound boneless turkey breast pieces, such
as steaks, slices, or tenderloins
1 tablespoon olive oil or cooking oil
1 teaspoon lemon-pepper seasoning
4 ounces Muenster or Monterey Jack
cheese, sliced
1 loaf Tomato-Basil Bread (see right) or
one 1-pound loaf unsliced French bread
1 recipe Tomato Mayonnaise
(see right) or mayonnaise
2 cups torn mixed greens (such as mesclun)
or torn spinach
½ of a red onion, thinly sliced

If using whole tenderloins, use a sharp knife to cut each in half horizontally, making four ½-inch-thick steaks. Rinse turkey; pat dry. Brush with oil. Sprinkle with lemon-pepper seasoning. Place turkey on the unheated rack of a broiler pan. Broil 4 to 5 inches from the heat for 4 minutes. Turn and broil for 4 to 5 minutes more or till tender and no longer pink. Top with cheese; broil 1 minute more or till cheese melts.

Use a serrated knife to cut bread. Spread bottom layer with about 2 tablespoons of the Tomato Mayonnaise or mayonnaise. On bottom half layer greens, turkey, and onion.

as much of the remaining all-purpose flour as you can.

On a floured surface, knead in enough remaining all-purpose flour to make a moderately stiff dough that is elastic (8 minutes). Shape into a ball. Place in a greased bowl; turn. Cover and let rise in a warm place till double (about 1 hour). Punch dough down. Turn out onto a lightly floured surface. Divide in half. Cover; let rest for 10 minutes.

Grease a baking sheet. Sprinkle with cornmeal. Roll each dough half into a 15x10-inch rectangle. Roll up from a long side. Moisten edge with water; seal. Taper ends. Place, seam down, on baking sheet. Brush with egg white and water mixture. Cover; let rise till double (45 minutes).

With a sharp knife, make 4 shallow diagonal cuts across top of each loaf. Bake in a 375° oven for 20 minutes. Brush with egg white mixture. Continue baking for 15 to 20 minutes or till bread sounds hollow when tapped. (If necessary, cover loosely with foil the last 15 minutes of baking to prevent over-browning). Remove from the baking sheet; cool on a wire rack. Makes 2 loaves (32 slices).

Nutrition facts per slice: 85 cal., 2 g total fat (0 g sat. fat), 1 mg chol., 157 mg sodium, 15 g carbo., 1 g fiber, 3 g pro.

◆ Chicken Tortilla Sandwich

Chicken Tortilla Sandwich

12 ounces boneless, skinless chicken breasts
⅓ cup bottled lemon-pepper
marinade for chicken
1 to 2 teaspoons chili powder
4 8- to 10-inch flour tortillas

4 ounces Gruyère or Monterey Jack cheese,
shredded (about 1 cup)
1 avocado, seeded, peeled, and thinly sliced
2 tablespoons snipped fresh cilantro
1 small tomato, chopped
½ cup dairy sour cream
1 tablespoon canned or fresh jalapeño
peppers, seeded and chopped

Cut chicken into ½-inch-wide strips. In a nonmetal bowl combine chicken, marinade, and chili powder. Cover; marinate in refrigerator for 4 to 6 hours. Preheat a skillet over medium-high heat; add undrained chicken. Cook for 2 to 3 minutes or till no longer pink.

Brush one side of tortillas with oil. Place, oil side down, on a baking sheet. Divide half of cheese, the avocado, chicken, tomato, and 1 tablespoon cilantro atop one-half side of each tortilla. Top with remaining cheese. Fold tortilla over filling. Bake in a 450° oven for 6 to 8 minutes.

Serve sandwiches with a mixture of sour cream, remaining cilantro, and jalapeños. Makes 4 servings.

Nutrition facts per serving: 477 cal., 29 g total fat (9 g sat. fat), 87 mg chol., 879 mg sodium, 24 g carbo., 7 g fiber, 30 g pro.

September
161

◆ Tabbouleh Pita

Tabbouleh Pita

½ cup bulgur
¼ cup snipped parsley
1 tablespoon sliced green onion
1 tablespoon lemon juice
1 tablespoon olive oil
¼ teaspoon salt
2 whole wheat pita bread rounds,
cut in half crosswise
Romaine lettuce leaves
1 orange, peeled and thinly sliced, and/or
1 small tomato, thinly sliced
1 recipe Hummus (see below)
¼ cup chopped cashews

For tabbouleh, soak bulgur in 1 cup hot water for 1 hour. Drain well; squeeze out excess water. Stir in parsley, onion, lemon juice, oil, and salt. Cover; chill several hours.

Line each pita bread half with lettuce leaves, orange, and/or tomato slices. Stir together tabbouleh, Hummus, and nuts; spoon into pockets. Makes 4 servings.

Hummus: In a food processor bowl combine 1 cup *canned garbanzo beans* (drained), 1 clove *garlic,* 2 tablespoons *lemon juice,* 1 tablespoon *olive oil,* ½ teaspoon *dried mint,* ½ teaspoon *sesame oil,* ¼ teaspoon *salt,* and a dash *pepper.* Cover; process till smooth. Cover; chill before serving. Makes ¾ cup.

Nutrition facts per serving: 343 cal., 14 g total fat (2 g sat. fat), 0 mg chol., 448 mg sodium, 49 g carbo., 8 g fiber, 10 g pro.

Prize Tested Recipes

Apricot-Date Loaves With Rosemary

SURPRISE! BET YOU NEVER THOUGHT THE HERB ROSEMARY WOULD TASTE SO GOOD IN A SWEET LOAF.

1½ cups apricot nectar
1½ cups snipped pitted dates
(one 8-ounce package)
½ cup dried apricots, snipped
1 tablespoon finely shredded orange peel
1¼ teaspoon dried rosemary, crushed
2¼ cups all-purpose flour
1½ teaspoons baking soda
½ cup margarine or butter
1 cup sugar
1 egg
⅓ cup evaporated milk

Lightly grease eight 4½x2½x1½- or four 5½x3x2- or three 7½x3½x2-inch loaf pans; set aside. In a medium saucepan bring nectar, dates, and apricots to boiling. Reduce heat; simmer, covered, for 5 minutes. Remove from heat. Stir in orange peel and rosemary; cool slightly. Meanwhile, in a small mixing bowl stir together flour and baking soda; set aside.

In a large mixing bowl beat margarine or butter with an electric mixer on medium speed about 30 seconds or till softened. Gradually add sugar, beating till fluffy. Beat in egg and milk. Alternately add flour mixture and date mixture, beating just till combined after each addition. Spread batter evenly in prepared baking pans.

◆ Apricot-Date Loaves with Rosemary

Bake in a 375° oven till a toothpick inserted near the center comes out clean, allowing about 25 minutes for the 4½x2½-inch pans, about 35 minutes for the 5½x3-inch pans, and about 40 minutes for the 7½x3½-inch pans. Cool in pans for 10 minutes. Remove from pans; cool completely on wire racks. Wrap and store bread overnight before slicing. Makes 32 servings (1 slice per serving).

Nutrition facts per slice: 116 cal., 3 g total fat (1 g sat. fat), 7 mg chol., 95 mg sodium, 21 g carbo., 1 g fiber, 2 g pro. Daily Values: 7% vit. A, 7% vit. C, 1% calcium, 4% iron.

$200 WINNER
Audrey Thibodeau
Mesa, Arizona

◆ Feta-Mint Rice

Feta-Mint Rice

TEAM THIS GREEK-INSPIRED RICE DISH WITH GRILLED LAMB OR BEEF.

¼ cup chopped onion
1 tablespoon olive oil
1 cup long grain rice
2 cups chicken broth
2 ounces crumbled feta cheese (½ cup)
3 tablespoons snipped fresh mint
½ teaspoon pepper
Fresh mint (optional)

In a large saucepan cook onion in hot oil till tender but not brown. Add uncooked rice; cook and stir for 1 minute. Slowly add chicken broth. Bring to boiling; reduce heat. Cover; simmer for 15 to 20 minutes or till rice is tender and liquid is absorbed. Stir in feta cheese, mint, and pepper. Serve warm. If desired, garnish with fresh mint leaves. Makes 6 side-dish servings.

Nutrition facts per serving: 194 cal., 7 g total fat (2 g sat. fat), 9 mg chol., 366 mg sodium, 26 g carbo., 0 g fiber, 5 g pro. Daily Values: 1% vit. A, 3% vit. C, 5% calcium, 14% iron.
$200 WINNER
Sandy Szwarc
Albuquerque, New Mexico

Two-Grain Vegetable Casserole

BARLEY, BULGUR, AND VEGETABLES CREATE A FIBER-RICH SIDE DISH OR VEGETARIAN ENTRÉE.

2 medium carrots, halved lengthwise
and thinly sliced
1 cup fresh small mushrooms, quartered
1 cup canned black beans, rinsed
and drained
1 8-ounce can whole kernel corn, drained,
or 1 cup frozen whole kernel corn
1 cup vegetable broth
½ cup pearl barley
⅓ cup snipped parsley
¼ cup bulgur
¼ cup chopped onion
¼ teaspoon garlic salt
½ cup shredded cheddar cheese

In a 1½-quart casserole combine all ingredients except cheese. Cover and bake in a 350° oven about 1 hour or till barley and bulgur are tender, stirring once halfway through the baking time. Sprinkle with cheese. Cover and let stand about 5 minutes or till cheese is melted. Makes 6 side-dish servings or 4 main-dish servings.

To make ahead: Prepare and cook casserole as directed, except do not add cheese. Cool, cover, and freeze for up to a month. To reheat, bake, covered, in a 350° oven for 55 to 60 minutes or till heated through, stirring once. Stir again. Sprinkle with cheese. Cover and let stand about 5 minutes or till the cheese is melted.

Nutrition facts per side-dish serving: 173 cal., 4 g total fat (2 g sat. fat), 10 mg chol., 478 mg sodium, 30 g carbo., 7 g fiber, 9 g pro. Daily Values: 61% vit. A, 13% vit. C, 8% calcium, 12% iron.
$100 WINNER
Shirley Auman
Davis, California

◆ Two-Grain Vegetable Casserole

◆ Pepper Twists

Pepper Twists

THESE BREADSTICKS BITE BACK. GAUGE
YOUR TOLERANCE FOR HEAT AND PICK
YOUR PEPPER LEVEL ACCORDINGLY.

2 cups all-purpose flour
1 tablespoon baking powder
1 to 1½ teaspoons cracked black pepper
¼ teaspoon salt
⅓ cup margarine or butter
⅔ cup beef or chicken broth

In a medium mixing bowl stir together flour, baking powder, pepper, and salt. Cut in margarine or butter till mixture resembles coarse crumbs. Make a well in the center. Add broth; stir just till dough clings together.

Turn dough out onto lightly floured surface. Knead gently for 10 to 12 strokes. Divide dough into 8 portions; divide each portion into fourths. Roll each portion into a 10-inch-long rope. Fold each rope in half and twist the rope 2 or 3 times.

Arrange twists on an ungreased baking sheet. Bake in a 450° oven for 5 minutes; turn and bake for 5 to 6 minutes more or till brown. Serve warm, or cool completely on a wire rack before serving. Makes 32 breadsticks.

Nutrition facts per breadstick: 44 cal., 2 g total fat (1 g sat. fat), 5 mg chol., 54 mg sodium, 6 g carbo., 0 g fiber, 1 g pro. Daily Values: 1% vit. A, 0% vit. C, 0% calcium, 2% iron.

$100 WINNER
Hunter Marlo
Salisbury, New York

October

American Harvest

5 Menus to Celebrate Autumn

Prize Tested Recipes

Banana Daiquiri Cheesecake, Spicy Pecan Pork,
Yogurt-Mint Pork Kabobs, Peanut Butter 'n' Banana Bread

American Harvest

BY JULIA MALLOY

Brilliant red cranberries float on marshy bogs. Acres of pumpkins and squash ripen to burnished gold and orange. From coast to coast, fields and orchards are turning into a colorful feast of plenty. What better time than fall harvest to gather friends and family for a fabulous fall meal? Celebrate our bounty with one or all five of these tantalizing menus, each with hints to keep the cooking simple and wine suggestions to match.

◆ Apple Cranberry Salad, top left; Wild Rice Oven Pilaf and Roast Duck with Wild Mushroom Sauce, bottom right

Colonial Feast

Celebrate the taste discoveries of our forefathers—cranberries, maple syrup, and wild rice—in an easygoing oven dinner.

Apple-Cranberry Salad

◆ ◆ ◆

Roast Duck with
Wild Mushroom Sauce

◆ ◆ ◆

Wild Rice Oven Pilaf

◆ ◆ ◆

Steamed green beans

◆ ◆ ◆

Maple Cream with Pecan Snaps

◆ ◆ ◆

Sparkling water

◆ ◆ ◆

Wine suggestions:

Serve a crisp meritage white blend (sauvignon blanc and sémillon) with the tangy salad. The duck goes well with a spicy zinfandel.

Creating a Colonial Feast

The day before:
- ◆ Make the salad dressing.
- ◆ Halve the cranberries.
- ◆ Bake the Pecan Snaps.
- ◆ Stir up the Maple Cream.

Up to 3 hours ahead:
- ◆ Prepare and roast the duck.
- ◆ Rinse the salad greens.

About 1½ hours ahead:
- ◆ Start cooking the rice.

About 1 hour ahead:
- ◆ Chill the white wine.
- ◆ Soak the mushrooms, then cook the sauce.
- ◆ Cook the green beans.
- ◆ Arrange the salads.
- ◆ Carve the duck.

YOUR GUIDE TO AMERICAN WINES

GRAPES ARE PART OF THE FALL HARVEST, PICKED FOR AWARD-WINNING, AMERICAN-STYLE WINES. TO HELP YOU LEARN MORE ABOUT OUR NATIVE WINES, WE'VE SUGGESTED SOME WINES TO SERVE WITH EACH DINNER MENU.

Alliance: This new red wine is a blend of sirah, grenache, and mouvédre grapes. It has a slightly smoky flavor.

Chardonnay (shard-n-AY): Pale and straw-colored, this popular white wine is medium to full bodied. It has a buttery, crisp flavor that is reminiscent of green apples.

Gewürztraminer (geh-vertz-trah-MEEN-er): Known for its perfumy aroma and its spicy, rich flavor, this soft white wine has a grapefruit flavor and the aroma of rose petals.

Meritage white (mir-i-TAHGE): Meritage wines are a blend of grapes, more in the style of French wines. The meritage white combines the sauvignon blanc and sémillon grapes. It has a full, spicy fruit flavor.

Pinot Noir (pee-no NWAR): Let this wine age several years before drinking. A good-quality pinot noir has a perfumy aroma and a smooth, rich, plum flavor.

Riesling (REEZ-ling): Young riesling has a floral aroma, a clean fruity taste, and a good balance of acidity and sweetness. Late-harvest riesling is fuller bodied, with a honey fragrance.

Sauvignon Blanc (SO-vee-nyawn BLAWN): This white wine has a spicy, slightly herblike flavor, with a note of fruitiness. It is usually on the dry side.

Zinfandel (ZIN-fan-dell): A grape originating in California, zinfandel creates rich, fruity red wines that range from light tasting to full bodied. This grape also is used to make a white zinfandel, a fruity, pale pink wine.

Apple-Cranberry Salad

PICK CRISP, BRIGHT EATING APPLES, SUCH AS GRANNY SMITH, RED DELICIOUS, OR MCINTOSH, FOR THIS TANGY SALAD.

¼ cup salad oil
¼ cup apple cider or apple juice
1 tablespoon cider vinegar
¼ teaspoon ground cinnamon
⅛ teaspoon ground cloves
¾ cup cranberries or seedless
red grapes, halved
3 tablespoons sugar (optional)
4 cups torn mixed greens
2 medium red and/or green apples,
cored and sliced

For dressing, in a screw-top jar combine oil, cider or juice, vinegar, cinnamon, and cloves. Cover and shake well to mix. Chill till needed.

If using cranberries, toss berries with 2 tablespoons of the sugar; let stand for 15 minutes. Toss with remaining 1 tablespoon sugar for a "frosted" look. (For grapes, which are sweeter, you can omit the sugar.)

Arrange greens on 4 salad plates. Top with apple slices. Shake dressing; pour over salads. Top with cranberries or grapes. Makes 4 to 6 side-dish servings.

Nutrition facts per serving: 204 cal., 14 g total fat (2 g sat. fat), 0 mg chol., 6 mg sodium, 21 g carbo., 2 g fiber, 1 g pro. Daily Value: 10% vit. A, 24% vit. C, 3% calcium, 6% iron.

Wine suggestion: Estancia Meritage White. The firm or tongue-tingling acidity of this white wine is a good match for the tart apples and cranberries. The round spicy fruit flavor echoes the spices and fruits. About $12.

Roast Duck with Wild Mushroom Sauce

LOOK FOR DOMESTIC DUCK IN YOUR SUPERMARKET FREEZER CASE. THAW IT IN THE REFRIGERATOR 24 HOURS BEFORE ROASTING.

1 4- to 6-pound domestic duckling
¼ cup broken dried mushrooms
1 cup frozen whole small onions, thawed
2 tablespoons margarine or butter
2 teaspoons sugar
4 teaspoons all-purpose flour
1½ cups beef broth
1 tablespoon tomato paste
½ teaspoon dried savory, sage, or
thyme, crushed
½ teaspoon Worcestershire sauce

Rinse duckling; pat dry with paper towels. Pull neck skin to back; fasten with a skewer. Tie drumsticks to tail. Twist wing tips under back. Place bird, breast side up, on a rack in a shallow roasting pan. Prick skin. Insert a meat thermometer into breast. Roast in a 375° oven for 1¾ to 3 hours (25 to 30 minutes per pound) or till 180° to 185°. The drumsticks should move easily.

Meanwhile, for sauce, pour enough boiling water over dried mushrooms to cover. Let stand for 30 minutes; drain.

In a saucepan cook mushrooms and onions in margarine or butter about 5 minutes or till tender. Stir in sugar. Cook and stir for 5 to 7 minutes or till vegetables are glazed. Stir in flour. Cook and stir for 3 to 5 minutes more or till flour is brown.

Add beef broth, tomato paste, herb, and Worcestershire sauce. Bring to boiling. Reduce heat; simmer, uncovered, for 10 to 15 minutes or till sauce is reduced to about 1⅔ cups.

To carve duck, remove the skin, if desired. With a sharp knife, slice duck along backbone. Slice downward, cutting meat from ribs. Remove wings and legs. Slice breast meat. Serve with sauce. Makes 4 to 6 main-dish servings.

Nutrition facts per serving without skin: 467 cal., 25 g total fat (8 g sat. fat), 155 mg chol., 483 mg sodium, 15 g carbo., 2 g fiber, 43 g pro. Daily Value: 12% vit. A, 10% vit. C, 3% calcium, 35% iron.

Wine suggestion: Fetzer Barrel Select Zinfandel. This hearty entrée demands a full-flavored wine. The spiciness of zinfandel and its rich, ripe berry flavor bring out the best in duck. About $10.

Wild Rice Oven Pilaf

THIS EASY BROWN-AND-WILD RICE COMBO BAKES IN THE OVEN ALONGSIDE THE DUCK.

2¼ cups boiling water
1 tablespoon margarine or butter
½ cup regular brown rice
½ cup wild rice
½ cup chopped onion
½ teaspoon salt
⅛ teaspoon pepper
½ cup shredded carrot
½ cup loose-pack frozen peas
¼ cup toasted chopped pecans

In a 1½-quart casserole combine boiling water and margarine or butter; stir till margarine is melted. Stir in brown rice, wild rice, onion, salt, and pepper. Cover; bake in a 375° oven for 70 minutes, stirring once.

Stir in carrot and frozen peas. Cover and bake about 10 minutes more or till rice is tender. Sprinkle pecans on top. Makes 4 to 6 side-dish servings.

Nutrition facts per serving: 258 cal., 8 g total fat (1 g sat. fat), 0 mg chol., 329 mg sodium, 41 g carbo., 3 g fiber, 7 g pro. Daily Value: 43% vit. A, 7% vit. C, 2% calcium, 9% iron.

Maple Cream With Pecan Snaps

SAVOR THE CARAMEL FLAVOR OF AMERICA'S NATIVE SWEETENER IN THIS CREAMY, MOUSSE-LIKE DESSERT.

1 tablespoon cold water
½ teaspoon unflavored gelatin
¾ cup whipping cream
2 tablespoons brown sugar
2 tablespoons maple syrup
¼ teaspoon maple flavoring (optional)
½ cup dairy sour cream
Pecan Snaps (see recipe, page 172)
(optional)

In a 1-cup glass measuring cup stir together the cold water and unflavored gelatin. Let stand for 2 minutes. Carefully place the measuring cup in a large saucepan of boiling water. Cook and stir about 1 minute or till the gelatin is completely dissolved.

In a chilled medium mixing bowl combine whipping cream, brown sugar, maple syrup, and, if desired, maple flavoring. Beat with an electric mixer on medium speed, gradually drizzling the dissolved gelatin over the cream mixture. Continue beating on medium speed just till soft peaks form (tips curl). Fold in

continued on page 172

continued from page 171

sour cream. Cover and chill for 1 to 2 hours or till the mixture mounds when spooned.

Spoon maple cream into 4 to 6 dessert goblets or dishes. Cover and chill overnight or till set. If desired, serve with Pecan Snaps; garnish with additional crushed Pecan Snaps. Serves 4 to 6.

Nutrition facts per serving: 249 cal., 21 g total fat (13 g sat. fat), 72 mg chol., 33 mg sodium, 15 g carbo., 0 g fiber, 2 g pro. Daily Value: 23% vit. A, 1% vit. C, 6% calcium, 2% iron.

Pecan Snaps

MAKE THESE CRISPY ROLLED WAFERS AHEAD AND STORE THEM BETWEEN LAYERS OF WAXED PAPER IN A COVERED CONTAINER. YOU CAN FREEZE THEM FOR UP TO 12 MONTHS.

¼ cup packed brown sugar
¼ cup margarine or butter
¼ cup maple syrup
½ cup finely ground pecans
⅓ cup all-purpose flour
1 tablespoon brandy or 1 teaspoon vanilla

◆ Maple Cream with Pecan Snaps

In a small saucepan combine brown sugar, margarine or butter, and maple syrup. Cook and stir over medium heat till the sugar is dissolved and the margarine is melted. Remove from heat. Stir in pecans, flour, and brandy or vanilla.

Line a cookie sheet with foil; lightly grease the foil with margarine or butter. Drop the batter from a level teaspoon about 5 inches apart onto the cookie sheet. (Only bake 4 or 5 cookies at a time because you need to shape them quickly before they harden.) Bake in a 350° oven for 8 to 10 minutes or till bubbly and deep golden brown.

Let stand on cookie sheet on wire rack for 1 minute. Immediately remove cookies from foil, flipping with a spatula onto the counter. With flat side to the inside, roll cookies around the greased handle of a wooden spoon, letting the bowl of the spoon hang over the edge of the counter (see photograph, page 173). Remove the wooden spoon, keeping the rolled shape.

Cool on a wire rack. (If cookies harden before you can shape them, return them to the hot oven for 1 minute or till softened.) Repeat with remaining batter. Makes about 3 dozen cookies.

Nutrition facts per cookie: 45 cal., 3 g total fat (0 g sat. fat), 0 mg chol., 19 mg sodium, 5 g carbo., 0 g fiber, 0 g pro. Daily Value: 1% vit. A, 0% vit. C, 0% calcium, 1% iron.

With the flat side of the warm cookie facing up, roll cookies around the greased handle of a wooden spoon. Cool on a rack.

Southern Sampler

DEVOTEES OF DIXIE WILL LOVE THE NEW FLAVOR TWISTS ON THEIR BELOVED PORK AND SWEET POTATOES. YOU'LL LOVE KNOWING THAT MOST OF THIS MENU CAN BE MADE AHEAD.

Fruit-Stuffed Pork Roast

♦♦♦

Sweet Potato Swirls
with Pineapple-Ginger Sauce

♦♦♦

Brussels sprouts

♦♦♦

Pear and Mincemeat Tart

♦♦♦

Iced tea

♦♦♦

Wine suggestions:

Try a fruity pinot noir or a lightly spiced gewürztraminer.

Making the Southern Sampler Menu

The day before:
◆ Bake the tart crust. Prepare the pears and grapes; chill.
◆ Prepare and freeze sweet potatoes.
◆ Fix pineapple sauce; chill.
◆ Butterfly and pound the roast.

About 4 hours ahead:
◆ Mix stuffing and assemble the pork roast; chill.
◆ Prepare the filling for the tart.
◆ Assemble the first two layers of the tart. Cover and chill.

2½ hours ahead:
◆ Put the roast in the oven.

About 45 minutes ahead:
◆ Chill the white wine.
◆ Bake the sweet potatoes.
◆ Cook the brussels sprouts.
◆ Reheat the sauce.

Before serving dessert:
◆ Garnish the tart.

Fruit-Stuffed Pork Roast

STARTING WITH PRECUT DRIED FRUIT MAKES THE STUFFING EASY TO STIR TOGETHER.

1 6-ounce package mixed dried fruit bits
½ cup finely chopped onion
1 tablespoon balsamic vinegar or vinegar
¼ cup fine dry bread crumbs
2 tablespoons margarine or butter, melted
¼ teaspoon salt
¼ teaspoon pepper
⅛ to ¼ teaspoon ground cloves
1 3- to 4-pound boneless pork top loin roast (double loin, tied)
Red currant jelly, melted (optional)
1 recipe Pineapple-Ginger Sauce (see recipe, page 174)
Fresh crab apples (optional)
Fresh thyme (optional)

To butterfly each pork loin, make one parallel slit to the right of the first cut and one parallel slit to the left. This means you will have 3 lengthwise cuts.

For stuffing, in a mixing bowl combine fruit, onion, and vinegar. Pour boiling water over to cover. Let stand for 30 minutes; drain well.

Add bread crumbs, margarine or butter, salt, pepper, and cloves to fruit. Toss gently to mix.

Untie roast to separate the two loins; trim fat. To butterfly each loin for stuffing, make a single lengthwise cut down the center of the loin, cutting to within ½ inch of the other side. Spread open. Make another lengthwise slit to the right of the first cut and a third slit to the left (see photograph above). Cover each loin with clear plastic wrap. Pound with a meat mallet to ½- to ¾-inch thickness.

Place the meat rectangles side by side with long sides overlapping about 1 inch. Sprinkle with salt and pepper. Spread stuffing onto meat. Starting from one long side, roll up the meat and stuffing jelly-roll style, rolling the second rectangle of meat into the first rectangle. Tightly retie the roast. Place the meat on *continued on page 174*

continued from page 173
a rack in a shallow roasting pan. Insert a meat thermometer.

Roast in a 325° oven for 1¾ to 2¼ hours or till 160° (medium) to 170° (well done). If desired, brush with jelly the last 15 minutes.

Cover meat with foil; let stand for 15 minutes before carving. Serve with Pineapple-Ginger Sauce; garnish with fresh crab apples and thyme, if desired. Makes 10 to 12 main-dish servings.

Nutrition facts per serving: 244 cal., 11 g total fat (4 g sat. fat), 61 mg chol., 184 mg sodium, 15 g carbo., 0 g fiber, 20 g pro. Daily Value: 6% vit. A, 1% vit. C, 1% calcium, 7% iron.

Red wine suggestion: La Crema Pinot Noir. Dried fruit in the stuffing cries for a not-too-sweet, full-bodied wine. The bright cherry fruit flavor with toasty oak overtones makes pinot perfect. About $12.

White wine suggestion: Joseph Phelps Gewürztraminer. The sweet-sour balance in the ginger sauce on the meat and potatoes needs a sweeter wine that will move on well to the dessert course, a spicy fruit tart. The Gewürztraminer has a slightly sweet flavor with a hint of exotic spiciness. About $10.

Sweet Potato Swirls

MAKE THESE UP TO A MONTH AHEAD OF YOUR DINNER AND FREEZE. OR, MAKE THEM EARLIER IN THE DAY AND CHILL.

4 medium sweet potatoes (about 2 pounds)
¼ cup margarine or butter
1 to 2 tablespoons milk (optional)
2 eggs
2 tablespoons margarine or butter, melted

Peel and quarter sweet potatoes. In a large saucepan cook potatoes, covered, in a small amount of boiling lightly salted water for 25 to 35 minutes or till tender. Drain well.

Transfer sweet potatoes to a medium mixing bowl. Mash with a potato masher or beat with an electric mixer on low speed. Beat in the ¼ cup margarine or butter. Add salt and pepper to taste. If sweet potato mixture is too stiff, gradually beat in milk. Cool slightly.

With the electric mixer running on low speed, beat eggs into cooled mixture. Using a decorating bag with a large star tip, pipe sweet potatoes into 8 mounds on a greased 15x10x1-inch baking pan (see photograph top right). (Or, spoon 8 mounds onto the baking pan.) If desired, cover the mounds loosely and chill or freeze at this point.

To bake, drizzle sweet potato mounds with melted margarine or butter. Bake refrigerated or frozen potatoes alongside the pork roast on a separate rack in a 325° oven for 10 minutes. Remove roast from oven. Increase oven temperature to 400°. Bake for 10 to 15 minutes more or till potatoes are light brown. Makes 8 side-dish servings.

Make-ahead directions: Prepare the sweet potatoes and pipe onto a baking sheet. Cover loosely; chill for up to 4 hours or freeze. Transfer frozen potatoes to a freezer container. Freeze for up to 1 month. Bake as directed.

Using a decorating bag fitted with a large star tip, pipe sweet potatoes into 8 mounds on a greased 15x10x1-inch baking pan.

Nutrition facts per serving: 186 cal., 10 g total fat (2 g sat. fat), 53 mg chol., 125 mg sodium, 22 g carbo., 3 g fiber, 3 g pro. Daily Value: 205% vit. A, 36% vit. C, 2% calcium, 3% iron.

Pineapple-Ginger Sauce

THIS SILKY SWEET-SOUR SAUCE IS PERFECT WITH THE ROAST PORK AND SWEET POTATOES, BUT YOU CAN ALSO SERVE IT WITH GRILLED CHICKEN OR VEGETABLES.

¾ cup packed brown sugar
2 tablespoons cornstarch
¾ cup unsweetened pineapple juice
¼ cup balsamic vinegar or white wine vinegar
1½ teaspoons grated gingerroot
¼ teaspoon salt
continued on page 176

◆ Fruit-Stuffed Pork Roast, Sweet Potato Swirls, Pineapple-Ginger Sauce

continued from page 174

In a medium saucepan stir together brown sugar and cornstarch. Stir in pineapple juice, balsamic or white wine vinegar, gingerroot, and salt. Cook and stir till thickened and bubbly. Cook and stir for 2 minutes more. Serve with Fruit-Stuffed Pork Roast and Sweet Potato Swirls. Makes about 1⅓ cups.

Make-ahead directions: Prepare the sauce as directed. Transfer to a storage container; cool slightly. Cover the surface with clear plastic wrap. Chill sauce till ready to use, for up to two days.

To reheat, transfer the sauce to a medium saucepan. Cook and stir over low heat till heated through. Serve as directed.

Nutrition facts per tablespoon: 42 cal., 0 g total fat (0 g sat. fat), 0 mg chol., 31 mg sodium, 11 g carbo., 0 g fiber, 0 g pro. Daily Value: 0% vit. A, 2% vit. C, 1% calcium, 1% iron.

Pear and Mincemeat Tart

PEEL THE PEARS BEFORE POACHING OR LEAVE THE RED OR YELLOW PEEL FOR MORE COLOR.

1 recipe Rich Pastry (see recipe, page 177)
½ cup whipping cream
1 8-ounce package cream cheese, softened
½ cup orange marmalade
⅔ cup orange juice
2 medium red or yellow pears
(such as Bartlett), sliced
1 cup canned mincemeat
1 cup seedless red or green grapes, halved
¼ cup orange marmalade or
apple jelly, melted

◆ Pear and Mincemeat Tart

Prepare and bake pastry.

For filling, chill a small mixing bowl and electric mixer beaters. In chilled bowl beat whipping cream on medium speed till soft peaks form; set aside. In a medium mixing bowl beat cream cheese and the ½ cup marmalade on medium speed till fluffy. Gently fold in whipped cream. Cover; chill up to 4 hours.

In a large skillet combine orange juice and pear slices. Bring to boiling; reduce heat. Cover and simmer for 6 to 8 minutes or just till pear is tender. Drain, discarding liquid. Cover and chill for 2 to 24 hours.

To assemble, spread mincemeat atop baked pastry. Top with cream cheese mixture. Cover and chill till ready to serve, up to 4 hours.

At serving time, arrange pear slices and grapes atop the cream cheese mixture. Brush with ¼ cup melted orange marmalade or apple jelly. Makes 8 to 10 servings.

Nutrition facts per serving: 563 cal., 29 g total fat (17 g sat. fat), 136 mg chol., 319 mg sodium, 74 g carbo., 3 g fiber, 6 g pro. Daily Value: 37% vit. A, 23% vit. C, 6% calcium, 15% iron.

Rich Pastry

THIS TART CRUST IS MORE LIKE A COOKIE THAN LIKE A REGULAR PIE PASTRY.

1¼ cups all-purpose flour
⅓ cup sugar
½ cup cold margarine or butter
2 beaten egg yolks
2 tablespoons cold water

In a medium mixing bowl stir together all-purpose flour and sugar. Cut in margarine or butter till pieces are the size of small peas.

In a mixing bowl combine egg yolks and cold water. Gradually stir yolk mixture into flour mixture. Gently knead the dough just till a ball forms. If necessary, cover with plastic wrap and chill for 30 to 60 minutes or till easy to handle.

On a lightly floured surface, slightly flatten the pastry dough. Roll dough from center to edges, forming a 13-inch circle. Wrap pastry around a rolling pin. Unroll pastry onto an 11-inch tart pan with a removable bottom or a 10-inch pie plate or quiche dish. Ease pastry into pan, being careful not to stretch it. Press pastry into the fluted sides of the pan; trim edges. Line pastry shell with a double thickness of foil.

Bake in a 375° oven for 10 minutes. Remove foil. Bake for 8 to 10 minutes more or till golden. Completely cool pastry shell in pan on a wire rack. Makes 1 pastry shell.

◆ Smoky Cheese Chowder

Pacific Coast Dinner

ENJOY A RELAXING NIGHT WITH GOOD FRIENDS AND A HEARTY MENU THAT SHOWCASES WEST COAST CREATIVITY. FRESH FISH, FRUITS AND VEGETABLES, AND ASIAN SEASONINGS ARE PREPARED SIMPLY.

Smoky Cheese Chowder
◆◆◆
Dilled Salmon
with Stir-Fried Vegetables
◆◆◆
Sourdough rolls
◆◆◆
Citrus Pumpkin Flan
◆◆◆
Coffee
◆◆◆
Wine suggestions:

With the smoky flavor of the chowder, try an alliance wine, a new blend of sirah, grenache, and mourvédre grapes. With the salmon, serve a full-bodied chardonnay (preferably one with apple overtones).

Pulling Together the Pacific Coast Dinner

The day before:
◆ Bake the pumpkin flans; cover and chill.
◆ Cut vegetables into strips; chill.
◆ Prepare the soup; chill.
About 30 minutes ahead:
◆ Chill the white wine.
◆ Reheat soup with cheese and pimiento.
◆ Broil the salmon.
◆ Stir-fry the vegetables.

continued on page 178

continued from page 177

Smoky Cheese Chowder

FOR THE SMOOTHEST SOUP, BE SURE TO USE A SMOKED PROCESS CHEESE.

*1 10-ounce package frozen
whole kernel corn
½ cup chopped onion
½ cup water
1 teaspoon instant chicken
bouillon granules
¼ teaspoon pepper
2½ cups milk
3 tablespoons all-purpose flour
1 cup shredded smoked process cheddar
cheese (4 ounces)
1 tablespoon diced pimiento, drained
Canned or frozen baby corn, sliced
lengthwise (optional)
Fresh chives (optional)
Chopped red sweet pepper (optional)*

In a saucepan combine corn, onion, water, bouillon, and pepper. Bring to boiling; reduce heat. Cover and simmer about 4 minutes or till corn is tender. Do not drain.

Stir together milk and flour; stir into corn mixture. Cook and stir till thickened and bubbly. Cook and stir for 1 minute more. Add cheese and pimiento; heat and stir till melted.

To serve, spoon into 4 soup bowls. If desired, garnish each serving with baby corn, chives, and red pepper. Makes 4 side-dish servings.

Make-ahead directions: Prepare chowder as directed, except do not add cheese and pimiento; cool. Transfer to a covered container; chill for up to 2 days. To reheat, in a saucepan heat and stir over low heat till heated through. Add cheese and pimiento. Serve as above.

Nutrition facts per serving: 223 cal., 5 g total fat (2 g sat. fat), 27 mg chol., 855 mg sodium, 32 g carbo., 0 g fiber, 15 g pro. Daily Value: 16% vit. A, 13% vit. C, 29% calcium, 6% iron.

Wine suggestion: R.H. Phillips Alliance. The light, smoky overtones of this soft, round red wine go well with the smoked flavor of the cheese soup. About $12.

Dilled Salmon with Stir-Fried Vegetables

TO SAVE TIME, CUT UP THE VEGETABLES AHEAD OF TIME AND SOAK THEM IN ICE WATER UNTIL YOU'RE READY TO STIR-FRY.

*1 pound fresh or frozen skinless
salmon fillets
¼ teaspoon salt
¼ cup apple jelly
3 tablespoons rice vinegar or white vinegar
2 tablespoons water
1 tablespoon soy sauce
1 teaspoon cornstarch
½ teaspoon dried dillweed
1 tablespoon cooking oil
3 cups julienne-cut carrots, parsnips,
turnips, and/or rutabagas
1 small red sweet pepper, seeded and cut
into julienne strips
4 green onions, thinly sliced lengthwise
and cut into 1½-inch-long strips
Cracked colored peppercorns
Fresh dill (optional)*

Thaw fish, if frozen. Cut into 4 serving-size pieces. Arrange on the greased rack of an unheated broiler pan. Sprinkle with salt. Broil 4 inches from heat till fish just flakes, allowing 4 to 6 minutes for each ½ inch of thickness.

For sauce, in a bowl stir together jelly, vinegar, water, soy sauce, cornstarch, and dillweed. Set aside.

Pour cooking oil into a hot wok or skillet. (Add more oil as necessary during cooking.) Preheat over medium-high heat. Stir-fry carrots, parsnips, turnips, and/or rutabagas for 3 to 4 minutes till crisp-tender. Remove and keep warm. Add red pepper and green onions to wok or skillet; stir-fry for 1 to 2 minutes or till crisp-tender. Add to other vegetables. Add the sauce to wok. Cook and stir till thickened and bubbly. Cook and stir for 2 minutes more.

To serve, spoon warm vegetables onto plates. Drizzle with some of the sauce. Top with salmon. Spoon any remaining sauce over salmon. Sprinkle with cracked peppercorns. If desired, garnish with fresh dill. Makes 4 main-dish servings.

Nutrition facts per serving: 246 cal., 7 g total fat (1 g sat. fat), 20 mg chol., 468 mg sodium, 28 g carbo., 4 g fiber, 18 g pro. Daily Value: 96% vit. A, 65% vit. C, 4% calcium, 12% iron.

Wine suggestion: Château Ste. Michelle Chardonnay, 1992. The buttery, ripe apple flavor of this chardonnay complements the richness of salmon and the fruitiness of the herb-apple glaze. About $9.

◆ Dilled Salmon with Stir-Fried Vegetables

◆ Citrus Pumpkin Flan

Quickly pour caramelized sugar into four 6-ounce custard cups. Tilt to evenly coat bottoms. Place cups in a baking pan.

Citrus Pumpkin Flans

THESE SYRUP-GLAZED CUSTARDS TASTE LIKE PUMPKIN PIE WITHOUT THE CRUST.

⅔ cup sugar
3 beaten eggs
¾ cup canned pumpkin
1 5-ounce can (⅔ cup) evaporated milk
¼ cup sugar
1 teaspoon pumpkin pie spice*
1 teaspoon finely shredded orange peel
1 teaspoon vanilla
Pomegranate seeds** (optional)

For caramelized sugar, in a medium heavy skillet melt the ⅔ cup sugar over medium-high heat. Do not stir sugar, just shake the skillet occasionally. When the sugar starts to melt, reduce heat to low. Cook, stirring frequently, till sugar is golden brown. Quickly pour sugar into four 6-ounce custard cups. Tilt to evenly coat the bottoms of the cups (see photograph top right).

Place cups in a baking pan. In a mixing bowl stir together eggs, pumpkin, milk, the ¼ cup sugar, pumpkin pie spice, orange peel, and vanilla. Pour pumpkin mixture atop caramelized sugar in cups. Place the pan on the oven rack. Pour boiling water into pan around cups to a depth of 1 inch. Bake in a 325° oven for 40 to 45 minutes or till a knife inserted near the centers comes out clean. Remove cups from pan. Cool slightly. Chill, covered, 4 to 24 hours.

To serve, use a knife to loosen edges of flan, slipping the point of the knife down the sides of the flan to let in air. Invert flans onto individual dessert dishes, scraping the caramelized sugar onto the dish. If desired, top with pomegranate seeds. Makes 4 servings.

*Note: To make your own pumpkin pie spice, stir together ½ teaspoon *ground cinnamon*, ¼ teaspoon *ground ginger*, ⅛ teaspoon *ground nutmeg*, and ⅛ teaspoon *ground allspice*.

**Note: Look for hard-shelled, tomato-shaped pomegranates in the fall. Cut into them to get the glassy red seeds for eating or garnishing.

Nutrition facts per serving: 317 cal., 8 g total fat (3 g sat. fat), 174 mg chol., 100 mg sodium, 55 g carbo., 1 g fiber, 8 g pro. Daily Value: 111% vit. A, 6% vit. C, 13% calcium, 9% iron.

Southwest Supper

STARRING IN THIS HOT AND SPICY TEX-MEX STEW ARE BEANS, SQUASH, AND CORN, LONGTIME STAPLES OF NATIVE AMERICANS IN THE SOUTHWEST. BAKE THE PUDDING CAKE WHILE YOU EAT, THEN WATCH YOUR FAMILY GO PEANUTS OVER IT.

Bean and Squash Stew
◆◆◆
Sliced Avocado and Citrus Platter
◆◆◆
Chili-Corn Muffins
◆◆◆
Peanut Butter and Hot Fudge
Pudding Cake
◆◆◆
Sparkling water or milk

Quick-Cooking the Southwest Supper

One to two hours ahead, prepare dinner in the following order:
- ◆ Bake the pudding cake.
  - ◆ Prepare the salads.
    - ◆ Cook the stew.
- ◆ Bake the corn muffins.

Bean and Squash Stew

PUNGENT SOUTHWEST FLAVORS SPICE UP THIS HEARTY, MEATLESS MAIN-DISH SOUP.

2 cups water
1 cup butternut squash, peeled, seeded, and cut into ½-inch-thick cubes, or carrot, cut into ¼-inch-thick slices
1 15- or 15½-ounce can black beans or red kidney beans, rinsed and drained
1 14½-ounce can Mexican-style stewed tomatoes
1 cup frozen or canned baby corn, cut crosswise into ½-inch-long pieces
1 small onion, sliced and separated into rings
¼ cup tomato paste
1 vegetable bouillon cube

◆ Bean and Squash Stew, Sliced Avocado and Citrus Platter, Chili-Corn Muffins

1 to 2 teaspoons chili powder
¾ teaspoon dried oregano, crushed
1 clove garlic, minced
Dairy sour cream (optional)

In a 3-quart saucepan combine water and squash or carrots. Bring to boiling; reduce heat. Cover and simmer for 5 minutes. Add beans, tomatoes, corn, onion, tomato paste, bouillon cube, chili powder, oregano, and garlic. Bring to boiling; reduce heat. Cover and simmer

for 10 to 15 minutes. If desired, top each serving with sour cream. Makes 4 main-dish servings.

Nutrition facts per serving: 163 cal., 1 g total fat (0 g sat. fat), 0 mg chol., 785 mg sodium, 36 g carbo., 9 g fiber, 11 g pro. Daily Value: 34% vit. A, 50% vit. C, 5% calcium, 16% iron.

Pipe from a plastic bag or spoon the batter into lightly greased cactus-shaped, corn stick, or muffin cup pans, filling each two-thirds full.

◆ Peanut Butter and Hot Fudge Pudding Cake

Chili-Corn Muffins

CHOOSE YOUR MUFFIN SHAPE. USE A CACTUS-SHAPED PAN, A STICK PAN, OR THE TRADITIONAL MUFFIN CUP PAN.

1 cup all-purpose flour
1 cup yellow, white, or blue cornmeal
2 tablespoons sugar
2 teaspoons baking powder
¼ teaspoon baking soda
¼ teaspoon salt
2 slightly beaten eggs
1 cup buttermilk or sour milk*
¼ cup cooking oil
1 4-ounce can diced green chili peppers
2 tablespoons coarsely chopped, drained dried tomatoes (oil-pack) or chopped pitted ripe olives, drained

In a bowl stir together flour, cornmeal, sugar, baking powder, baking soda, and salt. In another bowl beat together eggs, buttermilk or sour milk, and oil. Add to flour mixture; stir just till batter is smooth (do not overbeat). Stir in undrained chili peppers and tomatoes or olives.

Pipe from a plastic bag or spoon batter into lightly greased cactus-shaped, corn stick, or muffin pans, filling pans ⅔ full (see photograph, above). Bake in a 400° oven for 15 to 18 minutes or till golden brown. Makes about 15 cactus-shaped or regular muffins or 24 corn sticks.

*Note: To make sour milk, stir 1 tablespoon *vinegar or lemon juice* into enough *milk* to make 1 cup total. Let stand for 5 minutes.

Nutrition facts per cactus-shaped muffin: 120 cal., 5 g total fat (1 g sat. fat), 29 mg chol., 167 mg sodium, 16 g carbo., 1 g fiber, 3 g pro. Daily Value: 2% vit. A, 5% vit. C, 5% calcium, 6% iron.

Peanut Butter and Hot Fudge Pudding Cake

TWO ALL-AMERICAN FLAVORS TEAM UP FOR ONE TUMMY-WARMING DESSERT.

½ cup all-purpose flour
¼ cup sugar
¾ teaspoon baking powder
⅓ cup milk
1 tablespoon cooking oil
½ teaspoon vanilla
¼ cup peanut butter
½ cup sugar
3 tablespoons unsweetened cocoa powder
1 cup boiling water
Vanilla ice cream
Fudge ice-cream topping (optional)
⅓ cup chopped peanuts

In a bowl combine flour, ¼ cup sugar, and baking powder. Add milk, oil, and vanilla; stir till smooth. Stir in peanut butter. Pour into ungreased 1½-quart casserole.

In the same mixing bowl stir together the ½ cup sugar and cocoa powder. Gradually stir in boiling water. Pour evenly over batter.

Bake in a 400° oven about 30 minutes or till a toothpick inserted in cake comes out clean.

Serve warm with ice cream and fudge sauce, if desired. Top with peanuts. Makes 4 servings.

Nutrition facts per serving: 421 cal., 18 g total fat (3 g sat. fat), 1 mg chol., 211 mg sodium, 57 g carbo., 2 g fiber, 10 g pro. Daily Value: 1% vit. A, 0% vit. C, 12% calcium, 12% iron.

Heartland Breakfast

OUR NATION'S BREADBASKET PRODUCES THE GREATEST VARIETY OF GRAINS IN THE WORLD. WHEAT, BUCKWHEAT, AND CORNMEAL COMBINE FOR A STACK OF WHOLESOME HOTCAKES.

Native-Grain Hotcakes with Cranberry Maple Syrup

♦♦♦

Canadian-style bacon

♦♦♦

Fresh fruit compote

♦♦♦

Milk

♦♦♦

Coffee or Tea

Preparing a Heartland Breakfast

About 30 minutes ahead in the following order:
- ◆ Fix a fresh fruit bowl.
- ◆ Heat Canadian-style bacon.
- ◆ Prepare the hotcakes.
- ◆ Heat the syrup.

Native-Grain Hotcakes with Cranberry Maple Syrup

STORE ANY LEFTOVER SYRUP IN THE REFRIGERATOR AND REHEAT FOR A FEW SECONDS IN THE MICROWAVE OVEN.

1 cup buckwheat flour
¼ cup all-purpose flour
¼ cup yellow cornmeal
1 teaspoon baking powder
½ teaspoon salt
¼ teaspoon baking soda
2 beaten eggs
1½ cups buttermilk or sour milk*(see page 182)

◆ Native-Grain Hotcakes with Cranberry Maple Syrup

2 tablespoons honey
1 tablespoon cooking oil
1¼ cups maple syrup
½ cup fresh cranberries or frozen blueberries
Margarine or butter (optional)

In a mixing bowl stir together buckwheat flour, all-purpose flour, cornmeal, baking powder, salt, and baking soda. Combine eggs, buttermilk or sour milk, honey, and oil. Add egg mixture to flour mixture all at once. Stir just till blended but still slightly lumpy.

For each hotcake, pour about ⅓ cup batter onto a hot, lightly greased griddle or into a heavy skillet. Cook over medium heat for 1 to 2 minutes on each side or till golden brown, flipping to cook the second sides when the hotcakes have a bubbly surface and slightly dry edges.

Meanwhile, in a saucepan heat maple syrup with cranberries or frozen blueberries over medium-high heat about 8 minutes or till berries begin to pop.

Serve hotcakes with margarine or butter and syrup. Makes 6 to 8 (5-inch) hotcakes.

Nutrition facts per hotcake with 1 tablespoon syrup: 249 cal., 5 g total fat (1 g sat. fat), 73 mg chol., 375 mg sodium, 45 g carbo., 3 g fiber, 8 g pro. Daily Value: 4% vit. A, 0% vit. C, 12% calcium, 12% iron.

Prize Tested Recipes

Banana Daiquiri Cheesecake

THIS YUMMY TROPICAL DESSERT IS A UNIQUE CROSS BETWEEN CAKE AND CHEESECAKE.

¾ cup all-purpose flour
1 4-serving-size package regular banana pudding mix
1 teaspoon baking powder
½ cup milk
3 tablespoons margarine or butter, softened
1 egg
2 medium bananas
1 8-ounce packge cream cheese, softened
⅓ cup sugar
2 tablespoons milk
1 tablespoon lime juice
½ teaspoon rum extract
Banana slices (optional)
Lime peel strips (optional)

◆ Banana Daiquiri Cheese Cake

Grease bottom and sides of an 8-inch springform pan; place on a baking sheet. In a large mixing bowl stir together flour, pudding mix, and baking powder; add the ½ cup milk, margarine or butter, and egg. Beat with an electric mixer on medium speed 2 minutes. Pour batter into prepared pan. Slice the 2 bananas; arrange slices atop batter. Set aside.

In a medium mixing bowl beat cream cheese, sugar, the 2 tablespoons milk, lime juice, and rum extract on medium speed till smooth. Spoon cream cheese mixture over bananas, carefully spreading mixture to cover.

Bake in a 350° oven for 30 to 35 minutes or till center is set. Cool in pan for 15 minutes on a wire rack. Loosen crust from sides of pan. Cool for 30 minutes more. Cover and chill at least 2 hours before serving. To serve, remove sides of springform pan; garnish cake with additional banana slices and lime peel strips. Makes 8 servings.

Nutrition facts per slice: 306 cal., 16 g total fat (8 g sat. fat), 59 mg chol., 373 mg sodium, 37 g carbo., 1 g fiber, 5 g pro. Daily Value: 20% vit. A, 5% vit. C, 8% calcium, 7% iron.

$200 WINNER
Ilona Schwab
Wilmette, Illinois

Spicy Pecan Pork

SATISFY A CRAVING FOR BREADED PORK TENDERLOIN WITH THIS NUT-COATED VERSION.

12 ounces boneless pork loin
1 egg, beaten
1 egg white, beaten
3 tablespoons Dijon-style mustard

◆ Spicy Pecan Pork

◆ Yogurt-Mint Pork Kabobs

¼ to ½ teaspoon ground red pepper
⅓ cup fine dry bread crumbs
⅓ cup toasted ground pecans
⅓ cup all-purpose flour
2 tablespoons cooking oil
Sliced fresh chili peppers (optional)

Slice pork loin crosswise into 4 equal slices. Place meat between 2 sheets of plastic wrap; pound with the flat side of a meat mallet to ¼-inch thickness. In a shallow bowl combine egg, egg white, mustard, and red pepper. In another bowl combine bread crumbs and pecans.

Coat pork in flour. Dip slices, one at a time, into the egg mixture, then coat with crumb mixture. In a 12-inch skillet heat oil over medium to medium-high heat. Add pork. Cook, uncovered, for 6 to 8 minutes or till tender and just slightly pink, turning once. If desired, top each serving with fresh hot peppers. Makes 4 servings.

Nutrition facts per serving: 326 cal., 21 g total fat (4 g sat. fat), 92 mg chol., 404 mg sodium, 16 g carbo., 1 g fiber, 18 g pro. Daily Value: 3% vit. A, 10% iron.

$200 WINNER
Lori Connors
Opelika, Alabama

Yogurt-Mint Pork Kabobs

CATHY SUGGESTS SERVING THESE WINNING KABOBS ON A BED OF HOT COOKED SAFFRON RICE (MADE FROM A MIX).

1 16-ounce container plain nonfat yogurt
2 tablespoons lemon juice
2 to 4 cloves garlic, minced
2 teaspoons dried oregano, crushed

1 teaspoon dried mint, crushed
1½ pounds boneless pork loin, cut
into 1-inch cubes
½ cup seeded, finely chopped tomato
½ cup seeded, finely chopped cucumber
4 cups desired fresh vegetables
(such as eggplant, zucchini, yellow summer
squash, red onion, and mushrooms)
cut into 1-inch pieces
Olive-oil-flavored nonstick spray coating

In a bowl combine yogurt, lemon juice, garlic, 1 teaspoon of the oregano, and mint. Divide mixture in half. Stir pork cubes into half of the yogurt mixture. Cover; chill meat and remaining yogurt mixture for 1 to 4 hours.

For sauce, up to 1 hour before serving, stir tomato and cucumber into the remaining half of the yogurt mixture. Cover and chill till serving time.

In a large bowl combine the desired vegetables. Lightly spray vegetables with nonstick spray coating, tossing to coat. Stir in remaining 1 teaspoon oregano. Set aside.

continued on page 186

◆ Peanut Butter 'n' Banana Bread

3 tablespoons cooking oil
1 teaspoon vanilla
1 egg, slightly beaten
1 6-ounce package milk chocolate pieces
(1 cup)
1 recipe Peanut Butter Frosting
(see recipe, below)

In a large mixing bowl stir together flour, sugars, baking powder, salt, and cinnamon. In another bowl combine mashed bananas, milk, peanut butter, oil, vanilla, and egg. Add to flour mixture, stirring just till combined. Stir in chocolate pieces. Pour batter into two greased 8x4x2-inch loaf pans.

Bake in a 350° oven for 50 to 55 minutes or till wooden toothpick inserted near the center comes out clean. Cool in pans for 10 minutes. Remove from pans; cool thoroughly on a wire rack. Wrap and store overnight before serving. To serve, frost with Peanut Butter Frosting. If desired, top with crushed peanuts and miniature semisweet chocolate pieces. Slice to serve. Makes 2 loaves (24 slices).

Peanut Butter Frosting: In a small saucepan melt 3 tablespoons *chunky peanut butter* and 2 tablespoons *margarine or butter*. Remove from heat; stir in 1 cup sifted *powdered sugar* and 1 teaspoon *vanilla*. Stir in 1 tablespoon *milk*. Add more *milk*, if necessary, till of spreading consistency. Makes about ½ cup.

Nutrition facts per slice: 235 cal., 10 g total fat (3 g sat. fat), 10 mg chol., 190 mg sodium, 33 g carbo., 1 g fiber, 5 g pro. Daily Value: 2% vit. A, 2% vit. C, 7% calcium, 7% iron.

$100 WINNER
Kelly Thornberry
La Porte, Indiana

continued from page 185
Drain pork. Alternately thread pork and vegetables onto twelve 6-inch-long skewers. Grill kabobs on the rack of an uncovered grill directly over medium coals for 12 to 14 minutes or till pork is tender and juices run clear, turning once halfway through grilling. Serve kabobs with sauce. Makes 6 servings.

Nutrition facts per serving: 207 cal., 8 g total fat (3 g sat. fat), 53 mg chol., 97 mg sodium, 13 g carbo., 2 g fiber, 22 g pro. Daily Value: 3% vit. A, 44% vit. C, 14% calcium, 9% iron.

$100 WINNER
Cathy A. Deppen
Memphis, Tennessee

Peanut Butter 'n' Banana Bread

PEANUT BUTTER LOVERS WILL ENJOY THE MIX OF FLAVORS IN THIS LOAF: BANANA, CHOCOLATE, AND PEANUT BUTTER.

2½ cups all-purpose flour
½ cup granulated sugar
½ cup packed brown sugar
1 tablespoon baking powder
¾ teaspoon salt
¼ teaspoon ground cinnamon
2 ripe large bananas, mashed (1 cup)
1 cup milk
¾ cup chunky peanut butter

November

Home for Thanksgiving

Festive Recipes for Your Holiday Feast

Prizewinning Cookies

Prize Tested Recipes

*Nutty Blue Cheese Rolls, Pesto-Artichoke Stuffing,
Oh-So-Good Cornbread Stuffing, Ginger Chicken-Bacon Bites*

Home for Thanksgiving

By Lisa Holderness

The spirit of Thanksgiving comes alive in us as we prepare for this annual home-coming of loved ones. Visions of golden roast turkey and pumpkin pie spur great anticipation! This year, complement your traditional fare with a few new recipes from our Thanksgiving collection. You'll find homebaked breads, family-pleasing side dishes, and fabulous desserts. Each festive dish keeps the cooking relaxed so the cook has time to join the fun.

◆ Roast Turkey with Fennel and Sausage Stuffing

Turkey Roasting Made Easy

BELOW YOU'LL FIND ALL THE INFOR-MATION NEEDED TO SUCCESSFULLY PREPARE AND ROAST YOUR HOLIDAY BIRD.

Buying: With a 12-pound or less bird, buy 1 pound per serving. If the bird is more than 12 pounds, buy 3⁄4 pound per serving.

Thawing: To thaw a whole frozen turkey, place the wrapped frozen bird on a tray in the refrigerator for 3 to 4 days (24 hours for every 5 pounds). Or, place in a sink of cold water. Change the water every 30 minutes. (Allow 30 minutes per pound.) Do not thaw at room temperature or in warm water.

When thawed, remove giblets and neck piece from cavities. Rinse and pat dry with paper towels. Do not stuff the bird until you're ready to roast it.

Stuffing: Just before roasting, spoon some stuffing loosely into neck cavity. Pull neck skin over stuffing; fasten to back with a short skewer. Loosely spoon stuffing into body cavity; do not pack. Spoon any remaining stuffing into a casserole; cover and chill till baking time. Tuck drumsticks under band of skin that crosses tail (or tie legs with string). Twist wing tips under back.

If you prefer not to stuff your turkey, place quartered onions and celery in the body cavity. Pull neck skin to back; fasten with a short skewer. Tuck drumsticks under band of skin that crosses tail. If there isn't a band, tie drumsticks to tail. Twist wing tips under back.

Open roasting: Place unstuffed or stuffed turkey, breast side up, on a rack in a shallow pan. If desired, brush with cooking oil. Place a meat thermometer into the center of an inside thigh muscle so the bulb doesn't touch the bone. Cover turkey loosely with foil, leaving some space between bird and foil. Press foil over drumsticks and neck.

Roast in a 325° oven till meat thermometer registers 180° to 185°; the stuffing should be at least 165°. When done, the turkey meat should be fork tender and juices should not run pink when a thigh is pierced with a fork.

If desired, baste the bird occasionally. When turkey is two-thirds done, cut skin or string between drumsticks. Remove foil the last 30 to 45 minutes to let the bird brown.

Remove roasted turkey from the oven and cover loosely with foil. Let stand for 15 minutes before carving.

Use these timings as a guide for roasting a stuffed turkey:

Weight	Time
8 to 12 pounds	3½ to 4½ hours
12 to 16 pounds	4 to 5 hours
20 to 24 pounds	5 to 6½ hours

For unstuffed turkeys of the same weight, reduce the total cooking time by 30 to 45 minutes.

Roasting in a bag: In a turkey-size oven cooking bag shake 1 tablespoon all-purpose flour (flour prevents the bag from bursting). Add bird to bag. Place bird, breast side up, in a large 2-inch deep roasting pan. Close the bag with a nylon tie. With a sharp knife, cut six 1⁄2-inch slits in the top of the bag to allow steam to escape. Insert a meat thermometer into the thigh muscle through a slit in the bag. Roast in a 350° oven till done.

Use these timings as a guide for roasting in a bag:

Weight	Time
12 to 16 pounds	2½ to 3 hours
16 to 20 pounds	3 to 3½ hours
20 to 24 pounds	3½ to 4 hours

Fennel and Sausage Stuffing

FENNEL ADDS A SUBTLE LICORICELIKE FLAVOR TO THIS BREAD STUFFING. THIS WINTER VEGETABLE HAS A BULB ON ONE END, STALKS LIKE CELERY, AND FEATHERY GREEN TOPS.

1 10-ounce package frozen chopped spinach, thawed
½ pound ground turkey sausage
1 medium fennel bulb with tops
1 cup chopped onion
⅓ cup margarine or butter
1 teaspoon dried sage, crushed
¼ teaspoon pepper
⅛ teaspoon salt
9 cups dry sourdough or French bread cubes
1 to 1⅓ cups chicken broth

Squeeze the thawed spinach in a colander to remove as much liquid as possible. Transfer the spinach to a large mixing bowl; set aside.

In a large skillet cook turkey sausage till brown. Drain off fat. Add the sausage to the spinach.

Remove green tops from fennel; snip enough of the tops to make 1 tablespoon. Set aside. Cut the fennel bulb into wedges, removing the core. Coarsely chop the fennel (you should have about 1¼ cups).

In the same skillet cook chopped fennel and onion in hot margarine or butter till tender but not brown. Stir in the snipped fennel tops, sage, pepper, and salt. Add the fennel mixture to sausage mixture. Stir in sourdough or French bread cubes. Drizzle with enough broth to moisten; toss gently to coat.

Use to stuff a 12- to 14-pound turkey. Spoon remaining stuffing into a casserole. Cover and chill till ready to add to

◆ Roast Turkey with Fennel and Sausage Stuffing

the oven. The last 30 to 45 minutes of turkey roasting, add the casserole and bake till heated through. Makes 12 to 14 side-dish servings.

Nutrition facts per serving: 175 cal., 9 g total fat (2 g sat. fat), 7 mg chol., 474 mg sodium, 17 g carbo., 0 g fiber, 8 g pro. Daily Value: 18% vit. A, 6% vit. C, 4% calcium, 9% iron.

Dilly Buns

THESE ROLLS COME TOGETHER TWICE AS FAST AS TRADITIONAL YEAST ROLLS BECAUSE THEY NEED ONLY ONE SHORT RISING.

2½ to 3 cups all-purpose flour
1 package fast-rising active dry yeast
2 teaspoons dillseed
¼ teaspoon baking soda
1 cup cream-style cottage cheese
¼ cup water
2 tablespoons margarine or butter
2 teaspoons sugar
½ teaspoon salt
¼ teaspoon pepper
1 egg
1 beaten egg
1 tablespoon water
Fresh dill sprigs (optional)

In a large mixing bowl combine ¾ cup of the flour, the yeast, dillseed, and baking soda.

In a medium saucepan heat and stir cottage cheese, ¼ cup water, margarine
continued on page 192

continued from page 191

or butter, sugar, salt, and pepper till warm (120° to 130°) and margarine is almost melted.

Add cheese mixture to flour mixture. Add the first egg. Beat with an electric mixer on low speed for 30 seconds, scraping the sides of the bowl constantly. Beat on high speed for 3 minutes. Using a spoon, stir in as much remaining flour as you can.

Turn dough out onto a lightly floured surface. Knead in enough of the remaining flour to make a moderately soft dough that is smooth and elastic (3 to 5 minutes total). Cover and let rest for 15 minutes.

Shape dough into 18 balls, pulling the edges under to make smooth tops. Place the balls about 2 inches apart on greased baking sheets. Cover and let rise in a warm place till nearly double (20 to 30 minutes).

Combine beaten egg and 1 tablespoon water. Top each bun with a dill sprig, if desired; brush with egg mixture. Bake in a 375° oven about 12 minutes or till golden. Makes 18.

To make cloverleaf rolls: Lightly grease eighteen 2½-inch muffin cups. After the 15-minute rest, shape the dough into 54 balls. Place 3 balls in each muffin cup. Let rise and bake as directed. Makes 18.

Make-ahead tip: Freeze cooled buns for up to 3 months in a freezer container. Thaw at room temperature for about 1 hour.

Nutrition facts per bun or roll: 93 cal., 2 g total fat (1 g sat. fat), 25 mg chol., 150 mg sodium, 14 g carbo., 1 g fiber, 4 g pro. Daily Value: 2% vit. A, 0% vit. C, 1% calcium, 6% iron.

For these turkey-shaped rolls, start with a flattened circle of dough. Cut slits for the tail feathers and a wedge to separate the head and tail.

Whole Wheat Gobblers

START WITH FROZEN BREAD DOUGH SO ALL YOU HAVE TO DO IS SHAPE AND BAKE THESE PLAYFUL ROLLS.

1 16-ounce loaf frozen whole wheat bread dough
1 tablespoon margarine or butter, melted
Poppy seed, sesame seed, and/or paprika (optional)

Thaw bread dough according to package directions. On a lightly floured surface, divide dough into 8 portions; shape into balls. Cover and let rest for 10 minutes.

For each gobbler, flatten or roll a ball into a 4-inch circle. Using kitchen scissors, snip 3 horizontal, rounded 1-inch-long slits on one side of the circle for the feathered tail. (See photograph, above.) Cut out a narrow wedge under

the last cut to separate the tail from the body. On the top edge of the circle, cut out a V, about 2 inches long, to separate the tail from the head. Transfer to a greased baking sheet. Using small scraps of dough, form a beak and wattle (loose

◆ Clockwise from top left: Dilly Buns, Dilly Cloverleaf Rolls, Tomato Rosemary Muffins, Whole Wheat Gobblers, Rye Anise Loaves

skin under beak). Use a little water to attach dough parts to the head. Form feet; attach to the body.

Brush rolls with melted margarine or butter. Sprinkle with poppy seed, sesame seed, or paprika, if desired. Bake in a 375° oven for 10 to 12 minutes or till golden. Cool on a wire rack. Serve warm. Makes 8.

Make-ahead tip: To freeze, place baked rolls in freezer containers. Freeze for up to 3 months. To serve, wrap frozen rolls in foil; reheat in a 300° oven for 15 minutes.

Nutrition facts per roll: 159 cal., 4 g total fat (0 g sat. fat), 0 mg chol., 332 mg sodium, 27 g carbo., 2 g fiber, 7 g pro. Daily Value: 1% vit. A, 0% vit. C, 0% calcium, 0% iron.

Rye-Anise Loaf

ANISEED AND ORANGE FLAVOR THIS HEARTY BREAD. CHOOSE FROM TWO SHAPING IDEAS.

2 to 2½ cups all-purpose flour
2 packages active dry yeast
¾ cup milk
¼ cup molasses
2 tablespoons margarine or butter
1 tablespoon sugar
2 teaspoons aniseed, slightly crushed
1½ teaspoons finely shredded orange peel
1 teaspoon salt
1 egg
1¼ cups rye flour
Milk
Poppy seed, sesame seed, and/or aniseed
(optional)

In a large mixing bowl stir together 1½ cups of the all-purpose flour and the yeast. Heat and stir milk, molasses, margarine or butter, sugar, aniseed, orange peel, and salt till warm (120° to 130°) and margarine is almost melted. Add to flour mixture. Add egg. Beat with an electric mixer on low speed 30 seconds, scraping the sides of the bowl constantly. Beat on high speed for 3 minutes.

Using a spoon, stir in rye flour and as much of the remaining all-purpose flour as you can. Turn out onto a lightly floured surface. Knead in enough remaining all-purpose flour to make a moderately stiff dough that is smooth and elastic (6 to 8 minutes total). Shape into a ball. Place in a greased bowl; turn once to grease surface. Cover and let rise in a warm place till double (1¼ to 1½ hours). Punch dough down. Cover; let rest for 10 minutes.

On a lightly greased large baking sheet, pat dough to a 14x8-inch oval*.

Tomato-Rosemary Muffins

1¾ cups all-purpose flour
⅓ cup grated Parmesan cheese
2 tablespoons sugar
2 teaspoons baking powder
½ teaspoon dried rosemary, crushed
¼ teaspoon baking soda
⅛ teaspoon garlic powder
⅛ teaspoon pepper
1 beaten egg
½ cup milk
½ cup tomato sauce
⅓ cup olive oil or cooking oil
Grated Parmesan cheese (optional)

In a bowl mix flour, ⅓ cup Parmesan cheese, sugar, baking powder, rosemary, baking soda, garlic powder, and pepper. Make a well in center. Combine egg, milk, tomato sauce, and oil. Add all at once to flour mixture. Stir just till moistened (the batter should be lumpy).

Lightly grease thirty-six 1¾-inch muffin cups;* fill ⅔ full. If desired, sprinkle with additional Parmesan cheese. Bake in a 350° oven about 15 minutes or till light brown. Remove from pans. Serve warm or cool. Makes 36 mini muffins.

*Note: To make 12 regular-size muffins, fill 12 greased 2½-inch muffin cups ⅔ full. Bake in a 350° oven for 20 to 24 minutes.

Make-ahead tip: Freeze cooled muffins for up to 3 months. Thaw at room temperature for 45 minutes.

Nutrition facts per mini muffin: 50 cal., 3 g total fat (1 g sat. fat), 7 mg chol., 70 mg sodium, 6 g carbo., 0 g fiber, 1 g pro. Daily Value: 1% vit. A, 0% vit. C, 3% calcium, 2% iron.

To shape the Rye-Anise Loaf, pat into a large oval and use kitchen shears to cut slits on each side.

Using kitchen shears, make 4 cuts, 2 inches long, on each long side of oval. (See photograph, above.) Separate cuts slightly. Cover; let rise in a warm place till nearly double (about 1 hour).

After rising, make several ¼-inch-deep vertical slits between the cuts on long sides of loaf. Brush with milk. Sprinkle with poppy seed, sesame seed, and/or aniseed.

Bake in a 350° oven for 25 to 30 minutes or till bread sounds hollow when tapped. Brush again with milk. Cool slightly. Serve warm. Makes 1 loaf (18 to 20 servings).

*Note: For a round loaf, as shown on page 193, pat dough to a 9-inch circle. Make 8 cuts almost to center. Twist each wedge slightly. Let dough rise and bake as directed.

Make-ahead tip: After shaping, brush the dough lightly with oil. Let rise, loosely covered, in the refrigerator for 4 to 24 hours. Uncover and let stand at room temperature for 30 minutes before baking.

Nutrition facts per serving: 219 cal., 4 g total fat (1 g sat. fat), 25 mg chol., 287 mg sodium, 40 g carbo., 3 g fiber, 6 g pro. Daily Value: 5% vit. A, 1% vit. C, 4% calcium, 15% iron.

Holiday Citrus Salad

IF RED BLOOD ORANGES ARE AVAILABLE IN YOUR SUPERMARKET, USE THEM FOR A FESTIVE HOLIDAY TOUCH. SHRED SOME ORANGE PEEL FOR THE DRESSING BEFORE PEELING THE ORANGES.

1 jicama, cut into julienne strips (2 cups)
2 medium red, yellow, and/or green sweet peppers, cut into julienne strips (2 cups)
1 recipe Caraway Dressing (see recipe, below)
8 cups torn mixed greens
2 medium oranges, peeled and sliced crosswise
4 or 5 chives, chopped

In a large bowl toss together jicama, sweet pepper strips, and half of the Caraway Dressing. Cover and chill the mixture in the refrigerator for 4 to 24 hours.

To serve, place the mixed greens in a serving bowl. Drizzle the remaining Caraway Dressing over the greens. Arrange orange slices around the edge of the bowl. Stir the chopped chives into the jicama mixture; spoon into the center. Serve immediately. Makes 8 side-dish servings.

Caraway Dressing: In a screw-top jar combine ⅓ cup *salad oil*; ¼ cup *white wine vinegar*; 2 tablespoons *honey*; 1 tablespoon *coarse-grain brown or* Dijon-style mustard; 1 teaspoon *caraway seed*, crushed; ½ teaspoon finely shredded *orange peel*; and ⅛ teaspoon freshly ground *pepper*. Cover; shake well. Store in the refrigerator for up to 1 week.

Nutrition facts per serving: 138 cal., 9 g total fat (1 g sat. fat), 0 mg chol., 50 mg sodium, 13 g carbo., 2 g fiber, 2 g pro. Daily Value: 35% vit. A, 95% vit. C, 4% calcium, 9% iron.

Potatoes and Carrots Au Gratin

THINLY SLICE THE POTATOES THE EASY WAY—WITH A FOOD PROCESSOR.

6 medium baking potatoes (2 pounds)
3 medium carrots, peeled and thinly sliced (1½ cups)
2 bay leaves
2 leeks, cut into ½-inch slices (1 cup)
2 tablespoons margarine or butter
2 tablespoons all-purpose flour
½ teaspoon salt
½ teaspoon ground nutmeg
¼ teaspoon white or black pepper
1 12-ounce can evaporated milk
¾ cup shredded Gruyère or Swiss cheese (3 ounces)
½ cup finely shredded Parmesan cheese (2 ounces)
¼ cup seasoned fine dry bread crumbs
2 tablespoons margarine or butter, melted

Peel potatoes; thinly slice. In a 3-quart saucepan combine potato, carrots, and bay leaves. Add water to cover. Bring to boiling; reduce heat. Cover and cook for 5 minutes.

Add leeks. Cook, covered, 3 minutes or till vegetables are just tender. Drain well; discard bay leaves. (At this point, *continued on page 196*

continued from page 195
you can cool vegetables, cover, and chill overnight.)

For sauce, in same saucepan melt the first 2 tablespoons margarine or butter. Stir in flour, salt, nutmeg, and pepper. Add milk. Cook and stir till thickened and bubbly. Cook and stir for 1 minute more. Remove from heat. Add ½ cup of the Gruyère cheese; stir till smooth.

Transfer the warm or chilled vegetables to a lightly greased 2-quart au gratin dish or rectangular baking dish. Carefully spoon the warm cheese sauce over the potato mixture; spread with the back of the spoon to coat all vegetables.

For crumb topping, in a small mixing bowl stir together grated Parmesan cheese, seasoned fine dry bread crumbs, and remaining 2 tablespoons melted margarine or butter. Sprinkle the topping over the potato mixture. If desired, cover and chill the casserole at this point for up to 2 hours.

At serving time, bake the casserole, uncovered, in a 350° oven for about 15 minutes (25 minutes if chilled) or till the cheese sauce is bubbly around the edges of the dish. Sprinkle with the remaining shredded Gruyère cheese. Bake about 5 minutes more or till the cheese is melted and the casserole is heated through. Makes 8 side-dish servings.

Nutrition facts per serving: 280 cal., 12 g total fat (6 g sat. fat), 26 mg chol., 286 mg sodium, 33 g carbo., 4 g fiber, 12 g pro. Daily Value: 79% vit. A, 17% vit. C, 26% calcium.

◆ Clockwise left to right: Holiday Citrus Salad. Potatoes and Carrots Au Gratin. Cranberry Conserve. Vegetable Strudel

Cranberry Conserve

JARS OF THIS WONDERFULLY TANGY RELISH MAKE GREAT HOLIDAY GIFTS. SERVE WITH ROAST TURKEY OR HAM.

⅓ cup packed brown sugar
⅓ cup margarine or butter
2 teaspoons vinegar
2 large onions, coarsely chopped
4 cups cranberries
½ cup raisins
¼ cup apple cider or apple juice
¼ teaspoon ground allspice
¼ teaspoon ground cloves
3½ cups granulated sugar
1 cup toasted broken pecans

mixture thickens, stir frequently to prevent sticking. Remove from heat; stir in the nuts.

Meanwhile, pour boiling water over clean half-pint jars; let stand in hot water till ready to fill. Ladle mixture into hot jars, leaving a ¼-inch headspace. (If you have any mixture left that doesn't make a full jar, cover and chill it for up to 1 week. Serve it first.) Wipe rims. Adjust lids. Process in a boiling-water canner for 15 minutes (start timing when the water boils).

Or, ladle into half-pint freezer containers, leaving a ½-inch headspace. Seal, label, and freeze for up to 1 year. Makes about 4 half-pints.

Nutrition facts per tablespoon: 46 cal., 1 g total fat (0 g sat. fat), 0 mg chol., 7 mg sodium, 9 g carbo., 0 g fiber, 0 g pro.

Vegetable Strudel

PURCHASED PHYLLO DOUGH, FROZEN VEGETABLES, AND A PACKAGE OF BÉARNAISE SAUCE ARE THE SECRETS TO THIS SHOWY SIDE DISH.

*1 10-ounce package frozen chopped
    broccoli, thawed and well drained
1 10-ounce package frozen whole kernel
    corn, thawed and well drained
2 plum tomatoes, seeded and
    chopped (½ cup)
¼ cup thinly sliced green onion
¼ teaspoon pepper
1 0.9-ounce package béarnaise sauce
6 sheets frozen phyllo dough
    (18x14-inch rectangles), thawed
3 tablespoons margarine or butter, melted*

continued on page 198

In a large skillet cook and stir brown sugar, margarine or butter, and vinegar over medium heat for 1 to 2 minutes. Add onions. Cook, uncovered, over low heat for 10 to 12 minutes or till onions are glazed and tender, stirring often. Set mixture aside.

In a 6- to 8-quart kettle or Dutch oven combine cranberries, raisins, apple cider or juice, allspice, and cloves. Bring to boiling over medium heat, stirring occasionally. Continue to cook, uncovered, over medium heat for 5 minutes.

Stir in onion mixture and granulated sugar. Return to boiling. Cook, uncovered, for 10 to 15 minutes more. As

continued from page 197

For filling, stir together the broccoli, corn, tomatoes, green onion, and pepper; set aside.

Prepare béarnaise sauce according to package directions, except use only 2 tablespoons margarine or butter. Stir ½ cup sauce into vegetable mixture. Cover; chill remaining sauce.

On a flat surface, brush 1 sheet of phyllo dough with some of the 3 tablespoons margarine. Keep remaining phyllo covered with a damp cloth. Top with another phyllo sheet; brush with margarine. Repeat with remaining phyllo and most of the margarine.

Spoon the filling along one of the long sides of the phyllo stack in a 3-inch-wide strip, to within 1 inch of the edges. Starting from long side with filling, roll up jelly-roll style. Fold ends under to seal. Place, seam side down, in an ungreased shallow baking pan. Brush with remaining margarine. Score top of strudel into 12 serving-size pieces.

Bake the strudel, uncovered, in a 425° oven for 18 to 20 minutes or till golden. Cool slightly.

Meanwhile, in a small saucepan heat and stir remaining sauce over very low heat. If necessary, thin the sauce with a little milk.

To serve, use a serrated knife to slice the phyllo roll. Serve with the warm sauce. Makes 12 side-dish servings.

Nutrition facts per serving: 117 cal., 6 g total fat (1 g sat. fat), 2 mg chol., 191 mg sodium, 14 g carbo., 1 g fiber, 3 g pro. Daily Value: 13% vit. A, 19% vit. C, 3% calcium, 4% iron.

◆ Left to right: Apple-Cranberry Struesel Pie, Old-Fashioned Pumpkin Torte, Gingerbread Trifle

Apple-Cranberry Struesel Pie

LOOK FOR DRIED CRANBERRIES IN SPECIALTY FOOD STORES OR IN THE GOURMET FOODS AISLE OF YOUR GROCERY STORE.

1 recipe Pastry for Single-Crust Pie (see recipe, page 199)
½ cup dried cranberries or dried tart cherries
6 large apples, peeled, cored, and sliced (6 cups)
¾ cup granulated sugar
3 tablespoons all-purpose flour
1 teaspoon apple pie spice
¼ teaspoon salt
⅓ cup half-and-half or light cream
⅓ cup all-purpose flour
⅓ cup toasted finely chopped pecans or walnuts
⅓ cup packed brown sugar
¼ teaspoon ground nutmeg
3 tablespoons margarine or butter
1 recipe Vanilla Icing (optional) (see recipe, page 199)

Prepare pastry. Line pastry with a double thickness of foil. Bake in a 450° oven for 8 minutes. Remove foil. Bake for 5 to 6 minutes more or till golden. Cool in pie plate on a wire rack. Reduce the oven temperature to 375°.

For filling, pour boiling water over cranberries. Let stand for 5 minutes; drain. Mix cranberries and apples; place in the pastry shell. Combine granulated sugar, the 3 tablespoons flour, apple pie spice, and salt. Stir in half-and-half or light cream. Pour over fruit.

For nut topping, combine the ⅓ cup flour, nuts, brown sugar, and nutmeg.

With a pastry blender, cut in margarine or butter till the pieces are the size of small peas. Sprinkle over filling.

Cover edge of pie with foil. Bake in the 375° oven for 25 minutes. Remove foil. Bake for 20 to 25 minutes more or till top is golden and fruit is tender. Cool pie for 45 minutes on a wire rack. If desired, drizzle with Vanilla Icing. Serve warm or cool. Store any leftover pie, covered, in the refrigerator. Makes 8 servings.

Make-ahead tip: The day before, bake the piecrust; cool thoroughly and wrap in plastic wrap. Store at room tem-

perature. The nut topping and Vanilla Icing can also be prepared the day before. Cover both and store in the refrigerator.

Pastry for Single-Crust Pie: In a medium mixing bowl stir together 1¼ cups *all-purpose flour* and ¼ teaspoon *salt*. Cut in ⅓ cup *shortening* till pieces are the size of small peas. Sprinkle 3 to 4 tablespoons *cold water*, a tablespoon at a time, over mixture, tossing gently till all is moistened. Form dough into a ball. On a lightly floured surface, roll dough to a 12-inch circle. Fit into a 9-inch pie plate. Trim to ½ inch beyond edge; fold under pastry and flute edge.

Vanilla Icing: Combine 1 cup sifted *powdered sugar,* 1 tablespoon *milk,* and ¼ teaspoon *vanilla.* Stir in additional milk, a teaspoon at a time, till of drizzling consistency.

Nutrition facts per slice: 422 cal., 18 g total fat (4 g sat. fat), 4 mg chol., 192 mg sodium, 65 g carbo., 3 g fiber, 4 g pro. Daily Value: 7% vit. A, 0% vit. C, 2% calcium, 12% iron.

Old-Fashioned Pumpkin Torte

THIS AUTUMN CAKE USES NUTS AND GRAHAM CRACKERS INSTEAD OF FLOUR.

2⅔ cups toasted slivered almonds
1 cup graham cracker crumbs
(about 15 square crackers)
1¼ teaspoons baking powder
1¼ teaspoons pumpkin pie spice
¾ teaspoon finely shredded orange peel
8 eggs, separated
1⅓ cups sugar
1 cup canned pumpkin
1½ teaspoons vanilla
1 recipe Apple-Date Filling
(see recipe, below right)
1 recipe Sweetened Whipped Cream
(see recipe, below right)
1 recipe Apricot Roses (optional)
(see recipe, below right)

Grease and flour three 8x1½-inch round baking pans; set aside. In a food processor bowl or blender container, cover and process or blend almonds in small batches till finely ground but not oily. Transfer to a mixing bowl. Stir in the graham cracker crumbs, baking powder, pumpkin pie spice, and orange peel; set aside.

In a small mixer bowl beat the egg yolks and ⅔ cup of the sugar with an electric mixer on high speed for 6 minutes. Stir in pumpkin and vanilla. Fold in nut mixture.

Wash beaters. In a large mixer bowl beat egg whites on medium speed till soft peaks form (tips curl). Gradually add remaining ⅔ cup sugar, 2 tablespoons at a time, beating till stiff peaks form (tips stand straight). Fold about 1 cup of the egg white mixture into the pumpkin mixture. Fold the pumpkin mixture into remaining egg white mixture. Spread evenly in prepared pans.

Bake in a 350° oven for 20 to 25 minutes or till light brown. Cool on racks for 10 minutes. Remove from pans; cool thoroughly on wire racks. If desired, wrap each cake layer with freezer wrap and freeze for up to 3 months. Thaw before using.

To assemble torte, split each cake layer in half horizontally. Place the bottom of 1 split layer on serving plate. Spread with about ⅔ cup of the Apple-Date Filling. Repeat with remaining cake layers and filling, ending with top cake layer. Spoon Sweetened Whipped Cream on top layer. If desired, garnish with Apricot Roses. Serve immediately or cover and chill up to 4 hours. Serves 16.

Apple-Date Filling: In a small mixer bowl beat two 8-ounce packages *cream cheese*, softened, with an electric mixer on medium speed till fluffy. Add ⅔ cup packed *brown sugar*, 2 teaspoons *vanilla*, and ½ teaspoon *pumpkin pie spice*; beat well. Stir in ⅔ cup finely chopped pitted *dates or raisins* and ½ cup *chunk-style applesauce*. Cover; chill up to 48 hours. Makes about 3 cups.

Sweetened Whipped Cream: In a chilled small mixing bowl beat ½ cup *whipping cream*, 2 teaspoons *sugar*, and ½ teaspoon finely shredded *orange peel* with an electric mixer on medium speed just till stiff peaks form. Makes about 1 cup.

Apricot Roses: Roll dried apricot halves between waxed paper to ⅛-inch-thick circles. Cut in half. For center of each rose, roll 1 half-circle into a cone shape. For petals, press on as many half-circles around center as desired, curving rounded edges outward and overlapping petals. Trim bottom. Hold together with half of a wooden toothpick.

Nutrition facts per serving: 433 cal., 26 g total fat (10 g sat. fat), 148 mg chol., 184 mg sodium, 44 g carbo., 3 g fiber, 10 g pro. Daily Value: 54% vit. A, 3% vit. C, 11% calcium.

Gingerbread Trifle

A GINGERBREAD MIX AND PURCHASED PUDDING GIVE YOU A HEAD START ON THIS ELEGANT DESSERT.

1 14- or 14½-ounce package gingerbread
mix
⅓ or ½ cup packed brown sugar*
2 tablespoons cornstarch
½ teaspoon ground cinnamon
1½ cups cherry-cranberry drink or
cranberry juice cocktail
1½ cups frozen pitted tart red cherries
1 29-ounce can pear slices, drained
1 recipe Easy Lemon Cream
(see recipe, page 201)

Prepare and bake gingerbread mix according to package directions. Cool. Cut into 1-inch cubes.

Meanwhile, for the cherry sauce, in a medium saucepan combine brown sugar (*use ½ cup if using the cranberry juice cocktail option), cornstarch, and cinnamon. Stir in fruit drink. Add frozen cherries. Cook and stir till thickened and bubbly. Cook and stir for 2 minutes more. Cover and cool without stirring. (To make ahead, transfer to a covered container and chill up to 3 or 4 days.)

To assemble the trifle, in a 3-quart clear glass bowl or soufflé dish spoon a

Coffee by the fire marks the close of yet another wonderful Thanksgiving holiday. To romance this finale, set out a fireside collection of coffee accompaniments, such as flavored syrups, sugar cubes, whipped cream, grated chocolate, cinnamon sticks, and candy stirs. Let guests dress up their own coffee. Include a tray of truffles and candies for those who crave one last bite of sweet.

third of the Easy Lemon Cream. Add a third of the cherry sauce. Sprinkle with half of the gingerbread. Spoon another third of the lemon cream over gingerbread. Top with another third of the cherry sauce. Arrange half of the sliced pears atop the cherry sauce (cover and chill remaining pears). Layer with remaining gingerbread, lemon cream, and cherry sauce. Cover and chill for 2 to 24 hours. To serve, arrange the remaining pear slices atop the trifle. Makes 10 to 12 servings.

Easy Lemon Cream: Beat 1 cup *whipping cream* and 1 teaspoon *vanilla* just till soft peaks form. Fold in 1 cup purchased *lemon pudding* and stir gently till combined. For creamier texture, stir in 1 tablespoon *lemon juice or milk.*

Nutrition facts per serving: 377 cal., 15 g total fat (8 g sat. fat), 33 mg chol., 338 mg sodium, 59 g carbo., 1 g fiber, 3 g pro. Daily Value: 12% vit. A, 17% vit. C, 3% calcium, and 12% iron.

Prizewinning Cookies

BY
LISA HOLDERNESS

Holiday cookies are rich with tradition, often passed from generation to generation. Thousands of readers shared their most treasured cookies by entering our holiday cookie contest last winter. After plenty of sampling, we chose 12 best-tasting recipes and three top decorating ideas as winners. These cookies are so special, we think you'll want to make them a part of your holiday baking tradition.

◆ Shimmering Snowflakes
  Grand Prize, Decorating
  Cheryl Bohen,
  Pendleton, New York
  (Recipe page 204)

◆ Mini Peanut Butter Cups
  2nd Place, Decorating
  Thelma Hoagland,
  Fort Wayne, Indiana
  (Recipe page 204)

◆ **Pistachio Nut Stars of India**
Grand Prize, Recipe
Wolfgang H. M. Hanau,
North Miami, Florida
(Recipe page 205)

◆ **Triple Hanukkah Stars**
3rd Place, Decorating
Vicki Hulbert,
Palos Verdes Estates,
California
(Recipe page 204)

Shimmering Snowflakes

OUR GRAND-PRIZE DECORATING WIN-
NER, CHERYL BOHEN, USES HER
FAVORITE SUGAR COOKIE RECIPE TO
MAKE THESE SNOWFLAKE STARS. THE
ROLLED SUGAR COOKIE DOUGH RECIPE
AT RIGHT WORKS GREAT TOO.

*1 recipe Rolled Sugar Cookie Dough (see
recipe, right) or sugar cookie recipe
8 ounces vanilla-flavored candy coating,
cut up, or semisweet chocolate pieces
3 tablespoons shortening
Edible glitter (optional)
Green and red jelly beans halved
(optional)
Vanilla-flavored candy coating or
semisweet chocolate, melted (optional)*

On a lightly floured surface, roll a portion of chilled cookie dough ⅛ inch
thick. With a 3- or 3½-inch star or
snowflake cookie cutter or stencil, cut
out cookies. Reroll the scraps. With a
smaller star or flower cutter (about ¾
inch in diameter), cut out a shape in the
center of each cookie, if desired. Use
¼-inch assorted-shaped cutters or a
sharp knife to cut smaller designs. Place
on ungreased cookie sheets.

Bake in a 375° oven for 7 to 8 minutes or till edges are firm and bottoms
are very lightly browned. Transfer cookies to wire racks; cool.

Heat and stir 8 ounces candy coating
or chocolate and shortening over very
low heat till mixture begins to melt.
Remove from heat; stir till smooth. Dip
cooled cookies, facedown, into melted
mixture, shaking cookies gently to
smooth any ripples in the coating.
Transfer cookies to wire racks. If desired,
sprinkle with glitter or decorate with
jelly beans, cut side down. Or, let the
chocolate on the cookies dry. With a
spoon, drizzle additional candy coating
or chocolate (in a contrasting color) onto
cookies. Makes 24 cookies.

Rolled Sugar Cookie Dough: In a
large mixing bowl beat ⅓ cup *butter* and
⅓ cup *shortening* with an electric mixer
on medium speed for 30 seconds. Add
1 cup *all-purpose flour,* ¾ cup *sugar,*
1 *egg,* 1 tablespoon *milk,* 1 teaspoon
baking powder, 1 teaspoon *vanilla,* and a
dash *salt.* Beat till combined. Beat in
1 cup *all-purpose flour.* Divide dough in
half. Cover; chill 3 hours. Use for
Shimmering Snowflakes (see recipe, left).

Nutrition facts per cookie: 175 cal.,
10 g total fat (3 g sat. fat), 9 mg chol.,
62 mg sodium, 20 g carbo., 0 g fiber, 2 g
pro. Daily Value: 3% vit. A, 0% vit. C,
3% calcium, 3% iron.

Mini Peanut Butter Cups

THELMA HOAGLAND DECORATES PEANUT
BUTTER COOKIES WITH FROSTING FLOW-
ERS SET IN MINI PEANUT BUTTER CUP
BASKETS.

*¾ cup peanut butter
½ cup shortening
⅓ cup granulated sugar
⅓ cup packed brown sugar
1 egg
2 tablespoons milk
1 teaspoon vanilla
1⅓ cups all-purpose flour
½ teaspoon baking soda
¼ cup granulated sugar
30 bite-size chocolate-covered peanut
butter cups, halved lengthwise
1 16-ounce can vanilla frosting
Food coloring*

In a large mixing bowl beat peanut
butter, shortening, ⅓ cup granulated
sugar, and the brown sugar with electric
mixer on medium speed till combined.
Add egg, milk, and vanilla; beat well.
Combine flour and baking soda; add to
egg mixture, beating well.

Shape dough into 1-inch balls. Roll in
the ¼ cup sugar; place 2 inches apart on
ungreased cookie sheets. Bake in a 350°
oven for 10 to 12 minutes or till lightly
browned. Remove from the oven.
Immediately press half of a peanut butter
cup, cut side down, into each cookie,
about ½ inch from bottom edge (cookies
will crack). Cool for 1 minute; transfer
cookies to racks. Cool.

To decorate, tint portions of frosting
with desired colors of food coloring.
Pipe a basket handle, flowers, leaves, and
berries above candy basket as desired.
Makes about 60 cookies.

Nutrition facts per cookie: 80 cal.,
5 g total fat (1 g sat. fat), 4 mg chol.,
41 mg sodium, 8 g carbo., 2 g pro.

Triple Hanukkah Stars

VICKI HULBERT'S KIDS LOVE TO HELP
MAKE THESE COLORFUL STARS.

*½ cup unsalted butter
1 cup sugar
1 egg
1 tablespoon brandy or water
½ teaspoon vanilla
½ teaspoon baking powder
¼ teaspoon salt
2 cups all-purpose flour
Blue paste food coloring
2 ounces white baking bar, chopped
1 teaspoon shortening*

In a large mixing bowl beat butter and sugar with an electric mixer on medium to high speed till combined. Add egg, brandy or water, and vanilla; beat on low speed till fluffy. Add baking powder and salt just till combined. Beat in as much of the flour as you can. Using a spoon, stir in remaining flour. Divide dough in half. Tint one half with blue food coloring. Wrap all dough in plastic wrap; chill for 2 to 3 hours or till easy to handle.

On a lightly floured surface, roll each portion of dough about 1/8 inch thick. Cut out dough stars, using three 6-pointed star cutters of varying sizes, rerolling scraps. (Or, make star patterns from clean cardboard. Use a knife to cut the dough around the patterns.) Place a large star of blue or plain dough on a lightly greased baking sheet. Top with a medium-size star of the other color, then add a small star of the first color. Repeat with the remaining stars, varying the color order.

Bake in a 325° oven for 14 to 15 minutes or till bottoms of cookies are lightly browned. Cool 1 minute on cookie sheet; transfer to racks.

Heat and stir baking bar and shortening over very low heat till bar just starts to melt. Remove from heat; stir till smooth. Cool slightly. Transfer to a clean, sealable sandwich bag and snip a small hole at one corner. Drizzle atop cookies. Let cookies stand till decorations are set. Makes 20 to 24 cookies.

Nutrition facts per cookie: 144 cal., 6 g total fat (4 g sat. fat), 23 mg chol., 42 mg sodium, 21 g carbo., 0 g fiber, 2 g pro. Daily Value: 4% vit. A, 0% vit. C, 1% calcium, 4% iron.

◆ Lime Zingers, 2nd Place, Rorie Kerns, Alameda, California (Recipe, page 206)

Pistachio Nut Stars of India

THESE GRAND PRIZE COOKIES BLEND SOME OF THE FLAVORS OF INDIA, INCLUDING CARDAMOM AND CINNAMON.

1 cup butter
1/2 cup granulated sugar
1/4 cup packed brown sugar
2 tablespoons vanilla yogurt
1 egg
2 1/2 cups all-purpose flour
1 teaspoon ground cinnamon
1/4 to 1/2 teaspoon ground cardamom
1/4 teaspoon salt
2 cups finely chopped pistachio nuts or almonds
2 lightly beaten egg whites
1/2 cup orange marmalade
1/4 cup powdered sugar

In a large mixing bowl beat butter, granulated sugar, brown sugar, and yogurt with an electric mixer on medium to high speed till creamy. Add whole egg; beat well. Beat in flour, cinnamon, cardamom, and salt. Stir in nuts. Divide dough in half. Cover; chill for 2 hours.

On a floured surface, roll each half of dough 1/8 inch thick. Using a 3-inch star cookie cutter, cut out 36 stars from each half of the dough, rerolling scraps as needed. Place on lightly greased baking sheets. With a small star-shaped cutter, cut stars from centers of half of the stars. Brush all cookies with egg whites.

Bake cookies in a 375° oven for 8 to 10 minutes or until lightly browned. Cool on wire racks.

To assemble cookies, spread dull side of each whole star with 1/2 teaspoon marmalade. Top each with a cut-out cookie, shiny side up. Press cookies together gently. Sift powdered sugar lightly atop. Makes 36 cookies.

Nutrition facts per cookie: 148 cal., 9 g total fat (4 g sat. fat), 20 mg chol., 73 mg sodium, 16 g carbo., 1 g fiber, 3 g pro.

Lime Zingers

FOR CHRISTMAS, DECORATE THESE TANGY COOKIES IN RED AND WHITE, AS SHOWN ON PAGE 187.

1 cup butter
½ cup granulated sugar
2 teaspoons finely shredded lime peel
¼ cup lime juice (2 limes)
1 teaspoon vanilla
2¼ cups all-purpose flour
¾ cup finely chopped Brazil nuts or hazelnuts
½ of an 8-ounce package cream cheese, softened
1 cup sifted powdered sugar
1 tablespoon lemon or lime juice
1 teaspoon vanilla
Food coloring

In a large mixing bowl beat butter with an electric mixer on medium to high speed for 30 seconds. Beat in sugar till combined. Beat in lime peel, the ¼ cup lime juice, and 1 teaspoon vanilla. Beat in as much flour as you can. Using a wooden spoon, stir in any remaining flour. Stir in nuts. Divide dough in half.

On a lightly floured surface roll each half of dough about ¼ inch thick. Cut into desired shapes using 1- or 2-inch cookie cutters. Place on ungreased cookie sheets. Bake in a 350° oven for 8 to 10 minutes or till light brown around the edges. Cool.

For frosting, beat cream cheese, powdered sugar, lemon or lime juice and vanilla with an electric mixer on medium speed till smooth; tint as desired with food coloring. Frost cookies. Pipe designs with contrasting colors of frosting, if desired. Makes 72 cookies.

◆ Mocha Caramel Trees, 3rd Place.
Rhonda Melnrick, Bothell, Washington

Nutrition facts per cookie: 62 cal., 4 g total fat (2 g sat. fat), 9 mg chol., 31 mg sodium, 6 g carbo., 1 g pro.

Mocha Caramel Trees

RHONDA MELNRICK COMBINED SHORTBREAD WITH HER FAVORITE COFFEE DRINK.

1 cup butter, softened
¾ cup sifted powdered sugar
3 tablespoons granulated sugar
1 teaspoon instant espresso coffee powder or coffee granules
1 tablespoon vanilla
3 tablespoons unsweetened cocoa powder
1⅔ cups all-purpose flour
½ cup semisweet chocolate pieces
1 teaspoon shortening
½ of a 14-ounce bag caramels
¼ cup butter
2 tablespoons milk

In a large mixing bowl beat butter and sugars with an electric mixer on medium speed till fluffy. Dissolve instant coffee in vanilla; add to butter mixture. Beat in cocoa powder. Beat in as much flour as you can. Stir in any remaining flour. Divide dough in half. Cover; chill about 1 hour or till firm.

On a floured surface, roll each half of dough ¼ to ⅜ inch thick. Cut into 3-inch trees, reindeers, or other shapes. Place cookies 1½ inches apart on greased cookie sheets. Bake in a 325° oven for 12 to 15 minutes or till set but not overbrowned. Cool 1 minute; transfer to wire racks. Cool completely.

Heat and stir chocolate pieces and shortening over low heat till chocolate begins to melt. Remove from heat; stir till smooth. Drizzle over cookies. Let stand till set.

Heat and stir the caramels, ¼ cup butter, and milk over very low heat till smooth. Cool slightly. Drizzle with a spoon over cookies. Makes about 30 cookies.

Nutrition facts per cookie: 150 cal., 9 g total fat (5 g sat. fat), 21 mg chol., 95 mg sodium, 16 g carbo., 0 g fiber, 1 g pro. Daily Value: 7% vit. A, 1% calcium, 3% iron.

Ultimate Bar Cookies

FOR YEARS, BURMA PIERCE AND HER DAUGHTER HAVE MADE THESE BARS, THEN PACKED UP A TIN FOR GRANDMA.

2 cups all-purpose flour
½ cup packed brown sugar
½ cup unsalted butter, softened
1 cup coarsely chopped walnuts
1 3.5-ounce jar macadamia nuts, coarsely chopped (1 cup)
1 6-ounce white baking bar, coarsely chopped (1 cup)
1 cup milk chocolate pieces
¾ cup unsalted butter
½ cup packed brown sugar

◆ Ultimate Bar Cookies, 4th Place
Burma Pierce, Chattanooga, Tennessee

In a medium mixing bowl beat flour, brown sugar, and butter with an electric mixer on medium speed till mixture forms fine crumbs. Pat firmly into an ungreased 13x9x2-inch baking pan. Bake in a 350° oven for 15 minutes or till lightly browned. Transfer the pan to a wire rack. Sprinkle nuts, white baking bar, and chocolate pieces over hot crust.

Heat and stir the ¾ cup butter and remaining brown sugar over medium heat till bubbly. Cook and stir for 1 minute more. Pour evenly over layers in pan. Bake 15 minutes more or till just bubbly around edges. Cool in pan on rack. Cut into desired shapes. Makes about 36 bars.

Nutrition facts per bar: 188 cal., 13 g total fat (6 g sat. fat), 18 mg chol., 12 mg sodium, 16 g carbo., 1 g fiber, 2 g pro. Daily Value: 6% vit. A, 0% vit. C, 2% calcium, 4% iron.

Crinkled Fudge Truffle Cookies

GLORIA BRADFIELD CALLS THIS THE UNDISPUTED "QUEEN OF COOKIES" BECAUSE IT IS HER MOST REQUESTED RECIPE.

◆ Crinkled Fudge Truffle Cookies, 5th Place, Gloria Bradfield, Spirit Lake, Iowa

3 4-ounce bars sweet baking chocolate, chopped
2 tablespoons butter-flavored shortening
1 teaspoon instant coffee granules
3 eggs
1¼ cups granulated sugar
1 teaspoon vanilla
1 cup chopped pecans
6 tablespoons all-purpose flour
1 teaspoon ground cinnamon
½ teaspoon baking powder
¼ teaspoon salt
Nonstick spray coating
Pecan halves (optional)
Powdered sugar (optional)

In a small saucepan heat and stir chocolate and shortening over very low heat till chocolate begins to melt. Remove from heat. Add coffee. Stir till smooth. Cool.

Beat eggs and sugar with an electric mixer on medium to high speed till light and lemon colored (3 to 4 minutes). Beat in chocolate mixture and vanilla. On low speed beat in pecans, flour, cinnamon, baking powder, and salt till combined.

Spray cookie sheets with nonstick coating. Drop teaspoons of dough 2 inches apart on cookie sheets. Place a pecan half atop each cookie, if desired. Bake in a 350° oven for 8 to 10 minutes or till just set on surface (do not overbake). Cool for 1 to 2 minutes; transfer to racks. Cool completely. If desired, sprinkle with powdered sugar. Makes 54 to 60 cookies.

Nutrition facts per cookie: 75 cal., 4 g total fat (2 g sat. fat), 12 mg chol., 17 mg sodium, 9 g carbo., 1 g fiber, 1 g pro. Daily Value: 0% vit. A, 0% vit. C, 0% calcium, 2% iron.

◆ Peanut Butter Puffs, 6th Place
Gloria Piantek, Plainsboro, New Jersey

Peanut Butter Puffs

KEEP A BATCH OF THESE IN THE FREEZER
FOR LAST-MINUTE HOLIDAY ENTERTAIN-
ING OR FOR GIFT GIVING. DECORATE
WITH CHOCOLATE JUST BEFORE SERVING.

½ cup peanut butter
½ cup sifted powdered sugar
2 tablespoons butter
1 teaspoon vanilla
7 sheets frozen phyllo dough
(18x14-inch sheets), thawed
⅓ cup butter, melted
½ cup semisweet chocolate pieces, melted
¼ cup chopped pecans (optional)

For cookie filling, stir together the
peanut butter, powdered sugar, butter,
and vanilla till well mixed. Set the
filling aside.

Brush 1 sheet of phyllo dough with
some of the melted butter. (Keep the
remaining sheets covered with a damp
towel to prevent them from drying out.)
Cut phyllo sheet lengthwise into 4 long
strips. Place a slightly rounded teaspoon
of the peanut butter filling about 1 inch
from one end of one of the strips.

◆ Almond-Fudge Brownies, 7th Place, Mary V. McCammon, Rolling Prairie, Indiana

Starting at the same end with the filling, fold a corner of the dough over
filling so it lines up with the other side
of the strip, forming a triangle. Continue
folding like a flag in a triangular shape,
using the entire strip. Repeat with the
remaining 3 strips. Repeat with remaining sheets of phyllo, butter, and filling.
Brush each triangle with melted butter.
Place on an ungreased cookie sheet, seam
side down. Bake in a 400° oven for 6 to
8 minutes or till golden. Cool on racks.

Pipe or drizzle the tops of cookies with
melted chocolate (thin chocolate with
melted shortening, if necessary). Or, if
desired, spread cookies with chocolate
and sprinkle with chopped pecans. Cool
till chocolate sets up. Serve immediately
or cover and chill for up to 2 days.
Makes 28 cookies.

Nutrition facts per cookie: 89 cal., 6
g total fat (2 g sat. fat), 8 mg chol., 75
mg sodium, 7 g carbo., 0 g fiber, 2 g
pro. Daily Value: 2% vit. A, 0% vit. C,
0% calcium, 2% iron.

Almond-Fudge Brownies

Nonstick spray coating
½ cup all-purpose flour
½ cup almonds, ground
½ teaspoon baking powder
½ cup butter
2½ ounces unsweetened chocolate, cut up
1 cup sugar
2 slightly beaten eggs
1 slightly beaten egg yolk
1 teaspoon vanilla
½ cup candy-coated semisweet
chocolate pieces

Spray only the bottom of a 2-quart
square baking dish with nonstick coating. In a bowl combine flour, almonds,
and baking powder.

Heat and stir butter and unsweetened
chocolate over medium heat till melted.
Stir in sugar, eggs, egg yolk, and vanilla.

Beat by hand till just combined. Stir into flour mixture. Spread mixture into prepared baking dish. Sprinkle with candy-coated pieces. Bake in a 350° oven 30 minutes. Cool in pan on a rack. Cut into squares. Makes 16 brownies.

Nutrition facts per brownie: 199 cal., 12 g total fat (5 g sat. fat), 55 mg chol., 112 mg sodium, 22 g carbo., 1 g fiber, 3 g pro.

Pumpkin Nut Cups

½ cup unsalted butter, softened
1 3-ounce package cream cheese, softened
1 cup all-purpose flour
½ cup packed brown sugar
¼ cup canned pumpkin
1 egg yolk
1 tablespoon half-and-half, light cream, or milk
4 teaspoons unsalted butter, melted
1 tablespoon rum or ¼ teaspoon rum flavoring
1 teaspoon vanilla
⅛ teaspoon ground cinnamon
⅛ teaspoon ground nutmeg
½ cup coarsely chopped pecans
¼ cup packed brown sugar
1 tablespoon unsalted butter, melted

In a medium mixer bowl beat the ½ cup butter and the cream cheese with an electric mixer till well blended. Stir in the flour. Divide dough into 24 balls, 1 inch in diameter, and press the dough evenly into bottom and up sides of twenty-four 1¾-inch muffin pans. Bake in a 325° oven for 10 minutes.

◆ Pumpkin Nut Cups, 8th Place,
Susan Drabic, Laurys Station, Pennsylvania

Combine the ½ cup brown sugar, pumpkin, egg yolk, cream or milk, the 4 teaspoons butter, rum or rum flavoring, vanilla, cinnamon, and nutmeg. Spoon into warm prebaked cups. Stir together nuts, remaining brown sugar, and remaining butter; sprinkle over pumpkin mixture.

Bake in a 325° oven 25 minutes. Cool in pans for 10 minutes. Loosen and remove cups from pans. Serve warm or cool. Makes 24 cookies.

Nutrition facts per cookie: 116 cal., 8 g total fat (4 g sat. fat), 26 mg chol., 14 mg sodium, 10 g carbo., 0 g fiber, 1 g pro. Daily Value: 13% vit. A, 0% vit. C, 1% calcium, 3% iron.

Sesame-Apricot Thumbprints

KAREN RESCINITI ROLLS THESE BUTTERY COOKIES IN SESAME SEED AND FILLS THEM WITH ASSORTED FLAVORS OF JAM.

1 cup unsalted butter
¼ cup packed brown sugar
2 cups all-purpose flour

◆ Sesame-Apricot Thumbprints, 9th Place,
Karen Resciniti, Tampa, Florida

1 teaspoon almond extract
¼ teaspoon salt
4 to 5 tablespoons sesame seed, toasted
Apricot preserves, currant jelly, and/or grape jelly

In a large mixer bowl beat butter and brown sugar with an electric mixer on medium speed till light and fluffy. Beat in the flour, almond extract, and salt till well combined. Shape into 1-inch balls; roll in sesame seed.

Place balls 1½ inches apart on lightly greased cookie sheets. Flatten cookies slightly and indent centers with thumb; fill with preserves, using about ½ teaspoon for each. Bake in a 375° oven about 10 minutes or till edges are firm. Cool cookies on wire racks. Makes 40 cookies.

Nutrition facts per cookie: 71 cal., 4 g total fat (2 g sat. fat), 9 mg chol., 15 mg sodium, 8 g carbo., 0 g fiber, 1 g pro. Daily Value: 3% vit. A.

◆ Cardamom Crescents, 10th Place.
Nanette L. Wesley, Jackson, Georgia

Cardamom Crescents
1 cup whole hazelnuts or blanched
almonds, finely ground
1 cup sugar
½ cup butter
1¾ cups all-purpose flour
2 eggs
1 teaspoon instant coffee granules
1 teaspoon ground cardamom
½ teaspoon baking powder
Nonstick spray coating
1 cup semisweet chocolate pieces
1 teaspoon shortening
1 cup hazelnuts or blanched almonds,
finely chopped

In food processor bowl* combine hazelnuts or almonds, sugar, and butter. Cover; process till fluffy. Add flour, eggs, coffee, cardamom, and baking powder. Cover; process till mixture forms a ball. Transfer to a bowl. Cover and chill for 1 hour.

Spray cookie sheets with nonstick coating. Form rounded teaspoonfuls of dough into 2-inch crescent shapes. Place the crescents 1 inch apart on prepared cookie sheets. Bake in a 350° oven for 12 to 15 minutes or till edges of cookies are golden. Cool on wire racks.

Heat and stir chocolate pieces and shortening over very low heat till chocolate begins to melt. Remove from heat and stir till smooth. Quickly dip one end of each crescent into chocolate and then into chopped nuts. Transfer cookies to racks over waxed paper to dry. Makes 60 cookies.

*Note: If you do not have a food processor, finely grind nuts, half at a time, in a blender. In a large mixer bowl beat sugar and butter with an electric mixer on medium speed till fluffy. Stir in nuts. Add eggs, coffee, cardamom, and baking powder. Beat till well combined. Beat in as much of the flour as you can. Stir in remaining flour. Cover and chill for 1 hour. Continue as directed.

Nutrition facts per cookie: 79 cal., 5 g total fat (1 g sat. fat), 11 mg chol., 21 mg sodium, 8 g carbo., 0 g fiber, 1 g pro. Daily Value: 1% vit. A, 0% vit. C, 1% calcium, 2% iron.

Merry Middles
INSTEAD OF ICING THESE CHOCOLATE-FILLED COOKIES, SIMPLY ROLL THEM IN COLORED SUGAR OR CANDY SPRINKLES, AS SHOWN ON PAGE 187.

½ cup butter
¼ cup butter-flavored shortening
1 egg
2 egg yolks
1 cup sugar
2 teaspoons vanilla
½ teaspoon baking powder
½ teaspoon salt

2½ cups all-purpose flour
⅓ cup sifted powdered sugar
2 tablespoons unsweetened cocoa powder
1 tablespoon melted butter
¼ teaspoon almond extract
½ cup semisweet chocolate pieces
2 teaspoons butter-flavored shortening
½ cup vanilla-flavored pieces

Beat butter and ¼ cup shortening with an electric mixer on medium to high speed for 30 seconds. Add egg, egg yolks, sugar, vanilla, baking powder, and salt. Beat till combined. Beat or stir in the flour.

Transfer ¾ cup of the dough to a small mixing bowl. Add powdered sugar, cocoa powder, and the 1 tablespoon melted butter. Beat well. Roll into 1-inch balls. Beat almond extract into the remaining dough.

For each cookie, mold about 1 tablespoon of the almond-flavored dough around each cocoa ball. Roll gently to make a smooth round ball. Place 2 inches apart on ungreased cookie sheets. Cover and chill for 1 hour.

Bake in a 375° oven for 10 to 11 minutes or till bottoms are lightly browned. Cool for 1 minute; transfer cookies to wire racks. Cool.

In a small heavy saucepan combine chocolate pieces and 1 teaspoon of the remaining shortening. Heat and stir over very low heat till chocolate begins to melt. Remove from heat; stir till smooth. In another pan, repeat with vanilla pieces and remaining shortening. Drizzle or pipe chocolate icing over cookies, then drizzle or pipe with vanilla icing. Makes about 30 cookies.

◆ Merry Middles, 11th Place, Kimberely Diehl, Idaho Falls, Idaho

◆ Hidden Treasure Cookies, 12th Place, Phyllis Briggs, Guilford, Maine

Nutrition facts per cookie: 150 cal., 8 g total fat (3 g sat. fat), 31 mg chol., 82 mg sodium, 19 g carbo., 0 g fiber, 2 g pro.

Hidden Treasure Cookies

SURPRISE! EACH FLUFFY MERINGUE IS FILLED WITH A STRIPED CANDY KISS.

1 cup all-purpose flour
3 tablespoons brown sugar
⅛ teaspoon salt
½ cup butter, softened
18 milk chocolate kisses with stripes and almonds
2 egg whites
¼ cup granulated sugar
1 teaspoon cornstarch
⅛ teaspoon baking powder
½ ounce grated semisweet chocolate (optional)

Combine flour, brown sugar, and salt. Cut in butter with pastry blender or work it in with your fingers till mixture forms a ball. Divide into 18 portions, about 1 inch each. Roll each into a ball. Place on ungreased cookie sheets. Press to 1½ inches in diameter with the bottom of a floured small glass. Bake in a 350° oven 12 to 15 minutes or till bottom is lightly browned. Cool for 1 minute. Place one candy in the center of each cookie. Cool on cookie sheet till candy is firm.* Reduce oven temperature to 300°.

For meringue, in a small bowl beat egg whites, granulated sugar, cornstarch, and baking powder till stiff peaks form. Pipe or spoon meringue over each candy and onto the cookie base. Sprinkle with the grated chocolate. Bake in a 300° oven for 20 minutes or till lightly browned. Cool on racks. Makes 18 cookies.

*Note: You can make the cookies up to this point and store, covered, for up to 3 days. Once meringue is added, cookies do not store well.

Nutrition facts per cookie: 117 cal., 7 g total fat (4 g sat. fat), 15 mg chol., 80 mg sodium, 12 g carbo., 0 g fiber, 2 g pro. Daily Value: 5% vit. A, 1% calcium, 3% iron.

Prize Tested Recipes

Nutty Blue Cheese Rolls

MADE WITH REFRIGERATED PIECRUST, THIS FLAKY APPETIZER BELONGS IN YOUR FILE OF EASY-TO-MAKE RECIPES.

⅔ cup finely chopped walnuts
⅓ cup crumbled blue cheese
1 tablespoon finely snipped parsley
¼ teaspoon pepper
½ of a 15-ounce package folded
refrigerated piecrust (1 crust)
1 tablespoon milk
2 teaspoons grated Parmesan cheese
Finely snipped parsley

For filling, in a medium mixing bowl stir together walnuts, blue cheese, 1 tablespoon parsley, and pepper. On a lightly floured surface, unfold piecrust according to package directions. Spread filling evenly over the crust. Cut the pastry circle into 12 wedges. Starting at wide ends, loosely roll up wedges. Place rolls, tip side down, on a greased baking sheet. Cover; chill for up to 24 hours, if desired.

Before baking, brush rolls lightly with milk. Sprinkle with Parmesan cheese and additional parsley. Bake in a 425° oven about 15 minutes or till golden. Cool on a wire rack. Serve warm. Makes 12.

Nutrition facts per roll: 139 cal., 10 g total fat (1 g sat. fat), 8 mg chol., 130 mg sodium, 9 g carbo., 3 g fiber, 3 g pro. Daily Values: 1% vit. A, 1% vit. C, 2% calcium, 1% iron.

◆ Nutty Blue Cheese Rolls

$200 WINNER
Anne Evans
Southborough, Massachusets

Pesto-Artichoke Stuffing

ITALIAN-STYLE INGREDIENTS TURN ORDINARY STUFFING MIX INTO A SPECIAL HOLIDAY DISH.

1 6-ounce package chicken-flavored
stuffing mix
1 14½-ounce can pasta-style chunky
tomatoes

¼ cup margarine or butter
3 tablespoons pesto
2 tablespoons water*
1 14-ounce can artichoke hearts, rinsed,
drained, and chopped
¼ cup pine nuts or chopped almonds

In a 2-quart saucepan combine seasoning packet from stuffing mix, undrained tomatoes, margarine or butter, pesto, and water. Bring to boiling; add artichoke hearts. Reduce heat; cover and simmer for 6 minutes.

◆ Pesto-Artichoke Stuffing

Remove saucepan from heat. Stir in stuffing mix and pine nuts. Cover and let stand for 5 minutes. Fluff with a fork before serving. Makes 5 cups (about 8 servings).

*Note: For a moister stuffing, add 1 to 2 tablespoons more water after cooking.

Nutrition facts per serving: 233 cal., 13 g total fat (2 g sat. fat), 12 mg chol., 754 mg sodium, 25 g carbo., 1 g fiber, 6 g pro. Daily Value: 11% vit. A, 14% vit. C, 4% calcium, 11% iron.

$200 WINNER
Pat Ekas
Stockton, California

◆ Oh-So-Good Cornbread Stuffing

Oh-So-Good Cornbread Stuffing

USE LEFTOVER CORNBREAD OR BAKE A PACKAGE OF CORNBREAD MIX FOR THIS SOUTHERN-STYLE STUFFING.

2 cups chopped, peeled, raw sweet potatoes
1 cup chopped onion
1 cup sliced celery
¼ cup margarine or butter
1 tablespoon snipped cilantro
1 teaspoon ground ginger

5 cups coarsely crumbled cornbread
¾ cup chopped walnuts
2 to 4 tablespoons chicken broth

In a large skillet cook sweet potatoes, onion, and celery in hot margarine or butter 5 to 7 minutes or till just tender.

Spoon mixture into a large mixing bowl. Stir in cilantro and ginger. Add cornbread and walnuts; toss gently to coat. Add enough of the chicken broth to moisten.

Use to stuff one 8- to 10-pound bird or place the stuffing in a casserole. Bake the casserole, uncovered, in a 375° oven about 45 minutes or till heated through. Makes 6 cups stuffing (10 servings).

Nutrition facts per serving: 413 cal., 24 g total fat (2 g sat. fat), 27 mg chol., 476 mg sodium, 46 g carbo., 3 g fiber, 8 g pro. Daily Value: 95% vit. A, 22% vit. C, 9% calcium, 10% iron.

$100 WINNER
Carol Cavaner
Irvona, Pennsylvania

◆ Ginger Chicken-Bacon Bites

Ginger Chicken-Bacon Bites

IT'S A WRAP! WRAP BACON AROUND SOY-MARINATED CHICKEN AND SKEWER WITH A TOOTHPICK.

12 ounces boneless, skinless chicken breasts
¼ cup orange marmalade
2 tablespoons soy sauce
½ teaspoon ground ginger
⅛ teaspoon garlic powder
1 8-ounce can whole water chestnuts
12 slices bacon
Flowering kale (optional)
Carrot cutouts (optional)

Cut chicken breasts into 24 bite-size pieces. For marinade, in a medium mixing bowl combine marmalade, soy sauce, ginger, and garlic powder. Add chicken pieces; cover and chill for 30 minutes.

Meanwhile, arrange bacon slices on the unheated rack of a broiler pan; broil 4 to 5 inches from the heat for 1 to 2 minutes or till partially cooked but not crisp. Drain off fat. Cool. Halve bacon slices crosswise.

Cut water chestnuts in half crosswise. Drain the chicken pieces. Wrap each piece of bacon around a chicken piece and a water chestnut half; secure with a wooden pick. Place on the unheated rack of the broiler pan. Broil 4 to 5 inches from the heat for 3 to 5 minutes or till chicken is no longer pink in the center, turning once. Makes about 24.

Nutrition facts per serving: 46 cal., 2 g total fat (1 g sat. fat), 10 mg chol., 135 mg sodium, 3 g carbo., 0 g fiber, 4 g pro. Daily Value: 0% vit. A, 2% vit. C, 0% calcium, 1% iron.

$100 WINNER
Beth Hammell
Cedar Rapids, Iowa

December

From Hearth to Heart
Holiday Baking Around the World

Felicidad!
Celebrate, Southwestern Style

Hanukkah
A Time for Sharing

Prize Tested Recipes
*Apricot-Almond Chocolate Torte, Spiced Orange Mocha,
Hazelnut-Praline Dream, White Christmas Cake*

From Hearth To Heart
Holiday Baking Around the World

By Julia Malloy

Let the luscious breads, cakes, and cookies baked in other countries weave some magic into your holiday celebrations, just as they have in the Old World. Each of these treasured recipes brings from its homeland time-honored traditions that symbolize the true meaning of the season—the birth of Christ, the spirit of giving, and hope for the new year to come.

◆ Pepparkakor, Sweden

◆ Berliner Kranser, Norway

◆ Lucia Buns, Sweden

Lucia Buns
(Sweden)

ON ST. LUCIA'S DAY (DECEMBER 13), SWEDISH DAUGHTERS DON FLICKERING CROWNS OF CANDLES AND GREENERY AND SERVE THEIR PARENTS COFFEE AND THESE SPICED BUNS.

2½ to 3 cups all-purpose flour
1 package active dry yeast
¾ cup milk
⅓ cup sugar
¼ cup margarine or butter
½ teaspoon salt
¼ teaspoon ground cardamom
⅛ teaspoon ground saffron
1 egg
¼ cup light raisins
¼ cup slivered almonds, ground
(see note, page 227)
Light raisins
1 slightly beaten egg white
1 tablespoon water
Sugar

In a large mixing bowl stir together 1 cup of the flour and the yeast; set aside. In a small saucepan heat and stir milk, ⅓ cup sugar, margarine or butter, salt, cardamom, and saffron just till warm (120° to 130°) and margarine is almost melted. Add milk mixture to flour mixture. Add whole egg. Beat with an electric mixer on low to medium speed for 30 seconds, scraping the sides of the bowl constantly. Beat on high speed for 3 minutes more. Stir in the ¼ cup raisins, ground almonds, and as much remaining flour as you can.

Turn the dough out onto a lightly floured surface. Knead in enough of the remaining flour to make a moderately soft dough that is smooth and elastic (3 to 5 minutes total). Shape into a ball.

Place dough in a lightly greased bowl; turn once to grease the surface. Cover and let rise in a warm place till double (1 to 1¼ hours).

Punch dough down. Turn dough out onto a lightly floured surface. Divide in half. Cover and let rest for 10 minutes.

To shape buns, divide each dough portion into 12 equal pieces. Roll each piece of dough into a 12-inch-long rope. Place 3 inches apart on greased baking sheets. Form each rope into an S shape, coiling ends in a snail fashion. (If desired, make double buns by pressing the centers of 2 of the S-shaped pieces together to form a cross.) Press one raisin into the center of each coil. Cover and let rise in a warm place till nearly double (30 to 40 minutes).

Mix the slightly beaten egg white and water; lightly brush onto buns. Sprinkle with sugar. Bake in a 350° oven about 12 minutes or till golden. Remove from baking sheets. Serve warm or cool. Makes 24 single or 12 double buns.

Brown-and-Serve Lucia Buns: Prepare and shape Lucia Buns as above; let rise till nearly double (30 to 40 minutes). Do not brush with egg white mixture or sprinkle with sugar. Bake in a 325° oven 10 minutes (do not brown). Remove from pan and cool thoroughly. Transfer to freezer bags. Seal, label, and freeze for up to 4 months.

To serve, open bag. Let stand at room temperature for 15 minutes. Uncover; place on a greased baking sheet. Brush with egg white mixture; sprinkle with sugar. Bake in a 375° oven for 8 to 10 minutes or till brown. Remove from baking sheets. Serve warm or cool.

Nutrition facts per single-S bun: 97 cal., 3 g total fat (1 g sat. fat), 9 mg chol., 76 mg sodium, 16 g carbo.,

1 g fiber, 2 g pro. Daily Value: 3% vit. A, 0% vit. C, 1% calcium, 4% iron.

Berliner Kranser (Butter Knot Cookies)
(Norway)

THIS RICH BUTTERY COOKIE IS BUT ONE OF MANY SERVED WITH COFFEE ON CHRISTMAS EVE IN SCANDINAVIA.

1 cup butter
½ cup sifted powdered sugar
1 hard-cooked egg yolk, sieved
1 raw egg yolk
1 teaspoon vanilla
2¼ cups all-purpose flour
1 slightly beaten egg white
2 to 3 tablespoons pearl sugar or
coarse sugar

In a large mixing bowl beat butter with an electric mixer on medium to high speed till softened. Add powdered sugar; beat till fluffy. Beat in egg yolks and vanilla. Beat in flour till combined. Cover and chill dough 1 hour or till firm enough to handle. (Chilling longer may make dough too firm to roll.)

Using about 1 tablespoon dough for each cookie, roll into 6-inch-long ropes. On an ungreased cookie sheet shape each into a ring, overlapping about 1 inch from ends. Brush with egg white; sprinkle with pearl or coarse sugar.

Bake in a 325° oven 18 to 20 minutes or till edges are light brown. Cool on cookie sheet for 1 minute. Remove; cool completely on a rack. Makes about 36.

Nutrition facts per cookie: 83 cal., 5 g total fat (3 g sat. fat), 25 mg chol., 54 mg sodium, 8 g carbo., 0 g fiber, 1 g pro. Daily Value: 6% vit. A, 0% vit. C, 0% calcium, 2% iron.

Pepparkakor
(Ginger Snaps)
(Sweden)

HEARTS, STARS, MEN, AND GOATS ARE THE FAVORED SHAPES FOR THESE SPICY SWEDISH COOKIES.

½ cup sugar
½ cup light molasses
¼ cup shortening
¼ cup butter or margarine
1 beaten egg
1 teaspoon ground cinnamon
½ teaspoon finely shredded orange peel
½ teaspoon ground allspice
½ teaspoon ground nutmeg
¼ teaspoon salt
¼ teaspoon baking soda
¼ teaspoon ground cardamom
¼ teaspoon ground cloves
2½ cups all-purpose flour
Finely chopped, slivered, or sliced nuts
(optional)
Candied cherries, quartered
(optional)

In a 2-quart saucepan combine sugar, molasses, shortening, and butter or margarine. Bring to boiling; reduce heat. Cook and stir over low heat till boiling. Cook and stir for 2 minutes more. Remove from heat; cool for 45 minutes.

Add egg, cinnamon, orange peel, allspice, nutmeg, salt, baking soda, cardamom, and cloves to saucepan, stirring well to mix. Add flour, one-third at a time, stirring well after each addition. Divide dough in half. Wrap and chill dough for 2 to 24 hours or till firm enough to handle.

On a well-floured surface, roll each portion of dough to ⅛-inch thickness. Cut into desired shapes (such as hearts or stars) with a 2½- to 3-inch cookie cutter. Arrange on a lightly greased cookie sheet. If desired, top with nuts or candied cherries.

Bake in a 375° oven for 5 to 6 minutes or till edges are light brown. Transfer cookies to a wire rack to cool. Makes 3 to 4 dozen (2½- to 3-inch) cookies.

Nutrition facts per cookie: 77 cal., 3 g total fat (1 g sat. fat), 9 mg chol., 39 mg sodium, 12 g carbo., 0 g fiber, 1 g pro. Daily Value: 1% vit. A, 0% vit. C, 0% calcium, 4% iron.

◆ Lingonberry Meringue Torte

Lingonberry
Meringue Torte
(Austria)

A MERINGUE IS THE TRADITIONAL TOPPER FOR THIS ALPINE WONDER, BUT FOR A SHORTCUT, YOU CAN FROST THE CAKE LAYERS WITH SWEETENED WHIPPED CREAM AND SKIP THE BROWNING STEP.

1 cup butter
4 eggs
2 cups all-purpose flour
1 teaspoon baking powder
¼ teaspoon ground nutmeg (optional)
1 cup sugar
1 teaspoon vanilla
½ cup water

continued on page 220

continued from page 219
¼ cup sugar
¼ cup light rum
¾ cup lingonberry or
raspberry preserves
4 egg whites
¼ teaspoon cream of tartar
⅓ cup sugar
1½ cups sugar
¼ cup water

For cake, allow butter and 4 eggs to stand at room temperature for 30 minutes. Grease and lightly flour a 9-inch springform pan or two 9-inch round cake pans; set aside. In a small mixing bowl stir together flour, baking powder, and nutmeg, if desired; set aside.

In a large mixing bowl beat butter with an electric mixer on medium speed for 30 seconds.

Gradually add 1 cup sugar to butter, 2 tablespoons at a time, beating on medium to high speed about 6 minutes or till very light and fluffy. Add vanilla. Add eggs, one at a time, beating for 1 minute after each addition, scraping the bowl often. Gradually add flour mixture to butter mixture, beating on low to medium speed just till combined.

Pour batter into the prepared pan(s); spread evenly. Bake in a 325° oven till a toothpick inserted near the center comes out clean, allowing about 50 minutes for the springform pan or 25 to 30 minutes for the 9-inch round pans. Cool in pan on a wire rack for 10 minutes.

Remove sides from springform pan or remove layers from cake pans. Cool completely on a wire rack. If using a springform pan, cut the cooled cake horizontally into 2 layers; do not remove bottom layer from pan base. (At this point, the cake layers can be wrapped

◆ Crostata, Italy

and frozen for up to 3 months. Thaw before assembling cake.)

For rum syrup, in a saucepan bring the ½ cup water and ¼ cup sugar to boiling; boil, uncovered, for 2 minutes. Remove from heat; stir in rum. Cool.

To assemble, place one cake layer on the bottom of a springform pan without sides. Place the cake on a baking sheet or on an ovenproof platter. With the tines of a fork, poke holes in cake; spoon half of the syrup over cake. Spread with preserves. Top with second cake layer; spoon remaining syrup over cake.

For meringue, let the 4 egg whites stand in a large mixing bowl at room temperature 30 minutes. Add cream of tartar. Beat with an electric mixer on medium speed till soft peaks form (tips curl). Gradually add ⅓ cup sugar, 1 tablespoon at a time, beating on high

speed till stiff peaks form and sugar is almost dissolved (5 to 6 minutes). Set meringue aside.

In a small saucepan combine 1½ cups sugar and ¼ cup water; cook and stir till boiling. Cook, without stirring, to 248° on a thermometer. Remove from heat. Immediately add hot syrup in a steady stream to egg whites while beating on low speed. Beat till cool, about 4 minutes. Spread meringue over cake. Using a pastry bag fitted with a large star tip, pipe any remaining meringue to decorate cake. Bake in a 450° oven for 5 minutes or till light brown. Chill, loosely covered, till ready to serve, up to 24 hours. Makes 12 servings.

Nutrition facts per slice: 499 cal., 17 g total fat (10 g sat. fat), 112 mg chol., 228 mg sodium, 81 g carbo., 1 g fiber, 6 g pro. Daily Value: 17% vit. A, 4% calcium, 9% iron.

Twist each pastry wedge twice at the narrow end, then place atop the apples and figs, arranging in a circle with the wide ends toward the edge.

Crostata
(Italy)

THE SECRET TO SHAPING THE TWISTS OF
RICH TART PASTRY LIES IN KEEPING THE
DOUGH CHILLED UNTIL YOU'RE READY
TO SHAPE IT. IF THE DOUGH BECOMES
TOO WARM, JUST POP IT BACK INTO THE
REFRIGERATOR FOR A FEW MINUTES.

2 cups all-purpose flour
⅓ cup sugar
1½ teaspoons baking powder
⅓ cup margarine or butter
1 slightly beaten egg
⅓ cup milk
1 teaspoon vanilla
4 cups sliced, peeled apples
½ cup snipped dried figs
⅔ cup apricot or peach preserves
Milk
Sugar

In a medium mixing bowl stir together flour, sugar, and baking powder. Cut in margarine or butter till mixture resembles coarse crumbs. Combine egg, milk, and vanilla; add to flour mixture. Mix well. Shape into a ball.

On a lightly floured surface, knead dough gently for 10 to 12 strokes or till smooth. Wrap and chill one-third of the dough. Pat remaining dough onto the bottom and up the sides of a 10- or 11-inch tart pan with removable bottom.

Arrange apple slices and figs on pastry in tart pan. Stir and spoon preserves evenly over fruit.

On a lightly floured surface, roll the chilled pastry into a 9- or 10-inch circle. Cut into 12 wedges. Twist each wedge twice at the narrow end; arrange in a circle atop apples. Brush with milk. Top with sugar.

Bake in a 375° oven for 40 to 45 minutes or till fruit is tender. If necessary, to prevent overbrowning, cover loosely with foil the last 10 to 15 minutes of baking. Remove sides of pan before serving. Serve warm. Makes 8 to 10 servings.

Nutrition facts per slice: 365 cal., 9 g total fat (2 g sat. fat), 28 mg chol., 176 mg sodium, 68 g carbo., 3 g fiber, 5 g pro. Daily Value: 11% vit. A, 6% vit. C, 9% calcium, 14% iron.

Rum Babas
(Russia)

THE BABA MOLDS TRADITIONALLY USED
FOR THESE INDIVIDUAL RUM-SOAKED
SPONGE CAKES ARE TALL AND NARROW.
MUFFIN OR POPOVER PANS MAKE GOOD
SUBSTITUTES.

2 cups all-purpose flour
1 package active dry yeast
⅓ cup milk
1 tablespoon sugar

◆ Rum Babas. Russia

½ teaspoon salt
4 eggs
½ cup margarine or butter
½ cup light raisins
1 teaspoon finely shredded orange peel
1½ cups water
¾ cup sugar
⅓ cup rum
½ cup apricot preserves
1 tablespoon water
¾ cup whipping cream (optional)
¾ cup dairy sour cream (optional)

In a bowl stir together 1½ cups of the flour and the yeast; set aside. In a small saucepan heat and stir milk, the 1 tablespoon sugar, and salt just till warm (120° to 130°).

Add milk mixture to flour mixture. Add eggs. Beat with an electric mixer on low to medium speed for 30 seconds, scraping the bowl constantly. Beat on

continued on page 222

continued from page 221

high speed for 3 minutes more. Using a spoon, stir in as much of the remaining flour as you can. (The batter will be soft and sticky.) Cut margarine or butter into small pieces; place atop batter. Cover; let rise in a warm place till double (about 1 hour).

Grease twelve ½-cup baba molds, twelve 2½-inch muffin cups, or 8 popover pan cups. Set aside.

Stir margarine or butter, raisins, and orange peel into the batter. Divide the batter among molds or cups, filling each ½ to ⅔ full. Cover and let rise in a warm place for 20 to 30 minutes or till the batter fills the molds or cups. (Or, cover and refrigerate overnight.)

Bake in a 350° oven for 15 to 20 minutes or till golden. (If dough is made ahead and chilled, let it stand at room temperature for 20 minutes before baking.) Remove the baked babas from mold. Cool on a wire rack with waxed paper underneath the racks.

For the sugar syrup, in a small heavy saucepan stir together the 1½ cups water and the ¾ cup sugar. Cook and stir over medium heat till the sugar is dissolved. Bring to boiling. Boil, uncovered, without stirring, for 5 minutes. Remove from heat; cool slightly. Stir in the rum.

Using the tines of a large fork, prick babas all over. Dip babas, top sides down, into the sugar syrup 2 or 3 times or till moistened. Return to rack. Spoon any remaining syrup over babas.

For glaze, if necessary, snip any large pieces of apricot in the preserves. In a small saucepan combine the preserves and the 1 tablespoon water. Heat and stir over low heat till preserves are melted. Brush some of the glaze onto the babas.

◆ Florentines, Italy

For cream sauce, if desired, in a small mixing bowl stir together whipping cream and sour cream.

To serve, spoon cream sauce onto 8 or 12 dessert plates. Place a baba on each plate. Makes 8 or 12 babas.

Nutrition facts per baba baked in a baba mold or muffin pan: 291 cal., 10 g total fat (2 g sat. fat), 72 mg chol., 206 mg sodium, 44 g carbo., 1 g fiber, 5 g pro. Daily Value: 13% vit. A, 1% vit. C, 2% calcium, 9% iron.

Florentines
(Italy)

A SWIRL OF WHITE CHOCOLATE GIVES A NEW TWIST TO THE DARK CHOCOLATE THAT TRADITIONALLY COATS THESE CHEWY CHRISTMAS COOKIES.

6 tablespoons butter
⅓ cup milk
¼ cup sugar
2 tablespoons honey
1 cup sliced almonds
*½ cup finely chopped candied
mixed fruits and peel*

¼ cup all-purpose flour
¾ cup semisweet chocolate pieces
2 tablespoons shortening
2 ounces white baking bar
2 teaspoons shortening

In a medium saucepan combine butter, milk, sugar, and honey. Bring to a full rolling boil, stirring occasionally. Remove from heat (mixture will appear curdled). Stir in almonds and candied fruits and peels. Stir in flour.

Drop batter by level tablespoons at least 3 inches apart onto a greased and lightly floured cookie sheet (do not use an insulated cookie sheet). Using the back of a spoon, spread the batter into 3-inch circles. Bake in a 350° oven for 8 to 10 minutes or till the edges are light brown.

Cool on a cookie sheet 1 minute. Carefully transfer to waxed paper. Cool thoroughly.

Repeat with the remaining batter, greasing and flouring the cookie sheet between batches.

In a small heavy saucepan heat semisweet chocolate pieces and 2 tablespoons shortening over low heat till melted, stirring occasionally. Spread the bottom of each cookie with about 1 teaspoon of the chocolate mixture.

In another small saucepan melt white baking bar and the 2 teaspoons shortening. Drizzle white chocolate onto dark chocolate. To marble, draw the tines of a fork through the white chocolate. Store, covered, in the refrigerator. Makes about 24 cookies.

Nutrition facts per cookie: 131 cal., 9 g total fat (3 g sat. fat), 8 mg chol., 33 mg sodium, 13 g carbo., 0 g fiber, 2 g pro. Daily Value: 2% vit. A, 0% vit. C, 2% calcium, 3% iron.

Three Kings' Ring
(Mexico)

ON JANUARY 6 (EPIPHANY), MEXICAN AND SPANISH FAMILIES GATHER TO FEAST ON THIS FRUIT-AND-NUT-FILLED YEAST BREAD AND SIP ON COFFEE, HOT CHOCOLATE, OR LIMEADE.

3¼ to 3¾ cups all-purpose flour
1 package active dry yeast
⅔ cup milk
⅓ cup margarine or butter
⅓ cup granulated sugar
½ teaspoon salt
2 eggs
3 tablespoons margarine or butter, softened
¼ cup granulated sugar
2 teaspoons ground cinnamon
¾ cup diced candied mixed fruits and peel
½ cup chopped toasted almonds
1 cup sifted powdered sugar
¼ teaspoon vanilla
1 to 2 tablespoons orange juice
Ground cinnamon
Finely shredded orange peel
(optional)

◆ Three Kings' Ring, Mexico

In a large mixing bowl stir together 1½ cups of the flour and the yeast; set aside. In a small saucepan heat and stir milk, the ⅓ cup margarine or butter, the ⅓ cup granulated sugar, and salt just till warm (120° to 130°) and margarine or butter is almost melted. Add milk mixture to flour mixture; add eggs.

Beat with an electric mixer on low speed for 30 seconds, scraping the sides of the bowl constantly. Beat on high speed for 3 minutes more. Using a spoon, stir in as much of the remaining flour as you can.

Turn the dough out onto a lightly floured surface. Knead in enough of the remaining flour to make a moderately soft dough that is smooth and elastic (3 to 5 minutes total).

Shape the dough into a ball. Place in a lightly greased bowl; turn once to grease the surface. Cover and let rise in a warm place till double (1 to 1½ hours).

Punch dough down. Turn out onto a lightly floured surface. Cover; let rest 10 minutes. Roll dough into a 20x12-inch rectangle. Spread with the 3 tablespoons softened margarine or butter.

For filling, in a small mixing bowl combine the ¼ cup granulated sugar and cinnamon. Add mixed fruits and peel and almonds; toss gently to coat. Sprinkle the mixture onto the surface of the dough.

Beginning at a long side, loosely roll up the dough jelly-roll style. Moisten edges; pinch firmly to seal. Place roll, seam side down, on a greased baking sheet. Bring ends together to form a ring. Moisten ends; pinch together to seal ring. Flatten slightly. Using a sharp knife, make 12 cuts around the edge of the dough at 1½-inch intervals, cutting about two-thirds of the way to the center. Cover and let rise in a warm place till nearly double (30 to 40 minutes).

Bake in a 350° oven for 25 to 30 minutes or till bread sounds hollow when tapped. Cover with foil after 20 minutes, if necessary, to prevent overbrowning. Remove from baking sheet; cool on a wire rack.

For icing, in a small mixing bowl combine powdered sugar and vanilla. Stir in enough orange juice (about 4 teaspoons) to make an icing of drizzling consistency. Spoon icing over ring. Before icing dries, sprinkle with cinnamon and orange peel, if desired. Makes 1 ring (12 servings).

Nutrition facts per slice: 335 cal., 12 g total fat (2 g sat. fat), 37 mg chol., 200 mg sodium, 53 g carbo., 2 g fiber, 6 g pro. Daily Value: 12% vit. A, 1% vit. C, 4% calcium, 13% iron.

◆ Christopsomo Bread, Greece

Christopsomo Bread
(Greece)

THIS BREAD IS DECORATED WITH A CROSS OF DOUGH TO REPRESENT CHRIST. IN SOME REGIONS, BAKERS LEAVE A HAND IMPRINT IN THE TOP, TELLING THEIR CHILDREN THAT JESUS BLESSED THE LOAF WHILE IT WAS BAKING. OTHER BAKERS SHAPE THE BREAD TO SYMBOLIZE THE FAMILY'S PROFESSION.

2¾ to 3¼ cups all-purpose flour
1 package active dry yeast
¾ cup milk
¼ cup margarine or butter
¼ cup sugar
½ teaspoon salt
1 egg
½ cup snipped dried apricots or light raisins
½ cup chopped walnuts
1 teaspoon finely shredded lemon peel
4 unshelled walnuts
1 beaten egg
1 tablespoon water
1 teaspoon sesame seed

In a small mixing bowl stir together 1½ cups of the flour and the yeast; set aside. In a medium saucepan heat and stir milk, margarine or butter, sugar, and salt just till warm (120° to 130°) and margarine or butter is almost melted. Add milk mixture to flour mixture; add the first egg. Beat with an electric mixer on low speed 30 seconds, scraping sides of bowl constantly. Beat on high speed for 3 minutes more. Using a spoon, stir in apricots or raisins, chopped walnuts, lemon peel, and as much of the remaining flour as you can.

Turn dough out onto a lightly floured surface. Knead in enough of the remaining flour to make a moderately soft dough that is smooth and elastic (3 to 5 minutes). Shape dough into a ball. Place in a greased bowl; turn once to grease the surface. Cover and let rise in a warm place till double (1¼ to 1½ hours).

Punch dough down. Turn out onto a lightly floured surface. Divide dough into thirds. Cover; let rest 10 minutes. Remove one-third of the dough; divide into 8 pieces. Roll 4 pieces to four 14-inch-long ropes; roll 4 pieces to four 12-inch-long ropes. Twist together 2 ropes of the same length; repeat with the remaining ropes, making 4 twisted ropes total.

Shape the 2 remaining portions of dough into one ball; flatten to a 6-inch round loaf. Place on a lightly greased baking sheet. Wrap 2 long twisted ropes around the base, one on each side, pinching ends together to seal. Lay the 2 shorter twisted ropes across the top to form a cross. Press one unshelled walnut at the four points where the ends of the cross meet the base of the bread. Cover;

◆ Baklava, Greece

let rise in warm place till nearly double (30 to 45 minutes).

Brush the dough with a mixture of 1 beaten egg and water. Sprinkle with sesame seed. Bake in a 350° oven for 30 to 35 minutes or till the bread sounds hollow when tapped. Cover loosely with foil the last 15 minutes to prevent over-browning, if necessary. Remove from pan; cool completely on a wire rack. Makes 1 loaf (16 servings).

Make-ahead directions: Bake the loaf as directed. Cover tightly and freeze for up to 4 months.

Nutrition facts per slice: 161 cal., 6 g total fat (1 g sat. fat), 27 mg chol., 115 mg sodium, 22 g carbo., 1 g fiber, 4 g pro. Daily Value: 8% vit. A, 0% vit. C, 2% calcium, 9% iron.

Baklava
(Greece)

TO PREVENT THE PAPER-THIN PHYLLO DOUGH FROM DRYING OUT, KEEP THE UNUSED DOUGH COVERED WITH A SLIGHTLY DAMP TOWEL UNTIL YOU'RE READY TO USE IT.

4 cups (1 pound) walnuts, finely chopped
2 cups sugar
1 teaspoon ground cinnamon
1¼ cups margarine or butter, melted
1 16-ounce package frozen phyllo dough
(about twenty 18x14-inch sheets), thawed
1 cup water
¼ cup honey
½ teaspoon finely shredded lemon peel
2 tablespoons lemon juice
2 inches stick cinnamon
Grape leaves (optional)

For filling, in a large mixing bowl stir together chopped walnuts, ½ cup of the sugar, and ground cinnamon. Set aside.

Brush the bottom of a 15x10x1-inch baking pan with some of the melted margarine or butter. Unfold phyllo dough. Keep phyllo covered, removing sheets as you need them. Layer one-fourth (about 5) of the phyllo sheets in the pan, generously brushing each sheet with melted margarine or butter as you layer, and allowing phyllo to extend up the sides of the pan. Sprinkle about 1½ cups of the filling on top of the phyllo. Repeat layering the phyllo sheets and filling twice.

Layer remaining phyllo sheets atop the third layer of filling, brushing each sheet with margarine or butter before adding the next phyllo sheet. Drizzle any remaining margarine or butter over the top layers. Trim edges of phyllo to fit the pan. Using a sharp knife, cut through all the layers to make 60 diamond-, triangle-, or square-shaped pieces.

Bake in a 325° oven for 35 to 45 minutes or till golden. Slightly cool baklava in the pan on a wire rack.

◆ Cake of Kings, France

Meanwhile, for syrup, in a medium saucepan combine remaining 1½ cups sugar, the water, honey, lemon peel, lemon juice, and stick cinnamon. Bring to boiling; reduce heat. Simmer, uncovered, for 20 minutes. Remove cinnamon. Pour honey mixture over slightly cooled baklava in the pan. Cool completely. If desired, serve on a grape-leaf-lined platter. Makes about 60 pieces.

Nutrition facts per piece: 138 cal., 9 g total fat (1 g sat. fat), 0 mg chol., 82 mg sodium, 13 g carbo., 0 g fiber, 2 g pro. Daily Value: 4% vit. A, 0% vit. C, 0% calcium, 3% iron.

Cake of Kings
(France)

THIS SIMPLE ALMOND PASTRY REIGNS IN FRANCE AT TWELFTH NIGHT CELE-BRATIONS (TWELVE NIGHTS AFTER CHRISTMAS). ON THIS NIGHT, THE FRENCH HERALD THE VISIT OF THE THREE KINGS WHO BORE GIFTS TO THE HOLY INFANT. THE PASTRY IS OFTEN TOPPED WITH CROWNS OR KINGS TO SYMBOLIZE THE ROYAL VISITORS.

1 17¼-ounce package frozen
puff pastry (2 sheets)
4 ounces (½ of an 8-ounce can)
almond paste*
1¼ cups sifted powdered sugar
1½ teaspoons lemon juice
Water
Toasted sliced almonds
Cut-up candied red and green cherries
Chopped candied pineapple

Let folded pastry stand at room temperature for 20 minutes to thaw. Unfold. Cut out one 9-inch round from each sheet. If desired, cut pastry trimmings into small designs, such as hearts, stars, or triangles.

Place almond paste between 2 sheets of waxed paper; roll into a 9-inch round, evening edges with a knife if necessary. Remove top sheet of waxed paper.

On a baking sheet, place 1 round of puff pastry. Invert the round of almond paste onto pastry; remove waxed paper. Top with remaining round of puff pastry. If desired, for decoration, score the vertical sides of pastry with a table knife to make a scalloped edge. Bake in a 375° oven till golden brown, allowing 20 to 25 minutes for large rounds and 10 minutes for small cutouts. Remove from baking sheet; cool completely on a rack.

For icing, stir together powdered sugar, lemon juice, and enough water (1 to 2 teaspoons) to make an icing of drizzling consistency. Place waxed paper under rack. Spoon icing over pastry and cutouts, allowing icing to drizzle down sides. Top with sliced almonds, candied

continued on page 226

continued from page 225
cherries, and pineapple. Transfer to a platter. If desired, place cutouts around pastry. Cut into wedges to serve. Makes 12 servings.

*Note: This recipe was tested with almond paste containing just almonds and sugar. If the almond paste contains added corn or glucose syrup or fructose, your final results may be softer.

Nutrition facts per slice: 272 cal., 16 g total fat (0 g sat. fat), 0 mg chol., 154 mg sodium, 30 g carbo., 0 g fiber, 3 g pro. Daily Value: 0% vit. A, 0% vit. C, 2% calcium, 2% iron.

Kolacky
(Czechoslovakia)

FOR THE JUICY FRUIT FILLING IN KOLACKY (KOH-LAH-CHEE), CHOOSE EITHER TANGY APRICOT OR EASY CHERRY.

3¾ to 4¼ cups all-purpose flour
1 package active dry yeast
1 cup milk
¾ cup margarine or butter
½ cup sugar
½ teaspoon salt
4 egg yolks
1 recipe Apricot Filling or Cherry Filling
(see recipes, right)
2 tablespoons melted margarine or
butter, or milk
Powdered sugar

In a large mixing bowl stir together 2 cups of the flour and the yeast; set aside. In a medium saucepan heat and stir the 1 cup milk, the ¾ cup margarine or butter, sugar, and salt just till mixture

◆ Kolacky, Czechoslovakia

is warm and the margarine or butter is almost melted (120° to 130°).

Add milk mixture to the flour mixture. Add egg yolks. Beat with an electric mixer on low to medium speed for 30 seconds, scraping the sides of the bowl constantly. Beat on high speed for 3 minutes more. Using a wooden spoon, stir in as much of the remaining flour as you can.

Turn the dough out onto a lightly floured surface. Knead in enough of the remaining flour to make a moderately soft dough that is smooth and elastic (3 to 5 minutes total). Shape the dough into a ball. Place dough in a lightly greased bowl; turn once to grease the surface. Cover and let rise in a warm place till double (1 to 1½ hours).

Meanwhile, prepare the Apricot or Cherry Filling. Punch the dough down. Turn dough out onto a lightly floured surface. Divide in half. Cover and let rest for 10 minutes.

Shape each dough portion into 12 balls, pulling the edges under to make smooth tops. Place the balls 3 inches apart on greased baking sheets. Flatten each ball to rounds that are 3½ inches in diameter. Cover and let rise till nearly double (about 35 minutes).

Using your thumb or fingers, make a 2-inch-wide indentation in the center of each dough circle. Spoon about 2 teaspoons of Apricot or Cherry Filling into each indentation. Lightly brush the 2 tablespoons melted margarine or milk around the edges.

Bake in a 375° oven for 10 to 12 minutes or till golden. Transfer to a wire rack to cool. Sift powdered sugar over tops before serving. Makes 24 rolls.

Apricot Filling: In a small saucepan combine 1 cup snipped *dried apricots* and enough *water* to cover apricots by about 1 inch. Bring to boiling; reduce heat. Cover and simmer for 10 to 15 minutes or till apricots are very soft. Drain, reserving 2 tablespoons of the cooking liquid.

In a blender container or food processor bowl place apricots, reserved liquid, ¼ cup *sugar*, 1 teaspoon *lemon juice*, ¼ teaspoon *ground cinnamon*, and ⅛ teaspoon *ground nutmeg*. Cover and blend or process till smooth, stopping to scrape the sides as necessary. Cool before using. Makes 1 cup.

Cherry Filling: In a mixing bowl stir together 1 cup *canned cherry pie filling*, ⅛ teaspoon *ground cardamom or allspice*, and ¼ teaspoon *rum extract*. Makes 1 cup.

Nutrition facts per Kolacky with Apricot Filling: 178 cal., 8 g total fat (2 g sat. fat), 36 mg chol., 130 mg sodium, 24 g carbo., 1 g fiber, 3 g pro. Daily Value: 18% vit. A, 0% vit. C, 2% calcium, 8% iron.

Hazelnut Torte
(Austria)

AUSTRIAN BAKERS PRIDE THEMSELVES ON RICH, FLOURLESS CAKES. IN THIS FABULOUS TIERED TORTE, FINELY GROUND NUTS REPLACE THE FLOUR.

6 egg yolks
¾ teaspoon ground cinnamon
1 cup sugar
2 teaspoons finely shredded lemon peel
6 egg whites
1 teaspoon cream of tartar
3 cups very finely ground* hazelnuts
(filberts) or almonds
½ cup fine dry bread crumbs
1 recipe Mocha Butter Frosting
(see recipe, right)
½ cup chopped hazelnuts
(filberts) or almonds
Whole hazelnuts (filberts)

Grease and lightly flour the bottom of a 9-inch springform pan or two 9-inch round cake pans.

In a medium mixing bowl beat egg yolks and cinnamon with an electric mixer on high speed about 6 minutes or till very thick and light colored. Gradually add ½ cup of the sugar, 1 tablespoon at a time, beating till sugar is dissolved. Stir in lemon peel. Set aside.

Wash beaters. In a large mixing bowl beat egg whites and cream of tartar on high speed till soft peaks form (tips curl). Gradually add the remaining ½ cup sugar, 1 tablespoon at a time. Beat till stiff peaks form (tips stand straight).

Fold egg yolk mixture into egg whites. Stir together the 3 cups ground nuts and

◆ Hazelnut Torte, Austria

the bread crumbs. Sprinkle about one-third of the nut mixture over egg mixture. Using a rubber spatula, gently fold nuts into egg mixture. Fold in remaining nut mixture, about one-third at a time. Turn batter into prepared springform pan or divide evenly between cake pans; spread evenly.

Bake in a 325° oven till the top springs back when lightly touched, allowing 55 to 60 minutes for the springform pan or about 30 minutes for the 9-inch cake pans. The cake may have a slight dip. Remove from oven; cool in the pan on a wire rack for 15 minutes.

Using a narrow metal spatula, loosen the sides of the cake from the springform pan. Remove sides of springform pan. Invert cake onto a wire rack; carefully remove bottom of pan. (Or, remove cake from baking pans.) Cool cake completely on wire racks. Wrap cake tightly with plastic wrap; chill overnight.

To frost, slice the cake from the springform pan horizontally into 2 equal layers or use the two 9-inch cake layers. Spread 1 layer with 1 cup of the Mocha Butter Frosting. Top with remaining cake layer. Set aside 1 cup of the frosting for piping. Frost the top and sides with remaining frosting.

To decorate, press the ½ cup chopped nuts onto sides of cake. Using a decorating bag fitted with a medium star tip, pipe reserved frosting around top edge and base. Garnish top with whole hazelnuts. Cover; chill overnight. Let stand for 15 minutes before serving. Makes 14 to 16 servings.

Mocha Butter Frosting: Dissolve 1 tablespoon *instant coffee crystals* in 3 tablespoons *milk*. In a small mixing bowl beat ¾ cup softened *butter* with an electric mixer on medium speed till light and fluffy. Beat in 2 ounces *unsweetened chocolate*, melted and cooled.

Gradually add 3 cups sifted *powdered sugar*, beating till combined. Beat in coffee mixture; 2 tablespoons *cognac, brandy, or orange juice;* and 1 teaspoon *vanilla*. Gradually beat in 1 cup sifted *powdered sugar*. Beat for 1 minute on high speed till light and fluffy. Beat in more *milk or powdered sugar,* if necessary, to make a frosting of spreading or piping consistency.

*Note: Grinding nuts can be tricky because nuts form a paste if ground too much. To prevent this, grind the nuts in small batches with a food grinder, blender, or food processor. If using a blender or food processor, try adding 1 tablespoon of the sugar from the recipe for each cup of nuts, then quickly start and stop the appliance for better control.

Nutrition facts per slice: 508 cal., 32 g total fat (9 g sat. fat), 118 mg chol., 156 mg sodium, 52 g carbo., 3 g fiber, 8 g pro. Daily Value: 23% vit. A, 1% vit. C, 6% calcium, 11% iron.

Felicidad!
Celebrate, Southwestern Style

By Joy Taylor

Inside the holiday home of Margaret and Ray Burns, the heady scent of roasting peppers mingles with that of pine. In the kitchen, pots of homemade tamales, posole, and chili sauce simmer while empanadas cool on the counter. And, outdoors, the brilliant farolitos beckon friends. It is these familiar fragrances and sights that herald the approach of Christmas in Taos, New Mexico.

Tamales
*1 2½ pound boneless pork shoulder or butt
roast, trimmed of excess fat and cut up
10 cups water
1 medium onion, quartered
3 cloves garlic, minced
1½ teaspoons salt
1 recipe Red Chili Sauce (4 cups)
(see recipe, page 229)
¾ cup shortening
6 cups masa harina
1½ teaspoons baking powder
2 teaspoons salt
About 50 dried corn husks
(about 8 inches long)*

In a 4½- to 5-quart Dutch oven bring pork, water, onion, garlic, and the 1½ teaspoons salt to boiling. Simmer, covered, for about 2¼ hours or till meat is very tender. Remove meat from broth; cool meat and broth. Using two forks, shred meat, discarding fat. (You should have 3½ to 4 cups shredded meat.) Strain broth; reserve 5 to 6 cups broth. In a 3-quart saucepan heat the Red Chili Sauce; add shredded meat. Simmer, covered, about 10 minutes.

◆ Tamales

For masa, in a large bowl beat shortening with a mixer on medium speed for 1 minute. Stir together masa harina, baking powder, and the 2 teaspoons salt. Alternately add masa harina mixture and broth to shortening, beating well after each addition. Add just enough broth to make a thick, creamy paste. Soak corn husks in warm water 5 minutes; rinse to remove any corn silks and debris. Drain.

To assemble each tamale, spread 2 tablespoons masa mixture in the center of a husk. (Each husk should be about 8 inches long and 6 inches wide at the top. If husks are small, overlap two small husks to form one. If husks are large, tear off a small piece from side.) Place about 1 tablespoon meat sauce in middle of masa. Fold in sides of husk, then fold up bottom.

Place a mound of extra corn husks (or a foil ball) in center of a steamer basket placed in a Dutch oven. Add water to Dutch oven just below basket. Lean tamales in basket, open end up. Bring water to boiling; reduce heat. Cover; steam 40 minutes, adding more water as necessary. Makes about 50 tamales.

To make Tamales ahead: Up to 2 days before serving, cook, shred, and chill the meat in a covered container. Prepare the Red Chili Sauce; chill in a covered container.

The day of assembling Tamales, prepare masa. In a saucepan combine shredded meat and sauce; heat through.

You can also freeze the assembled Tamales. Lay Tamales in single layers on baking sheets; freeze. Transfer Tamales to freezer storage bags. Freeze for up to 2 months. To steam, arrange frozen Tamales in steamer basket as directed below left. Steam for 50 to 60 minutes or till heated through, adding additional water to pot as necessary.

Per tamale: 125 cal., 6 g fat (2 g sat. fat), 15 mg chol., 68 mg sodium, 12 g carbo., 1 g fiber, 5 g pro.

Red Chili Sauce

LOOK FOR DRIED LARGE PEPPERS THAT ARE LABELED CALIFORNIA, NEW MEXICO, ANAHEIM, OR PASILLA. YOU CAN PREPARE THIS SAUCE WITH ONE OR MORE PEPPER VARIETIES. MARGARET FIXES A MILDLY HOT SAUCE USING 6 ANAHEIM (OR NEW MEXICO), 7 CALIFORNIA, AND 2 PASILLA CHILI PEPPERS (WHICH ADD THE HEAT).

15 dried large chili peppers
(such as Anaheim, New Mexico,
California, or pasilla)
4 to 5 large cloves garlic
2 teaspoons ground cumin
1 teaspoon salt
2 tablespoons all-purpose flour
2 tablespoons bacon drippings, olive oil, or
melted shortening

Remove stems and seeds from dried chili peppers*. Place peppers in a single layer on a baking sheet. Roast in a 350° oven for 2 to 5 minutes or till they have

◆ Red Chili Sauce

a sweet roasted aroma, checking frequently to avoid burning. (Try to avoid deep inhaling.) Remove from oven; soak peppers in enough hot water to cover (about 5 cups) about 30 minutes or till cool. Transfer the peppers and 2½ cups of the soaking liquid to a blender container; add garlic, cumin, and salt. (Reserve remaining liquid.) Cover and blend till smooth.

In a 2-quart saucepan cook and stir flour in bacon drippings or oil over medium heat till light brown. Carefully stir in pureed chili mixture. Simmer, uncovered, for 5 to 10 minutes or till slightly thickened, being careful of splatters. If sauce is too thick, stir in additional soaking liquid (up to 1 cup) to make of desired consistency. Use this sauce for Tamales (see recipe, page 228) and to serve with Posole (see recipe, page 230). Makes 4 cups sauce.

*Note: When working with hot peppers, wear plastic gloves to protect your skin from the oils in the peppers. Avoid direct contact with your eyes. When finished, wash hands thoroughly.

Nutrition facts per tablespoon: 7 cal., 0.5 g total fat (0 g sat. fat), 34 mg sodium. Daily Value: 19% vit. C.

◆ Posole

◆ Chiles Rellenos Casserole

Note: For a richer tasting Posole, add 1 to 2 tablespoons butter to the soup, as Margaret does, along with the hominy.

Nutrition facts per serving: 250 cal., 12 g total fat (4 g sat. fat), 74 mg chol., 587 mg sodium, 13 g carbo., 1 g fiber, 21 g pro. Daily Value: 0% vit. A, 2% vit. C, 2% calcium, 11% iron.

Posole (Hominy and Pork Soup)

1 2-pound boneless pork shoulder roast, trimmed of fat and cut into chunks
2 medium onions, chopped
1 teaspoon garlic powder
1 teaspoon salt
1 teaspoon instant beef or chicken bouillon granules
½ teaspoon pepper
6 cups water
2 16-ounce cans white hominy, drained
1 recipe Red Chili Sauce (see recipe, page 229) (optional)
Lemon slices (optional)
Green onion tops or sliced green onion (optional)
Dried oregano, crushed (optional)

In a 4-quart Dutch oven combine pork, onions, garlic powder, salt, bouillon granules, and pepper; add water. Bring to boiling; reduce heat. Cover; simmer for 1½ to 2 hours or till meat is very tender. Remove meat from broth; cool. Cover broth; set aside. When meat is cool enough to handle, use two forks to shred meat; discard excess fat. Skim fat from broth. Return meat to broth. Add hominy; heat through. Ladle soup into bowls; top each serving with Red Chili Sauce, a lemon slice, green onion, and dried oregano as desired. Serves 8.

Chiles Rellenos Casserole

4 4-ounce cans whole green chili peppers, rinsed and drained
1 cup shredded cheddar cheese
1 cup shredded Monterey Jack cheese (4 ounces)
4 beaten eggs or 1 cup frozen egg product, thawed
1 12-ounce can (1½ cups) evaporated skim milk
2 tablespoons all-purpose flour
½ teaspoon seasoned salt
½ teaspoon garlic powder
½ teaspoon ground cumin
¼ teaspoon dried cilantro, crushed (optional)
¼ teaspoon ground black pepper
Flour tortillas (optional)
Crushed red pepper or paprika
Sliced green onion (optional)

Grease a 2-quart rectangular baking dish. To remove any excess moisture, pat the drained peppers with paper towels. Halve peppers lengthwise; remove seeds, if desired. Place half of the chili peppers in the bottom of the dish. Sprinkle with half of both cheeses. Place remaining chili peppers in the dish; sprinkle with the remaining cheese. Combine eggs or egg product, milk, flour, seasoned salt, garlic powder, cumin, cilantro, if desired, and black pepper; beat with a wire whisk or rotary beater till smooth. Pour over chili peppers and cheese.

Bake, uncovered, in a 350° oven for 30 to 35 minutes or till set in the center. Stack tortillas; wrap in foil. During the last 10 minutes of baking, place tortillas in oven to soften.

Before serving, sprinkle casserole with crushed red pepper or paprika and green onion, if desired. Pass warm tortillas. Makes 8 main-dish servings.

Nutrition facts per serving: 201 cal., 13 g total fat (7 g sat. fat), 135 mg chol., 482 mg sodium, 9 g carbo., 0 g fiber, 15 g pro. Daily Value: 18% vit. A, 31% vit. C, 34% calcium, 8% iron.

Cleo's Empanadas

USE THE RICH PRUNE FILLING TO MAKE EMPANADAS (EM PA NA DAHS), MEXICAN DESSERT TURNOVERS, OR A 9-INCH PIE (SEE PHOTO, PAGE 231).

1 12-ounce package pitted prunes
1½ cups water
1 cup sugar
2 teaspoons lemon juice
1 teaspoon ground cinnamon
1 teaspoon vanilla
2 15-ounce packages folded refrigerated unbaked piecrust (4 crusts)
Beaten egg white

◆ Cleo's Empanadas and pie

For filling, in a saucepan combine prunes and water. Bring to boiling; reduce heat. Simmer, covered, 20 to 25 minutes or till very tender; partially cool.

Using a slotted spoon, transfer prunes to a bowl, reserving liquid. Mash prunes with a fork. Stir sugar, lemon juice, cinnamon, and vanilla into mashed prunes to make a thick paste, adding some of the reserved cooking liquid if necessary.

On a floured surface, unfold one pastry crust. Roll to a 13-inch circle. Using a floured 4½-inch cookie cutter, cut dough into 8 circles, rerolling scraps as necessary. Spoon 1 tablespoon filling in the center of a dough round. Fold dough in half, pinching edges together to seal. Flute edges, if desired. Repeat to make 32 empanadas total.

Arrange on a greased baking sheet. Prick tops with a fork. Brush with egg white. Bake in a 375° oven for 18 to 20 minutes or till golden. Cool. Makes 32.

Nutrition facts per empanada: 182 cal., 8 g total fat (0 g sat. fat), 8 mg chol., 108 mg sodium, 28 g carbo., 1 g fiber, 2 g pro.

Biscochitos (Anise Cookies)

IN NEW MEXICO, BISCOCHITOS (BISS KO CHEAT OHS) ARE SERVED YEAR-ROUND.

3 cups all-purpose flour
1½ teaspoons aniseed, crushed
1 teaspoon baking powder
½ teaspoon salt
1¼ cups butter-flavored shortening
1 egg
½ cup sugar
3 tablespoons frozen orange juice concentrate, thawed, or brandy
1 teaspoon vanilla
Cinnamon-sugar (optional)
Crushed aniseed (optional)

Combine flour, 1½ teaspoons aniseed, baking powder, and salt; set aside. In a bowl beat shortening with an electric mixer on medium speed till fluffy. Add egg, sugar, orange juice or brandy, and vanilla, beating till mixture is light. Beat or stir in the flour mixture (dough will be stiff). Divide dough into 2 portions.

On a lightly floured surface, use a floured rolling pin to roll dough to ¼-inch thickness. Using a cookie cutter, cut into 2½-inch rounds. If desired, sprinkle cutouts with cinnamon-sugar and additional crushed aniseed. Arrange on greased cookie sheets; bake in a 350° oven about 9 minutes or till golden on bottoms. Cool. Makes about 3 dozen.

Nutrition facts per cookie: 114 cal., 7 g total fat (2 g sat. fat), 6 mg chol., 42 mg sodium, 11 g carbo., 0 g fiber, 1 g pro.

Sopa (Bread Pudding)

2 cups sugar
2½ cups water
6 tablespoons margarine or butter
1½ teaspoons ground cinnamon

◆ Sopa

1 teaspoon vanilla
1 16-ounce loaf white bread, toasted and cut into cubes (about 10 cups)
2 cups shredded cheddar cheese
¾ cup raisins
½ cup peanuts
Whipped cream (optional)

Place the sugar in a 3-quart heavy saucepan. Cook over medium-high heat, without stirring, till sugar starts to melt. Reduce heat to low; cook till golden brown, stirring frequently. Remove from heat. Carefully add 2½ cups water (it will splatter). Return saucepan to heat. Bring to boiling, stirring to melt hardened lumps. Remove from heat. Stir in margarine, cinnamon, and vanilla.

In a 3-quart rectangular baking dish layer half of the bread cubes. Sprinkle half of the cheese and all of the raisins over bread cubes. Top with the remaining bread cubes, remaining cheese, and nuts. Pour caramelized sugar mixture over all. Bake, uncovered, in a 350° oven for 30 minutes or till top is golden and syrup is absorbed. Serve warm with whipped cream and orange slices, if desired. Makes 16 servings.

Nutrition facts per serving: 315 cal., 12 g total fat (4 g sat. fat), 15 mg chol., 294 mg sodium, 46 g carbo., 1 g fiber, 7 g pro.

Hanukkah
A Time for Sharing

BY JULIA MALLOY

As she reaches out to light the menorah this year, Elizabeth Hart will cherish the moment more than ever. It's the last time she'll light the candles at her family's annual Hanukkah party. When she leaves for college next year, her younger brother Aaron will take her place.

"I know I'll miss lighting the menorah," she says.

Elizabeth and Aaron barely remember their family's first Hanukkah party over 15 years ago. On a whim, their parents, Florence and Peter Hart, invited a few friends and neighbors for a Hanukkah potluck. The Harts never dreamed their cozy gathering would mushroom into a major annual event. Their Washington, D.C., home is now the focal point of the Hanukkah season for the family and about 100 friends and neighbors.

As big as the party has become, one thing never changes—the meal is still a potluck. Florence knows that if she provides the setting, the food will almost magically appear. "I never know what the menu will be," she says. "Some people show up with an old favorite year after year. Others like to surprise us."

When the doorbell rings on the first day of Hanukkah, it could be David Osterhout holding his hearty brisket or Eli Cohen from next door with his homemade challah bread. Eli was one of the children invited to the original celebration and has baked the challah every year since. Sooner or later, Richard Perle appears with his apron and a sack of potatoes. After a spirited tasting several years ago, Richard was crowned the best latke maker. He now makes a command performance every year.

"The food is wonderful," says Florence, "but Hanukkah is really for the children. We have a special ceremony and small gifts for them."

The ceremony begins with Elizabeth lighting the menorah. Each child takes a turn reading from a dog-eared book about the first Hanukkah. The familiar story unfolds of how the ancient Jewish

people defeated a powerful enemy after a miracle provided them with enough lamp oil to light battle preparations.

When the last child finishes reading, Florence makes note of the graduations, anniversaries, and bar mitzvahs that her guests have celebrated during the year.

"In this busy group, where friends can lose track of each other, this is the moment to pause, reflect, and show support for one another," she says.

When Florence finishes her reflections on the past year, everyone gathers around the dining room table. Now it's time for these friends and neighbors to share more laughter and the dinner they've been waiting all year to taste.

Potato Latkes

THIS RECIPE FOR CRISPY, GOLDEN POTATO PANCAKES IS SIMILAR TO THE ONE USED BY RICHARD PERLE. SERVE THE LATKES WITH YOGURT, SOUR CREAM, OR APPLESAUCE.

4 medium potatoes
1 slightly beaten egg
1 small onion, finely chopped
2 tablespoons all-purpose flour

½ teaspoon salt
¼ teaspoon pepper
Cooking oil

Peel potatoes. Coarsely shred and place potatoes in cold water as you work to prevent darkening. Drain potatoes well. Pat dry with paper towels.

In a large mixing bowl combine potatoes, egg, onion, flour, salt, and pepper. Mix well.

In a 12-inch skillet heat 1 tablespoon cooking oil over medium-high heat.

Drop potato mixture by tablespoonfuls into hot oil. Fry for 2 to 3 minutes till edges are crisp; turn. Cook 2 to 3 minutes more till golden brown. Drain on paper towels; cover and keep warm. Repeat with remaining potato mixture, adding oil as necessary. Makes 20 latkes.

To make ahead: Drain cooked latkes on paper towels; cover and chill. To reheat, arrange on an ungreased baking sheet. Bake, uncovered, in a 400° oven for 10 to 12 minutes, turning once.

Nutrition facts per latke: 53 cal., 3 g total fat (0 g sat. fat), 11 mg chol., 58 mg sodium, 6 g carbo., 0 g fiber, 1 g pro.

Hanukkah Brisket

1 3- to 4-pound fresh beef brisket
¼ teaspoon seasoned pepper
Dash salt
1 tablespoon all-purpose flour
3 medium carrots, chopped
3 stalks celery, chopped
3 medium onions, chopped
1 7½-ounce can tomatoes, cut up
½ cup port wine
1 envelope regular onion soup mix
1 teaspoon dried basil, crushed
2 bay leaves

◆ Hanukkah Brisket, Green Beans in Yellow Pepper Butter, Potato Latkes

Trim excess fat from brisket; sprinkle meat with seasoned pepper and salt. Place flour in a large oven cooking bag and shake; add brisket. Set the bag in a roasting pan. Combine carrots, celery, onions, undrained tomatoes, wine, soup mix, basil, and bay leaves; pour atop brisket. Close bag; cut slits in top of bag; seal bag.

Roast in a 325° oven 2½ to 3 hours or till tender. Remove bay leaves. Slice meat across the grain into ¼-inch-thick slices. Skim fat from pan juices; serve with meat. Makes 12 main-dish servings.

To make ahead: Cool meat in bag; cover and chill overnight. To reheat, remove meat from bag; thinly slice. Place slices in a 3-quart rectangular baking dish. Skim fat from juices; pour over meat. Cover; heat in a 300° oven about 50 minutes or till hot. Serve as above.

Nutrition facts per serving: 257 cal., 11 g total fat (4 g sat. fat), 78 mg chol., 416 mg sodium, 10 g carbo., 2 g fiber, and 26 g pro.

Green Beans in Yellow Pepper Butter

1 tablespoon margarine or butter
1 medium yellow sweet pepper, coarsely shredded
6 tablespoons margarine or butter, softened
¼ cup pine nuts
1 tablespoon lemon juice
¼ teaspoon salt
⅛ teaspoon pepper
1½ pounds green beans, trimmed
1 large yellow sweet pepper, cut into julienne strips (1 cup)

In a small saucepan melt the 1 tablespoon margarine or butter. Add shredded yellow pepper. Cook over medium-high heat 5 minutes or till crisp-tender; set aside.

In a blender container or food processor bowl combine softened butter and pine nuts. Cover and blend or process till almost smooth. Add cooked shredded pepper, lemon juice, salt, and pepper. Cover and blend or process till almost smooth. Set aside.

Cook beans, covered, in a small amount of boiling water for 12 minutes. Cook pepper strips in a small amount of boiling salted water for 3 minutes. Drain beans and peppers.

To serve, transfer beans to a serving bowl. Arrange pepper strips around edge. Add butter mixture. Serve warm. Before serving, toss to coat. Makes 8 side-dish servings.

Nutrition facts per serving: 159 cal., 13 g total fat (7 g sat. fat), 27 mg chol., 71 mg sodium, 11 g carbo., 2 g fiber, 3 g pro. Daily Value: 16% vit. A, 180% vit. C, 4% calcium, 10% iron.

Prize Tested Recipes

◆ Apricot-Almond Chocolate Torte

Apricot-Almond Chocolate Torte

A LAYER OF ALMOND PASTE NESTLES BENEATH THE FROSTING. CHOOSE AN ALMOND PASTE WITHOUT ADDED CORN SYRUP OR FRUCTOSE FOR THIS RECIPE.

3 cups all-purpose flour
2 cups sugar
¾ cup unsweetened cocoa powder
2 teaspoons baking soda
½ teaspoon salt
1 cup water
1 cup cooled coffee
⅔ cup cooking oil
1 teaspoon vanilla
½ cup margarine or butter, cut up
6 ounces semisweet chocolate, cut up
1 tablespoon light corn syrup
1 cup apricot preserves
5 ounces almond paste (⅔ cup)

Grease and lightly flour two 9x1½-inch round baking pans; set aside. In a mixing bowl stir together flour, sugar, cocoa powder, baking soda, and salt. Add water, coffee, oil, and vanilla. Beat with an electric mixer on low to medium speed just till combined. Pour batter into prepared pans. Bake in a 350° oven for 35 minutes or till done. Cool in pans on wire racks for 10 minutes. Remove from pans; cool completely on racks.

For glaze, in a saucepan combine margarine or butter, chocolate, and corn syrup. Stir over low heat till melted. Remove from heat. Let stand till glaze begins to thicken.

Cut cake layers in half horizontally. Place 1 layer on a platter; spread with one-third of the preserves. Repeat 2 more times. Top with fourth cake layer.

Place almond paste between 2 sheets of waxed paper; roll till thin (about a 9-inch diameter). Remove top sheet of paper. Place almond paste atop cake, paper side up; remove paper. Trim almond paste even with cake edge. Spread top and sides of cake with chocolate glaze. (If glaze becomes too firm, stir in a few drops of hot water.) If desired, garnish with chocolate curls. Serves 16.

Nutrition facts per slice: 472 cal., 21 g total fat (3 g sat. fat), 0 mg chol., 288 mg sodium, 69 g carbo., 1 g fiber, 5 g pro. Daily Value: 7% vit. A, 0% vit. C, 6% calcium, 15% iron.

$200 WINNER
Annemarie Latimer
Columbia, New Jersey

◆ Spiced Orange Mocha

Spiced Orange Mocha

CAPPUCCINO GOES A STEP BETTER. SIMMER COFFEE, CHOCOLATE, ORANGE, AND SPICES INTO THIS MELLOW BREW.

1 medium orange
2 inches stick cinnamon
7 whole cloves
2 cups water
2 cups milk
½ cup packed brown sugar
¼ cup unsweetened cocoa powder
2 tablespoons instant coffee crystals
¼ teaspoon rum extract

Using a vegetable peeler or sharp knife, remove peel from orange; set aside. Squeeze juice from orange; add water, if necessary, to equal ⅓ cup. Set aside. For spice bag, place orange peel, cinnamon, and cloves in a double layer square of 100% cotton cheesecloth. Bring up corners; tie with string.

◆ Hazelnut-Praline Dream

In a blender container combine ice cream, milk, and liqueur. Cover and blend till smooth. Serve immediately in 4 glasses. Makes 4 (6-ounce) servings.

Nutrition facts per serving: 295 cal., 14 g total fat (9 g sat. fat), 51 mg chol., 91 mg sodium, 33 g carbo., 0 g fiber, 5 g pro. Daily Value: 18% vit. A, 2% vit. C, 15% calcium, 0% iron.

$100 WINNER
Kristine Feher
Passaic, New Jersey

In a large saucepan combine orange juice, spice bag, water, milk, brown sugar, cocoa powder, and coffee crystals. Bring to boiling; remove from heat. Cover and let stand for 10 minutes. Remove spice bag. Stir in rum extract. Makes 6 (6-ounce) servings.

Nutrition facts per serving: 136 cal., 2 g total fat (1 g sat. fat), 6 mg chol., 51 mg sodium, 26 g carbo., 0 g fiber, 4 g pro. Daily Values: 5% vit. A, 14% vit. C, 13% calcium, 6% iron.

$200 WINNER
Melissa Gilbert
Frederick, Maryland

Hazelnut-Praline Dream

EGGNOG LOVERS EVERYWHERE WILL GO FOR THIS EASY ICE-CREAM DRINK.

1 pint caramel-swirled vanilla ice cream
with pralines, butter brickle ice cream, or
butter pecan ice cream
1⅓ cups milk
¼ cup hazelnut liqueur

White Christmas Cake

WHY DREAM OF A WHITE CHRISTMAS WHEN YOU CAN HAVE THIS HEAVENLY WHITE-CHOCOLATE CAKE?

1½ cups margarine or butter
4 ounces white chocolate baking
bar, chopped
1½ cups buttermilk
4 eggs, slightly beaten
¼ teaspoon rum extract
3½ cups all-purpose flour
1 cup toasted chopped pecans
2¼ cups sugar
½ cup flaked coconut
1 teaspoon baking soda
1 teaspoon baking powder
1 recipe White Chocolate Frosting
(see recipe, right)

In a large saucepan bring margarine or butter and ¾ cup water to boiling, stirring constantly. Remove from heat. Add baking bar; stir till melted. Stir in buttermilk, eggs, and rum extract; set aside. Stir together ½ cup of the flour and the pecans; set aside.

In an extra-large bowl stir together remaining 3 cups flour, sugar, coconut, soda, and powder. Stir in margarine mix-

◆ White Christmas Cake

ture. Fold in pecan mixture. Pour into 3 greased and floured 9x1½-inch round baking pans. Bake in a 350° oven for 25 to 30 minutes or till done. Cool in pans on wire racks for 10 minutes. Remove from pans; cool on racks.

To assemble, place a cake layer on a platter. Spread with ½ cup frosting. Repeat layers. Top with remaining cake layer. Frost top and sides with remaining frosting. If desired, garnish with toasted coconut and/or pecan halves. Serves 16.

White Chocolate Frosting: Melt 4 ounces chopped *white chocolate baking bar.* Cool 10 minutes. In a large mixing bowl beat ½ cup softened *margarine or butter* and one 8-ounce and one 3-ounce package softened *cream cheese* with an electric mixer till combined. Beat in chocolate. Gradually add 6 cups sifted *powdered sugar,* beating till smooth.

Nutrition facts per slice: 776 cal., 41 g total fat (13 g sat. fat), 76 mg chol., 477 mg sodium, 98 g carbo., 1 g fiber, 8 g pro. Daily Value: 39% vit. A, 0% vit. C, 9% calcium, 12% iron.

$100 WINNER
Carol Gillespie
Chambersburg, Pennsylvania

Index

F-N

Index
238

Tips

Metric Cooking Hints

By making a few conversions, cooks in Australia, Canada, and the United Kingdom can use the recipes in Better Homes and Gardens® *Best Recipes Yearbook* with confidence. The charts on this page provide a guide for converting measurements from the U.S. customary system, which is used throughout this book, to the imperial and metric systems. There also is a conversion table for oven temperatures to accommodate the differences in oven calibrations.

Volume and Weight: Americans traditionally use cup measures for liquid and solid ingredients. The chart (top right) shows the approximate imperial and metric equivalents. If you are accustomed to weighing solid ingredients, here are some helpful approximate equivalents.

● 1 cup butter, caster sugar, or rice = 8 ounces = about 250 grams
● 1 cup flour = 4 ounces = about 125 grams
● 1 cup icing sugar = 5 ounces = about 150 grams

Spoon measures are used for smaller amounts of ingredients although the size of the tablespoon varies slightly among countries. However, for practical purposes and for recipes in this book, a straight substitution is all that's necessary.

Measurements made using cups or spoons should always be level, unless stated otherwise.

Product Differences: Most of the ingredients called for in the recipes in this book are available in English-speaking countries. However, some are known by different names. Here are some common American ingredients and their possible counterparts:
● Sugar is granulated or caster sugar.
● Powdered sugar is icing sugar.
● All-purpose flour is plain household flour or white flour. When self-rising flour is used in place of all-purpose flour in a recipe that calls for leavening, omit the leavening agent (baking soda or baking powder) and salt.
● Light corn syrup is golden syrup.
● Cornstarch is cornflour.
● Baking soda is bicarbonate of soda.
● Vanilla is vanilla essence.

Useful Equivalents

⅛ teaspoon = 0.5 ml	⅔ cup = 5 fluid ounces = 150 ml
¼ teaspoon = 1 ml	¾ cup = 6 fluid ounces = 175 ml
½ teaspoon = 2 ml	1 cup = 8 fluid ounces = 250 ml
1 teaspoon = 5 ml	2 cups = 1 pint
¼ cup = 2 fluid ounces = 50 ml	2 pints = 1 litre
⅓ cup = 3 fluid ounces = 75 ml	½ inch = 1 centimetre
½ cup = 4 fluid ounces = 125 ml	1 inch = 2 centimetres

Baking Pan Sizes

American	Metric
8x1½-inch round baking pan	20x4-centimetre sandwich or cake tin
9x1½-inch round baking pan	23x3.5-centimetre sandwich or cake tin
11x7x1½-inch baking pan	28x18x4-centimetre baking pan
13x9x2-inch baking pan	32.5x23x5-centimetre baking pan
2-quart rectangular baking dish	30x19x5-centimetre baking pan
15x10x2-inch baking pan	38x25.5x2.5-centimetre baking pan (Swiss roll tin)
9-inch pie plate	22x4- or 23x4-centimetre pie plate
7- or 8-inch springform pan	18- or 20-centimetre springform or loose-bottom cake tin
9x5x3-inch loaf pan	23x13x6-centimetre or 2-pound narrow loaf pan or paté tin
1½-quart casserole	1.5-litre casserole
2-quart casserole	2-litre casserole

Oven Temperature Equivalents

Fahrenheit Setting	Celsius Setting*	Gas Setting
300°F	150°C	Gas Mark 2
325°F	160°C	Gas Mark 3
350°F	180°C	Gas Mark 4
375°F	190°C	Gas Mark 5
400°F	200°C	Gas Mark 6
425°F	220°C	Gas Mark 7
450°F	230°C	Gas Mark 8
Broil		Grill

Electric and gas ovens may be calibrated using Celsius. However, increase the Celsius setting 10 to 20 degrees when cooking above 160°C with an electric oven. For convection or forced-air ovens (gas or electric), lower the temperature setting 10°C when cooking at all heat levels.